# The Incidental Feminist

# The Incidental Feminist

Friend, foe, femme fatale?
The truth about Thatcher

## TINA GAUDOIN

SWIFT PRESS

First published in Great Britain by Swift Press 2025

9 8 7 6 5 4 3 2 1

Copyright © Tina Gaudoin 2025

All rights reserved

The right of Tina Gaudoin to be identified as the Author of this Work has been asserted in accordance with the Copyright, Designs and Patents Act 1988.

Text design and typesetting by Tetragon, London
Printed and bound in Great Britain by CPI Group (UK) Ltd, Croydon, CR0 4YY

A CIP catalogue record for this book is available from the British Library.

We make every effort to ensure our products are safe for the purpose for which they are intended. Our authorised representative in the EU for product safety is Easy Access System Europe, Mustamäe tee 50, 10621 Tallinn, Estonia gpsr.requests@easproject.com

ISBN: 9781800753808
eISBN: 9781800753815

*For EE & TGE*

Dedicated to the memory of Dorothy Hodgkin.
So far, the only British woman to hold a Nobel Prize for science.
Tutor to Margaret Thatcher, Somerville College, Oxford, 1943-7.

# Contents

INTRODUCTION: Margaret Thatcher... What the Hell?     11
*Housekeeping*     15

PROLOGUE: We Need to Talk (Again) about Margaret     17
1   Autistic Glamour Puss?     21
2   The Mother Complex     61
3   Breaking the Class Ceiling     95
4   The Incidental Feminist     129
5   The Three Marketeers: Anatomy of an Icon     167
6   Warrior Queen, Gender Blender?     191
7   Onward Christian/Scientist     227
8   Madness, Madonna and MT:
      Pop, Profanity and Power under Thatcher     245
9   Knights, Rotters, Bounders and Cads     267
10  All the Prime Minister's Men     297

*Acknowledgements*     329
*Bibliography*     331
*Index*     339

Be sure that long patience and jealously hidden sorrows have hardened this woman of whom one cries out: She is made of steel! She is simply a woman and that is enough.

Colette, *La Vagabonde*

# INTRODUCTION

# Margaret Thatcher... What the Hell?

In the last three years of working on this book, I have, of necessity, become accustomed to hearing the above interrogative (give or take another four-letter expletive) when telling people about this project. It's not an unreasonable enquiry, especially when put to someone who did not actually vote for the woman in question. It's certainly one I have asked myself, many times. And yet there were unresolved issues, relating in particular to Margaret Thatcher's personality, which fascinated me. Why, for example, in the 35 years since Margaret Thatcher stepped down as PM, has she remained so indelibly lodged within the public consciousness? What aspects of her character and her leadership have been overlooked or ignored in the course of that history, which would render her a 'whole' person, rather than the two-dimensional character who has lived 'rent free' for so long in the minds of so many of us? What does it say about us that we still care (one way or the other) so much about her?

# THE INCIDENTAL FEMINIST

We are all familiar with the diametrically opposing Thatcher narratives: one endorses her as perhaps the greatest politician of the twentieth century and the other condemns her as the architect of a Britain dominated by privatising elites, blinded by greed and competitive consumerism, grown careless of the welfare of those less fortunate. What is so often forgotten, in the heat of debate, is the plain and simple fact that Margaret Thatcher was a woman, operating in what, at the time, was almost exclusively a male-dominated world. You might well say it still is. But what we experience these days is nothing compared to what she and millions of other women struggled with in their battle to achieve at least a level of parity with the opposite sex.

More than almost any other woman, we decontextualise Margaret Thatcher and her legacy, viewing both her achievements and her failures through the lens of today's societal values and norms. This was never more apparent than in the claim that she was 'not a feminist' – one I examine in greater detail in Chapter 4. Whether we like it or not, as women we all, to a greater or lesser extent, stand on her shoulders. We only have to look at the history books, read the novels and watch the movies of the 1950s, 60s and 70s, when she was making her political way, to understand that, for women, the past was truly a foreign country. And yet, we judge the first female leader of a G7 nation, her actions and her policies as if they were taking place in real time – today. Even less fathomable is our modern-day tendency to blame Margaret Thatcher for the ills of today's society – as though every one of our succeeding nine PMs somehow lacked intelligence, policy or agency.

I do not seek to rehabilitate Margaret Thatcher. Indeed, many would say she needs no redemption – for millions, particularly

# INTRODUCTION

outside the UK, she still offers a peerless example of supremely effective leadership. (When, in 1989, editor in chief Marc Burca of *Boardroom* magazine, interviewing New York businessman Donald Trump, asked: 'If you could meet anyone in the world, who would it be?' he was met with an immediate response: 'Margaret Thatcher.') My intention then, is to examine elements of Margaret Thatcher's personal and political life in a way that her (mostly) male biographers have not yet done. And that is to look at her as a woman first and a politician second. The fact that she was a female does not diminish her successes, nor for that matter does it excuse her failures. Rather it requires us, with the benefit of hindsight, to take another, more nuanced look at one of the most influential figures of the twentieth century.

# HOUSEKEEPING

This is not a soup-to-nuts biography – if that is what you seek then I recommend the many excellent works in the bibliography at the back of this book, the mother of them all being Charles Moore's peerless three-volume official biography of Margaret Thatcher (Penguin 2013/15/19). Vast numbers of documents relating to MT have been gathered by Chris Collins, the editor of the Margaret Thatcher Foundation, and made freely available online at margaretthatcher.org.

Because this book does not follow the narrative arc of a typical biography, it does not contain footnotes or endnotes. When a quote from a book is introduced, the book and its author are referenced. It follows, then, that any further quotes from this author are taken from the referenced book, unless otherwise noted. Quotes from interviews are in the present tense, unless otherwise noted. For ease of reading, throughout the book I have chosen to forgo the use of most honorary and inherited titles (of which there would be very many). I mean this as no disrespect. I refer to Margaret Thatcher, after her initial introduction, as MT, for the same reason.

Also provided at the close of the book is a list of acknowledgements. I should, however, like to take this early opportunity to posthumously thank the late Sir Julian Seymour, without whose help and guidance I could never have completed the task. Thanks also to my friend Jonathan Berger, who provided the initial connection, and to Andrew Riley and the team looking after the Thatcher Papers at the Churchill Archives Centre, Cambridge, without whom the writing of this book would not have been possible.

Writing a book about Margaret Thatcher is, as I have already mentioned, a tricky task. The volume of information about our former PM is so great and the accounts so conflicting that it has at times been necessary to accept versions of events which have received the most coverage or on which the greatest number of opinions or accounts appear to converge. There is little doubt that I have made some mistakes – any errors are mine, and for them I apologise in advance. MT's spelling and grammar was occasionally not on point. We have taken the decision to correct her mistakes, again for ease of reading.

Many people agreed to be interviewed for this book (both on and off the record). A few, despite more than one entreaty, did not respond. In such cases, I assumed they did not wish to be involved. Occasionally, a refusal to speak revealed more than an interview ever could. The two people who almost certainly owed their careers and positions in largest part to Margaret Thatcher – both ex-PMs: John Major and Theresa May – declined immediately. I cannot help but think that, had their situations been reversed, Margaret Thatcher would not have done the same.

# PROLOGUE

# We Need to Talk (Again) about Margaret

On 29 July 1981, at St Paul's Cathedral, London, the wedding of the Prince of Wales (now King Charles III) and Lady Diana Spencer brought together, under one seventeenth-century domed ceiling, the three most famous women in the world.

At approximately 11.20am, in front of 3,500 people in person, with another 750 million tuning in around the globe, Lady Diana Spencer, lost in acres of Suffolk taffeta, on the arm of her ailing father Earl Spencer, began a halting walk down the aisle and into the history books. The TV cameras had already captured the groom's mother, Her Majesty Queen Elizabeth II, pale and pensive in powder blue, white gloves and pearls. At a certain point in the procession, they seemed to pause momentarily. The object of their attention was the third woman in the troika: Prime Minister Margaret Hilda Thatcher in her Conservative-blue power suit and beribboned pillbox hat, standing ramrod straight, hands clasped in front of her, smiling benevolently, as the bride-to-be floated by. The contrast between the three women and their journey to global fame was never writ larger: one had been born into royalty; another, already ennobled, would emerge from the 90-minute wedding ceremony into global stardom. The third, who by the law of averages should never have been there in the first place, was a grocer's daughter from Grantham, the granddaughter of a cloakroom attendant, who had won her place in history as the first female Prime Minister of Great Britain, and one of the first global female leaders, the more conventional way: through hard work, grit, determination and sheer bloody-mindedness.

At least that was the way she and most political history books told it. The Margaret Thatcher legend charts a straight line from a modest flat above a grocery store in the desperately ordinary Midlands town of Grantham, to the shiny black door of No. 10 Downing Street, via a few other seemingly less meaningful stops: Somerville College, Oxford; the five constituencies where she was rejected; the Methodist chapel on City Road, Islington, where she married Denis Thatcher; Queen Charlotte's and Chelsea Hospital, where she gave birth to her twins Mark and Carol in 1953; Lincoln's Inn, where she was called to the Bar in 1954; and Finchley in North London, where she finally won her seat in 1959. And thence on to power.

In fact, the story of Margaret Thatcher is a good deal more nuanced than history so far dictates.

Margaret Thatcher was a paradox: a woman from the 'wrong' class, who succeeded in a world almost entirely dominated by upper-class men, whilst bringing few women along with her. An upright Christian with a Methodist upbringing, a curiously liberal

## PROLOGUE

approach to sex, a sense of humour bypass and absolutely no compunction about using her feminine wiles to get what she wanted, Thatcher was about as far removed from the tired trope of her as a man in woman's clothing as one could get. Rather, she relished her femininity, was addicted to the glamour of clothes, the seduction of Hollywood, and had a magpie eye for detail – political or otherwise. Margaret Thatcher was not, as is also commonly thought, simply a product of her time; rather she was an anomaly of her sex and class – a once-in-a-lifetime (or possibly a few lifetimes) phenomenon. This book analyses Margaret Thatcher as woman first and politician second.

# I

# Autistic Glamour Puss?

> Can you recommend any exercises or anything from the medical point of view particularly for reduction of the area of the seat and control of the tummy muscles – oh and also reduction and uplift of bust?
>
> Letter from MT to her sister Muriel, 20 August 1944

Margaret Thatcher had a long-lasting fascination with glamour, beauty and image in all of its guises, from film and fashion to music, poetry and lifestyle. The men she appreciated and would work best with were of the fine, upstanding Clark Gable variety (for which, see a certain American President and former actor); the women she most respected would be well dressed – from Queen Elizabeth II to her first 'dresser', the elegant Dame Guinevere Tilney; her design doyenne, Margaret King; her friend 'the Italian' Carla Powell; and her secret 'crush', Barbara Castle. Her musical preference was for Bach in all of his cantata splendour and her favourite poet was Rudyard Kipling, who constantly venerated the glossy opulence of the Raj. Perhaps the place she most appreciated geographically and politically was the USA; its 'can do' attitude and appearance-oriented culture played directly to her strengths and interests – particularly California, home to both Hollywood and the Reagans. An obsession with glamour on the part of Britain's first female PM is not an obvious topic to have troubled most biographers. Possibly this is because the majority of them thus far have been male? A notable exception is Charles Moore, Thatcher's official biographer, who pays heed in his comprehensive, three-tome biography (Penguin 2013/15/19): 'More striking, and more apparently at odds with her upbringing, was a strong interest in glamour, both in films and in fashion. Almost every letter to Muriel mentions the latest films to hit Grantham.'

The letters of which Moore speaks are the collection of roughly 150 missives, written between Margaret and her older sister Muriel Cullen, to which he and, later, I were granted access by Julian Seymour (director of MT's private office) and the Cullen family. Here, on greying lined exercise paper, raggedly torn from school books, on parchment stock from her father's grocery store – '*A. Roberts, Grocer and Provision Merchant,* THE MOST COMPREHENSIVE STOCK IN THE DISTRICT' – and later on cream Oxford University Conservative Association (OUCA) blue embossed letterhead, on husband Denis's own notepaper after they married (she crossed out his name) and finally on her own constituency letterhead, Margaret Thatcher the teenager and early twenty- and thirty-something writes, with what could at first be interpreted as a solipsistic focus, to her sister about school exam results, bossy teachers, Oxford flatmates, love interests and glamour with a capital G.

Over and above the gauche schoolgirl chat – 'Life in 6 Lower is not half as nice as life in form Va' and 'we are still doing worms in biology' – the main focus of the early letters, written in her distinctively firm, clear, grammar-schooled right hand, reveals an almost obsessive fascination with Hollywood and fashion, which as Moore points out were both ways to 'bring glamour to unexciting Grantham'. This was much called for. Once dubbed Britain's most boring town, Grantham was reputedly also the most bombed town of its size during the war. Remarkably, in the letters between the sisters, Thatcher rarely references the searing air-raid warnings and the ever-present threat of bombing raids, which would have marred her school and university days. What she does reference, though, is the punitive rationing, which continued long after the war was over and would see her counting down the days until she could use her next set of tokens, which naturally she puts towards her fashionable purchases: 'I also got a pink uplift bra, but they hadn't a white one so I am hoping to get that tomorrow with my remaining coupon.'

The experience of growing up in Grantham during the Second World War would nonetheless inform and shape the rest of MT's life. Her entry to Oxford in 1943, for example, was in part facilitated by the fact that, because of the war, more women than men would attend Oxbridge for the first time in the colleges' histories. In turn, this increased the possibilities for grammar-school girls like Margaret, who would, up until then, have stood little chance of acceptance. In her autobiography, she devotes five pages to the Great Depression of the thirties and the war itself: 'Well before war was declared we knew just what we thought of Hitler.' She also writes about the 'long queue waiting at the Labour exchange, seeking work or claiming the dole'. Her biggest impression, however, is the appearance of the children. 'I have never forgotten how neatly turned out the children of those unemployed families were.' Whilst black-and-white pictures reveal the devastation of wartime Grantham, with its bombed-out buildings and railway bridges, the young Margaret barely flinches. 'Last night I went fire watching at KGGS [Kesteven and Grantham Girls' School, her old school] with Miss Bowins... We slept in Harrowby House perfectly normally,' she writes, seemingly unfazed, to Muriel in 1944.

What is perhaps most interesting about these rarely seen letters is that they offer some early clues that Britain's first female PM possibly had a form of Autism Spectrum Disorder (or, as some campaigners would now prefer for it to be termed, Autism Spectrum Condition).

'You're not the first to suggest traits of autism in Margaret Thatcher's personality,' says one distinguished psychiatrist, 'but these would be at the mild end of the autism spectrum (which extends into normality).'

Autism, which is simply a neurological difference, tends to appear in childhood, but is now also increasingly diagnosed amongst adults, can make it difficult for people to understand social cues or express themselves to others. According to the National Autistic Society, 'Autism influences how people interact with the world.' Those with the condition may also often have 'intense interests, prefer order and routine, and use repeated movements or actions to calm [themselves] or express joy'.

I am, of course, indulging in armchair clinical psychology with my thesis; and it is impossible to conclusively diagnose individuals retroactively (though plenty have tried). However, the more one studies the letters, which contain MT's detailed, almost obsessive descriptions of her clothing and of the movies she has seen – and later the extensive, but painfully dull details of her exploits (such as they were at school, Oxford and beyond) – it's hard not to conclude that they represent what experts might term the 'special or restricted interests' that those with this kind of neurodevelopmental condition frequently display, often finding it hard to switch between topics. MT's infamous rigidity of thinking, her lack of a sense of humour, her awkwardness in social situations, what was perceived to be her rudeness, and her inability to sleep also to point to the condition. 'Her brief, seemingly uncharacteristic bouts of kindness, which have often been reported, were probably the results of masking,' says another psychiatrist, describing the tendency for those on the spectrum to overcompensate in certain forms of social interaction to 'fit in'.

For some people with an autism diagnosis the singularity of focus which this affords them may ultimately allow them to become brilliant at a specific subject or in a particular profession – for which, in MT's case, see politics. It should also be noted that often those who have the condition do not regard it as an 'affliction' but more as a 'difference' – and often a benefit. Conversely, those with severe autism may require full-time support and care.

Classifying autism is notoriously challenging. In the USA levels of intensity (1–3) are applied. By their measure, were MT diagnosed with autism today, she would almost certainly be classified as a level 1 on the Autism Spectrum Scale, meaning her symptoms allowed her to be 'fully functioning' with low support needs. (Until just over a decade ago, this mild form of autism was known as Asperger's and some campaigners or 'Aspies' argue that they'd like to return to the old terminology to promote a greater understanding of levels of neurodiversity.)

But Margaret Thatcher was born too early to receive any such diagnosis. The term 'autism' was first coined by Austrian-American psychiatrist Leo Kanner in 1943, the same year that she went up to Oxford.

Margaret was not popular at school. She found it hard to make friends and was 'perhaps a bit too eager and intense, inclined to be a know-it-all, her hand always up first in class', writes Robin Harris, one of Thatcher's speechwriters and advisors in *Not for Turning* (Bantam Press 2013). 'She never seemed to quite fit in with her peers,' says Penny Junor, who writes in the biography *Margaret Thatcher: Wife, Mother, Politician* (Sidgwick & Jackson 1983) that 'she tended to put a bit of a damper on their fun, to the extent that some of her classmates would walk a different route to school, so as not to meet up with her on the way'.

If the precocious Margaret was offended by other girls' behaviour towards her (she had notoriously thick skin), or she lacked the ability to read verbal and non-verbal clues, another characteristic prevalent amongst those on the autism spectrum, none of this makes it into her relentlessly detailed letters to Muriel. She writes to Muriel in September 1941:

> Last Thursday we went to see *Quiet Wedding* with Margaret Lockwood, a very amusing film. Also, we saw *This England* with Constance Cummings, Emlyn Williams and John Clements. We enjoyed it... although it was a historical film, for the greater part. With it was *Romance of the Rio Grande* with Cesar Romero and Patricia Morison... Most of the films you mention in your letter have been. *Bitter Sweet* is coming to the Picture House next week and *Pimpernel Smith* to the Savoy in the near future.

## AUTISTIC GLAMOUR PUSS?

> I have seen the film *Rebecca*. I thought it one of the best I have ever seen, with a well-concealed plot. It starred Joan Fontaine and Laurence Olivier.

In July 1944, she writes with similar focus to Muriel about clothes: 'Do you think that person who makes the handbags could make me one in maroon leather like your blue one? I have decided that maroon would be the best colour for my wardrobe as I am having that pinky dress made up.' And later in the same letter: 'Yesterday I went to Chambers and bought two underwear sets that I am very pleased with… I was hoping to buy some dark red court shoes in Lincoln tomorrow as two pairs of my shoes, a brown and a blue pair, have both suddenly worn out simultaneously.'

Often her single-minded passion for clothes led the teenage Margaret to be impulsive and secretive – revealing two other characteristic neurodivergent traits. For example, rather than telling her parents about her obsessive shopping habits, which she knows she can ill afford (she describes that summer holiday's tutoring of a 'not a very smart kid' as the 'hardest earned £2-2s I've ever had or hope to have in my life') she uses the excuse of changing trains in London, on her way back to Oxford, to indulge in some secret retail therapy: 'I went straight across to Paddington, dumped my suitcases and tubed to Oxford Circus,' she confides to her sister.

> I explored Oxford St, thoroughly looking in all the shops, also Regent St and Bond St – the latter I hadn't seen before. I had intended to do some shopping (though I didn't tell Mummy) so that was why I looked round thoroughly first. I got a pair of brown suede court shoes from Dolcis in Bond St – the last

pair they had in my size. They are an American shoe called 'Debutante Lovette' and are size 7½, American size of course.

Horrified by the price of an 'absolutely stunning' frock she tries on, she makes her way to the woollen department, where she tries on a 'fairly plain little frock with a Peter Pan collar two little pockets on the bodice and two to match on the skirt… looks much nicer on than off and underline it is absolutely pure wool through and through'. Cost: £3 16 shillings. Thrilled, she pronounces it 'one of the most worthwhile purchases I've ever made. I'll try and smuggle it home next time to show you without Mummy seeing it.' Later, in 1948, she writes to Muriel that 'I decided I couldn't possibly go to Llandudno with the "communal coat"'. So she rashly draws out some savings certificates, despite being short of money, and buys 'a fine lightweight black wool swagger'. She signs off with a cautionary plea: 'Don't mention new coat to parents. Love, Margaret.'

There are few of the conversational sister-to-sister niceties that you might expect from siblings four and a half years apart in age. And what quickly becomes clear are early signs of MT's inability to read social cues or to comprehend that her perspective might come across as arrogant or patronising. 'Margaret always brought to mind that old adage "I wish I was as sure about any one thing as she is of everything",' says David Howell (Secretary of State for Energy 1979–81 and then for Transport 1981–3), referencing the original William Lamb quote. 'She was overfull of theory and could be very rude and patronising.' Aged nine, MT famously told her primary school headmistress, who congratulated her on her luck at winning a prize: 'I wasn't lucky, I deserved it.' From

## AUTISTIC GLAMOUR PUSS?

Oxford she writes to Muriel that 'at a Conservative meeting I gave my paper on agricultural policy, which was a staggering success'. There is no tongue in her cheek as she writes (and surely Muriel, by then inured to Margaret's unusual responses, must have rolled her eyes?).

Charles Moore describes Margaret Thatcher as 'literal-minded' and that may have been so, but it was also yet another example of MT's 'different' take on the world. She was by all accounts incapable of telling anything but the truth, and she saw the world in black and white, without nuance. She admits this herself in her memoirs: 'I was perplexed by the metaphorical element of phrases like "Look before you leap". I thought it would be far better to say "Look before you cross".' The National Autistic Society points to differences in social interaction and communication as among the core characteristics of autism, such as 'being confused by metaphors and idioms, not always understanding hidden meanings or inference and taking phrases literally'.

In the most infamous example of this she fails to understand the witty rejoinder written into a speech for her by Ronald Millar, her speechwriter, making reference to the then PM James Callaghan, who, invoking Moses, had said that the nation would enter 'the promised land'. When Miller gives the kicker to her riposte – 'Keep taking the tablets' – she argues: 'Ronnie, nobody calls them tablets any more. We'll say "Keep taking the pills".' She famously had little or no conventional sense of humour and struggled to understand jokes, double entendre or implication. 'It was well known that she was resistant to humour, often had to have jokes explained to her. But she was also indifferent to most of the tricks of paradox, ambiguity, understatement and saying the opposite of what you mean, which pepper the talk of almost everyone else in the country,' according to Ferdinand Mount, one of her former speechwriters (*Cold Cream*, Bloomsbury 2008). Mount calls his time at No. 10, working for MT, a 'holiday from irony'.

Tim Bell, one of the three men responsible for Thatcher's image (the other two were Millar and PR man Gordon Reece), later detailed the delicate situation which arose when he was called upon to illuminate MT upon why she was never to use the term 'pussy' – as in 'The trouble with Mr Callaghan is he couldn't even organise pussy.' 'What's wrong with "pussy", dear? What do you think it means?' she asked Bell, to the delight of other ministers present (*Right or Wrong: The Memoirs of Lord Bell*, Bloomsbury 2014).

'The one thing she definitely lacked throughout her political career was a sense of humour,' agrees Jonathan Aitken (MP for Thanet East 1974–83 and South Thanet 1983–97). 'She was notorious for not getting the joke.' She was especially unamused when she heard on the grapevine that Aitken was making his own jokes at her expense, once dismissing her lack of foreign policy nous with an example, suggesting that the PM thought 'Sinai is the plural of sinus'. 'Erm, no. She most certainly did not find that funny,' Aitken says, ruefully, shaking his head.

Writing for *Psychology Today* (September 2021), Claire Jack PhD, an expert in women with Autism Spectrum Disorder, asserts that people with autism might struggle with certain types of humour because they take things literally and are less likely to engage in laughter purely for the sake of social interaction. 'Perhaps it's not so much that autistic people find things less funny – they may just not respond to the same social cues to laugh at things out of politeness or manners,' she writes.

## AUTISTIC GLAMOUR PUSS?

The unfiltered directness of people who are neurodiverse can sometimes cause them to be unintentionally cruel. Margaret's obsession with appearance often makes itself felt in the letters, with her unsparing descriptions of the way people looked or dressed: 'The new games mistress is not young as we have been used to having. Her name is Miss Dales and she looks about 30'; and 'the history mistress is very disappointing. She is quite middle-aged and very dowdy in dress.' In 1948, she writes about the Colchester landlady with whom she is living whilst working in her first job at British Xylonite (BX) Plastics in Manningtree, Essex: 'To our surprise Mrs Mac [Macaulay] looked completely out of place – in fact, she looked rather tarty – not so much in dress as in behaviour and of course her figure doesn't help.' Later in life MT's directness of approach would make others feel uncomfortable, but leave her unfazed. 'She was utterly incapable of feeling embarrassment. I've seen her say and do things that no other person would,' says Charles Powell, her Private Secretary and foreign policy advisor from 1983 to 1991. Her former press secretary, the irascible Bernard Ingham, once called her 'the most tactless woman I have ever met'. And he spoke as a loyal friend.

She was no more sparing of her sister Muriel's feelings. Many people with an autism diagnosis don't 'do' empathy, in the same way that they don't 'do' tears at the expected moments. (Even those closest to MT can count on one hand the number of times they saw her cry.) Writing to Muriel in November 1948, she references 'Eric… whom you thought was rather nice?' This is likely code for the fact that Muriel has, in modern-day parlance, 'the hots' for the aforementioned Eric. And yet Margaret fails to see how her subsequent words or actions might wound her sister.

'Well,' she continues triumphantly, 'he's coming to supper tomorrow evening.' On the 15th she writes to Muriel again with further details: 'Eric Derbyshire turned out to be a bit of a bore – he's rather inclined to talk as if he's in the pulpit half the time and he's very self-righteous.' A supreme irony indeed, given that this sentence sums up precisely the criticisms that many of her political opponents would level against Margaret, later in life.

These days, there is no shortage of information to suggest that MT may have been autistic. The biggest 'tell' is probably her inability to master social situations. 'Autistic people can find social situations difficult or overwhelming and struggle to make and maintain friendships, leading to social isolation,' says the website of the National Autistic Society. 'Rigidity in the way people with autism can think may make it difficult for them to compromise or cope with changes in routine,' says the charity Ambitious About Autism. According to the NHS, people with ASD may act in a 'different way to other people'. Another characteristic is that people with ASD often find it difficult to understand how other people think or feel.

Margaret's seeming lack of empathy or tact would mean her life would be a lonely one. 'You couldn't get close to her,' Betty Spice, a college mate, told Charles Moore, whilst another described her as 'not easy to know'. 'A great many of her relationships were transactional – she was like a sponge. She would learn all she could and then discard that person. She didn't seem to have a clue about the idea of friendship in the same way that most women would,' says one acquaintance of both Denis and Margaret. Another says that 'outside of politics, she was the embodiment of what young people today would call "awks". Her biggest problem socially, and sometimes politically, was that she could never "read the room".' Indeed, what sometimes came across as snobbish arrogance or coldness was often Margaret's inability to understand quite what to do or say in informal social situations. 'She wasn't one for small talk,' says her former private secretary Caroline Slocock (1989–91). 'But when she was meeting individual members of the public she would quickly get on their wavelength and she could be empathetic and kind to strangers, as I saw once when she was visiting dying AIDS patients.' Anne Hamilton, wife of Archie Hamilton (her former Parliamentary Private Secretary (PPS) and then Armed Forces Minister 1988–93), who spent a great deal of time with MT during her later years, agrees. 'She was actually very happy to chat, but you needed to get her onto something she actually had an interest in or passion for – that could have been anything from getting aid into Romania to historic houses or antique china.'

Throughout her life, MT had been famously short of that vital social emollient, 'small talk'. 'Her absence of small talk was so unusual that I could never quite believe it,' writes Mount. Her former daughter-in-law, Diane Burgdorf, described the entire Thatcher family's attitude to emotions as 'stiff upper lip' and said that MT could not make conversation on a one-to-one basis: 'She would change the conversation to clothes. When she asked me what label I was wearing... I'm not a clothes horse... I'd have to say, "I don't know."' Oliver Letwin, who worked for Thatcher in what he describes as a 'minor apparatchik role' between 1983 and 1986, says that she was in some 'obvious' ways impossible to deal with. 'She would talk over you all the time and you never got the sense she was listening to what you said. But you would later discover she had taken in exactly what you had said. And there were only important subjects. She had absolutely no small talk whatsoever. And I mean none.'

To compensate for her seeming inability to make friends at Oxford and throughout the rest of her life, Margaret would focus on her passions: politics, religion and – naturally – her appearance. This, too, irritated some of the other girls in her college. 'Her preoccupation with her appearance caused amusement. She went to the most expensive hairdresser in Oxford (Andreas) and spent the days during the vac combing the West End for suitable dresses,' complained one. Indeed, she did. And as far as the young MT was concerned there was nothing wrong with that. Alongside politics, fashion was always Margaret's way of making sense of the world. 'The essence of the well-dressed woman should never be exaggerated,' she later told *Vogue* in 1985 (she appeared in the magazine four times in total). 'Appearance is the first impression people get of you. And it does matter. It matters tremendously when you represent your country abroad.'

Another trait of a neurodivergent thinker is to use an obsession or fascination as a distraction or calming tool, in what they may perceive as a 'crazy', out-of-control world. Before what appears to be an important series of four Oxford (perhaps OUCA) evening events, MT writes, hurriedly and without nicety, to Muriel on an OUCA letterhead, which she embellishes with the emboldened acronym 'SOS', requesting, with obvious urgency,

> the pearls because I shall be wearing black two-piece for [event] one and three and black dinner frock for the second... the most important things are the pearls which will have to be sent off straight away – if they are to reach me by Friday. I have been to

a very smart dressmaker here with my velvet and she promised to make it up before the end of term.

'Send <u>*Vogue* when you have finished with it</u>,' she directs impatiently, finishing another letter to Muriel and underlining the imperative. Amanda Ponsonby, who was MT's unofficial lady-in-waiting and officially her Diary Secretary (1983–91), recalls that 'some of the best times were the very rare occasions when we kept her diary free for fittings of dresses and suits. After the sessions, which she loved, she would come down the stairs and be completely relaxed having enjoyed it immensely.' Towards the end of her prime ministerial term, whenever MT became seriously stressed, those closest to her would apparently discreetly place a call to Margaret King. Soon after, King would 'spontaneously' pay a visit to No. 10, under some spurious fashion pretence, to calm and distract the distressed PM. It was King who in effect dressed Thatcher for her final audience with the Queen and the press. 'Denis said, "Can you help? I can't get through to her." I went into her bedroom and she was sitting in a shocked daze. I distracted her with talk about what she should wear and how to do her make-up. She got back on her feet. Fashion always fortified her. It focused her. She loved it.'

Predictably, Margaret Thatcher was held to a different standard to every male politician who had gone before her (and for that matter to almost any male she came into contact with in her role as PM). With the headline 'Tories Choose Beauty' when she was nominated for the seat of Finchley in 1959, the *Evening Standard* opened the floodgates for commentary, judgement and hostility, based solely upon how Margaret Thatcher looked and what she wore, rather than on her policies or achievements. It was one thing for Her Majesty's Leader of the Opposition to be sporting a 'comb-over', but quite another for MT to be greying at the temples. 'I dye it myself,' she told an interviewer, which might have been partially true, but she also had it 'lifted' to an almost Monroe blonde as time wore on, by accomplished colourists. 'It was always to Paul [Allen] on Mondays for a wash and set, Thursdays it was a comb out – this was always in the diary and could not be moved. The colour she would have done in Kensington every six weeks,' says Ponsonby. There's a much-quoted story (which turns out to be apocryphal as far as I can tell) that, such was the hardwired sexism at No. 10 in the early days, MT's advisors decreed that the PM's diary entry should never read 'hairdresser', which they viewed as distinctly 'un-prime-ministerial' – so either Allen's name or simply 'Carmen' (code for Carmen rollers – the brand she used) was entered instead. In fact, the nervousness around her feminine 'toilette' appears to have prevailed only whilst she was in opposition. In her No. 10 diaries, the entry simply reads 'hair'. She herself always said she went blonde to hide the grey, but there was at least a nod to the fact that Denis preferred blondes. His first wife (also called Margaret) had been a blonde, and once MT changed her hair colour, the similarities between Margaret Thatcher and, by then, Lady Hickman, who divorced Denis after six years of marriage in 1948, were striking.

The pressure to 'dress for success' and to appear immaculate was not, and never had been, lost on Margaret Thatcher. From an early age she was the physical embodiment of the infamous Head & Shoulders shampoo advertisement: 'You Never Get a

Second Chance to Make a First Impression.' 'She dressed to kill. Every single day. She was a power dresser long before power dressing was fashionable and she never looked anything less than immaculate. She never for one moment considered the exploitation of her femininity to be a weakness,' says Virginia Bottomley, a Conservative MP from 1984 to 2005 and holder of a number of ministerial roles. But MT didn't always get it right. Her initial forays into the world of parliamentary dressing were less than successful. The reasons behind this were twofold. Firstly, she did not, for all of her slavish 'passion for fashion', come from the social milieu whereby sophisticated dressing was the norm; and secondly, as one of the first global female leaders (Sirimavo Bandaranaike of Sri Lanka, Indira Gandhi in India and Golda Meir in Israel notwithstanding) she was effectively a pathfinder for senior women in the workplace. 'Before there was Hillary Clinton, Michelle Obama or Kamala Harris there was Margaret Thatcher – she literally created the prototype for how a woman in power could and should dress,' says Shirley Soskin, businesswoman and image expert, who was involved with David Cameron's drive to get more women into politics. 'She was the original Boss,' says Robin Saunders, from the US, who became one of the most successful women from the financial sector in noughties Britain. 'We were all watching avidly from the USA – she literally created the "working woman's uniform" before our eyes. And she made us believe that anything was possible.'

In this there was an element of trial and error. For starters there was the hat. It wasn't her fault. When MT first ran for a seat in the 1950s it was still the custom for 'smart' women to wear hats. And wear them she did, from the dramatic black wool cloche she wore while canvassing in Dartford, to her sapphire-blue velvet wedding 'Duchess of Devonshire' number, complete with a vast ostrich feather, to the jaunty straw boater she was photographed outside Parliament wearing on her first day as Education Secretary. The nadir of Thatcher hat wearing came during the early 1970s, when she wore what was described at the time as a 'cream puff' at the state opening of Parliament. She repeated the look later in the year when she was pictured alongside Ted Heath at the party conference wearing a striking black-and-white-striped confection, which rested on the back of her head like a giant doughnut. The hats did nothing for her image – she was fast being labelled as what social historian Wendy Webster (*Not a Man to Match Her*, The Women's Press 1990) identifies as 'Tory Lady in a Hat'. Even with her blinkered focus on 'correctness', MT began to realise the way she was presenting herself would not help her win over her target market – what she termed as 'ordinary working people', and what pollsters and strategists would describe as the influential C1 and C2 sectors of British society. Until Margaret Thatcher came on the scene, these groups had been the Labour Party's bread and butter – the ambitious upper working and lower middle classes, whence she also originated.

It was Gordon Reece, the Tories' Director of Publicity, who finally banned the hats and began to help MT craft her appearance as a political powerhouse. 'Gordon was terrific,' MT explained to TV interviewer David Frost. 'He said my hair and my clothes had to be changed and we would have to do something about my voice. It was quite an education.' It was almost certainly Reece who managed to edge out Dame Guinevere Tilney, who was her unofficial 'dresser' until 1983. Tim Bell explained that 'Guinevere chose Margaret's clothes, which is why, in the early days, she looked like a sort of Victorian remnant, because that's how Guinevere dressed. Guinevere must have been 70 and Margaret was about 50, so you had this 20-year difference – it was hopeless.' This is harsh, even if there's an element of truth in Bell's analysis. In fact, Dame Guinevere, the daughter of Sir Hamilton Grant and the wife of a former Conservative MP, was something of a style icon in her day. She was also a distinguished human rights advocate at the United Nations, with a mission to end female circumcision and arranged marriages. She was introduced to MT in 1973 by Denis, who had apparently played golf with her husband. After Margaret became PM, Guinevere worked unpaid from a desk in the corridor of No. 10 until 1983. She was honoured by MT the following year.

Tilney's daughter-in-law, Juliet Hunter-Tilney, describes Dame Guinevere's relationship with MT as one of mutual respect. 'They liked one another. She advised Margaret on social niceties, etiquette, what to wear, things like that.' Thatcher made liberal use of Dame Guinevere's jewellery, which was generously made available to her, including brooches and a stunning necklace created out of an old tiara. (MT was never above borrowing from other people and later would appear at events wearing her own trademark pearls – a gift from Denis – having borrowed a brooch, a bracelet, a ring, or sometimes all three, from Margaret King.) Her standard jewellery – a large amethyst ring and a 'hard stone' pebble and gold bracelet – she wore with almost talismanic reverence, on her right hand and wrist, regardless of whether she was also wearing a borrowed Cartier diamond parure to a state banquet. 'Guinevere did think that Margaret had style, but she also thought it was not quite right. She was certainly not shy or retiring and I'm sure she gave Margaret a lot of unasked-for advice, which is probably what led to Margaret respecting her,' says Hunter-Tilney. The two went on diets together – famously one before MT's much publicised first tour of China, where she was photographed still wearing a vast broad-rimmed hat, but also deftly handling chopsticks. 'She had to slim down, so I had to show her how to do it,' commented Dame Guinevere. It was probably also Guinevere who suggested MT wear a daring long, floaty red chiffon Granville Proctor evening gown for a speech to the Finchley Conservatives on 31 January 1976, where she and her speechwriters had adroitly capitalised on a description of her by Yuri Gavrilov which had recently appeared in the Soviet newspaper the *Red Star* (and was later used by Tass). 'I stand before you tonight in my Red Star chiffon evening gown, my face softly made up and my fair hair gently waved, the Iron Lady of the Western World.'

Let it not be said that Margaret Thatcher merely 'wore' pussy-bow blouses. In the BMT (Before Margaret Thatcher) era pussy bows had been seen on a 1935 *Vogue* cover, in the designs of Coco Chanel and Yves Saint Laurent, and on movie stars from Ingrid Bergman to Grace Kelly. But it was MT who created the direct link between an innocently feminine twist of a silk or satin necktie and global power dressing. Since then, the pussy-bow blouse has been worn by everyone from Lady Diana Spencer to Nancy Reagan, Melania Trump and Kamala Harris (who wore her white version whilst accepting the first nomination of a black woman to the vice presidency in 2020). Samantha Cameron, wife of then PM David Cameron, even wore a stylish, modernised version of a Thatcher outfit from her own label Cefinn to MT's funeral as

## AUTISTIC GLAMOUR PUSS?

a mark of respect, complete with cream silk pussy-bow blouse. Meanwhile, in 2025 cutting-edge rapper, singer, producer and poet John Glacier wears a pussy-bow dress in the video for her single 'Ocean Steppin".

Thanks to MT, these days the pussy-bow blouse is a fashion metaphor, an item which says 'I mean business' with greater clarity than a sandwich board – or at least it did until Liz Truss wore it. MT apparently thought the bow a feminising and flattering addition to her increasingly monotone style of dressing, another Thatcher fashion choice which has been utilised by women across the globe, from Merkel to Meloni to Rayner and now Melania Trump. 'It's terribly important to have quite a wardrobe of attractive blouses,' MT told *TV-am* presenter Anne Diamond in an interview on 17 March 1984, which she gave during London Fashion Week specifically to show her support for the British fashion industry – she was the first PM ever to do so.

> I think we haven't quite taken it seriously enough. It is a very big employer. It's a very big exporter and with some very creative people doing excellent work. I want to show how much we appreciate them, how much we value them. Other governments do that. If you go to France, you know, you'll find all government ministers absolutely behind the fashion industry and we haven't somehow done it to quite the same extent here.

Thatcher's enthusiasm, which grew from childhood when she learned dressmaking skills at her seamstress mother's knee, is palpable on screen, as she and Diamond enter into a lively discussion on the PM's passion for clothes and she describes the 'enjoyment' of travelling to and from the dentist because, along the way, she's able to window-shop on Regent Street from her chauffeur-driven car.

Later that evening, she would throw open the doors of No. 10 for the first-ever Downing Street fashion week reception (a tradition which has been continued ever since). It was here that the PM, dressed strikingly in a long, black velvet two-piece, complete with chequerboard pussy-bow blouse, was introduced to a scruffy, trainer-wearing young designer called Katharine Hamnett, who was wearing a large T-shirt she'd smuggled into the reception (and then presumably changed into in the loo) bearing the slogan '58% Don't Want Pershing'. The incident was striking for many reasons, not least because Hamnett undermined the very premise of supporting her own industry by stealing the show and any available media coverage (which she ultimately then had to share with Thatcher). Whilst the papers portrayed it as an Extinction Rebellion-style 'action', reflecting a European opinion poll showing that 58 per cent of Brits did not want the American missiles stationed on British soil, Thatcher seized the moment with aplomb, shaking hands with Hamnett and beaming for the cameras. What did the two talk about? Hamnett later boasted that MT had let out a shriek of horror (which seems highly unlikely) and told her: 'We haven't got Pershing. But we've got cruise [missiles], my dear. So maybe you're at the wrong party?' Hamnett was either too preoccupied to pick up the masterful Thatcher put-down or it passed her by.

Long before Margaret King transformed MT into a style icon in 1987, MT had created for herself, by trial and error, a 'working woman's wardrobe' of a type that had never been seen, or called for, before. In this she was ably aided and abetted by her personal assistant and dresser Cynthia Crawford, whom Thatcher nicknamed 'Crawfie', possibly after Queen Elizabeth II's beloved nanny. Crawfie met Thatcher in 1978 whilst working for Conservative donor David Wolfson, and she swiftly became MT's 'mistress of the robes' and much more besides. It was Crawfie who began the ingenious practice of recording MT's outfits under the names of where they had first been worn, to differentiate them (there were, for example, many navy blue suits). 'We might say, "We'll take Waddesdon Navy"... Waddesdon was where she took Mitterrand, and they had a wonderful meal.' Thus, there was the Madrid Pink, the Prague Green, the Wogan Red and so on. It mattered not only what Margaret Thatcher wore, but how and when. People noticed. Other leaders noticed. Only two other women had ever had such sustained global political prominence: Elizabeth I and Elizabeth II. Whilst the former Queen had unrivalled political power, she was at least spared the unyielding glare of the media spotlight. The latter, meanwhile, lacked any political agency and thus could afford to dress and act as she pleased. It was Britain's good fortune that she chose to do both with such grace and style.

Margaret, meanwhile, was literally making it up as she went along and her biggest 'power dressing' inspiration was perhaps the redoubtable, perennially elegant redhead Barbara Castle (Labour cabinet minister, MP for Blackburn from 1945 to 1979 and ardent women's rights campaigner), who recorded in her diaries that 'in my political life I always found men vulnerable to a little femininity and many are unable to cope when it is combined with some mental ability and with what is considered a masculine strength of will'. Legend has it that Castle was once interviewed at home wearing pink fluffy mules and drawing seductively on a cigarette, complete with holder. She also owned a wig called 'Lucy' for days when she couldn't make it to the hairdressers. She had a penchant for skirt suits in strong colours, silk blouses, bows tied at the neck, statement jewellery and structured handbags. Sounds familiar? As well it might. In fact, MT had more than just female political advancement or fashion leadership to thank Barbara Castle for. Had it not been for her, a ladies' loo (infamously named 'Barbara's Castle') situated hard by the Commons chamber might not have been in existence by the time MT reached Westminster in 1959.

'There were chic working women before Margaret Thatcher – women like Barbaras Cartland and Castle in the 1950s and Marcia Falkender in the sixties. But really by the late 1970s there was still no workwear at all,' says Lisa Armstrong, Fashion Director of the *Daily Telegraph*. 'When Margaret Thatcher came to power the fashion was entirely inappropriate for her purposes, with the weird midi-length dresses and leg-of-mutton sleeves.' Armstrong adds that during her time in office, especially during the early days, people regarded MT as a frump. 'But now when you look at it you see that her look has aged incredibly well. Lots of women might even say that today her image is quite contemporary. Certainly, her style still influences fashion today.'

Margaret described the theory behind her working wardrobe to Anne Diamond as

> Suits with quite a lot of blouses and then also if you're travelling overseas and you arrive by aircraft, I do find it much easier to

arrive with a coat and dress outfit. For a very simple reason: the moment you get on the aircraft you hang up your coat and then you can put it on just before you get off and you're not full of creases. So that means I've got to go really for a basic wardrobe of good 'tailoreds'.

Think of almost any businesswoman, female politician or public figure and you'll find shades of Margaret Thatcher's theory of dressing somewhere within her outfit. From Sheryl Sandberg, the former Meta Platforms boss, to Christine Lagarde, Angelas Rayner and Merkel, Giorgia Meloni, Michelle Obama, Rachel Reeves, Ursula von der Leyen, Emily Maitlis, Victoria Beckham and the current Queen of the Pussy Bow, Catherine, Princess of Wales. The dilemma of what to wear to work is one with which any woman who has worked in a high- or even a low-profile job will be familiar. 'I have to be in my Sunday best seven days a week,' she told Diamond. 'If ever there was a day when I was wearing something old and not very nice, you can guarantee that would be the day someone important came to see me.'

Barack Obama alluded to the unique dilemma of all world leaders by admitting that he wore similar versions of grey or blue suits each day, because he was 'trying to pare down decisions'. Thatcher's appropriation of gendered 'male'-style suiting for her own means approached sartorial genius, whether you appreciated the way she did it or not. Critics criticised her 'manliness', which they saw reflected in her policies. It would, by this measure, have been quite acceptable for a man to look, behave and legislate in the same way as MT without fear of recourse or recrimination. 'What a lazy, easy option to describe or portray Margaret Thatcher as a man in woman's clothes,' says Shirley Soskin. 'It illustrates just how difficult it was to be a trailblazing woman at that time. And the criticism and satire didn't just come from men. Let's not forget that often women were not, and still are not, very good about supporting other women.'

Her style also presented a gift to Peter Fluck and Roger Law, creators of the immensely popular satirical puppet TV show *Spitting Image*, who portrayed her almost as a transvestite. 'As she became more strident, the puppet became more manic and manly… we were astonished how much outrageous stuff went to air with no problems,' Roger Law wrote in *The Guardian* (17 April 2013), which perhaps says more about the political persuasions of the powers that be at broadcaster ITV than it does about MT. Law also admitted to his own inverted snobbery. 'She was a lower-middle-class petit bourgeois. I come from a similar background and understood the enemy. She was, therefore, much easier to caricature than the bog-standard upper-class, self-deprecating, slippery politician.'

'That "handbag" became a verb during Margaret Thatcher's time as PM, and it became a verb that was pejoratively associated with female power, means that handbags became an important way for people to come to terms with the extraordinary power that Thatcher had. Extraordinary for a woman. Completely unextraordinary for a man,' commented historian and author Ludmilla Jordanova (*The Look of the Past*, Cambridge University Press 2012). Of course, it's likely that for MT a handbag (much as she liked and collected them) was just a handbag – in as much as it was an everyday part of her wardrobe – albeit one she once referred to as 'the only leakproof place in Downing Street' and on another

## AUTISTIC GLAMOUR PUSS?

occasion as her 'weapon'. Her speeches were written on paper specially sized for the handbag, and ministers were known to dread the moment when she popped the clasp and withdrew a note or a newspaper clipping. 'You'd give her a note and think she hadn't noticed it. It could be weeks and weeks and then suddenly you'd be in a meeting and she'd say, "I have here a note," and it would be the one you'd given her. Of course, then she'd quote liberally from it without acknowledging you at all,' says Oliver Letwin. Writing in *The Guardian* in 2013, Cynthia Crawford spoke about the IRA bomb which went off in the early hours of 12 October 1984 in the Grand Hotel, Brighton, targeting the Conservative government, including Thatcher, who were resident for the party conference.

> Everybody was in a terrible state. We were all just packing up. I think it went off at 2.50am. Somebody said: 'What are we going to do with the speech that she was due to give the next day?' We decided we would put it in the handbag – that was the safest place. Anything that was highly secretive or precious, we would put in her handbag because we knew she was never parted from it.

Was it a coincidence that MT's favourite handbags – made by Launer London – were also the choice of the monarch? Unlikely. She famously revered the Queen's no-nonsense style and restrained good taste, which reflected that of most upper-middle-class, headscarf-wearing, wellington-booted women, who carried their Launers in a particular way: straps over one arm, rather like a waiter would carry a napkin, exposing the tell-tale gold ampersand-style branding. In the two weeks after MT died, the company reported that sales of their Bellini and Adagio models (her favourites) had doubled. Most importantly for the British press, the handbag was a gift for lazy male cartoonists whose bread and butter during the Thatcher era was illustrating her in various locations, guises and states of undress, clobbering her enemies with a large handbag. 'Shall we start?' one wag is reported to have asked the entire cabinet, who were waiting impatiently around the table for MT to appear and staring at her Launer, which was already in situ: 'The bag is here.'

Jordanova's exploration of MT's handbag is part of a wider study in which she considers how historians might engage with pieces of visual and material evidence. The 'Thatcher handbag' of which she writes is housed at Churchill College, Cambridge – home to the archives of the man himself and by comfortable and credible association (since he was her hero) those of Margaret Thatcher too. This handbag – a workaday structured blue faux crocodile leather number – was not, as Margaret Thatcher's posthumous message states, 'used every day during my time at Downing Street'. We know from multifarious photographic evidence that this was not the case. However, the handbag, complete with its make-up bag containing a Clinique Colour Surge lipstick No. 211 Vintage Red, a Clinique green marble plastic compact with bronze powder and sponge still intact, two eyeliners (one unbranded in silvery brown, the other a black Boots No7), and two neatly pressed handkerchiefs – one white embroidered with grey silk thread, the other pink and edged with cream embroidery – offers an insight, not just into the daily routines of our first female PM, but also into the misogynistic, sexist narratives that still plague museums and archives, seeking to make choices around the preservation of historic women's items (fashionable or otherwise). As Jordanova points out, when the archive was first offered the handbag the then archivist was quoted as vehemently refusing it: 'This is a storm in a handbag. It is ridicule and reticule. We haven't got any handbags and as far as I know, we are not going to get any handbags. We are in the business of conserving documents.' Today, Margaret Thatcher's handbag is one of the most popular items in the archive and its metaphoric meaning is all too well understood, particularly since the term 'to handbag' (in the sense of to verbally assault) became a new Thatcher-generated verb, in or around 1987. The archives manager of the Thatcher Papers, the remarkably knowledgeable and helpful Andrew Riley, is these days only too happy to celebrate its place in global political history.

'Margaret Thatcher's handbag is almost certainly our best-known artefact – the allure of the bag and its contents seem to cut across all social and political boundaries,' says Riley. He estimates that the bag has been viewed by approximately 8,500 visitors to the Churchill Archive in the past two decades. Additionally, the loan of the bag to external organisations, in Cambridge, London and Germany, has generated some 350,000 further viewers. (The protective containers which allow for the safe viewing and storage of the handbag and its former contents have already been renewed three times.) 'Once unveiled, the handbag usually generates a buzz of excitement leading to the inevitable request for a photograph,' says Riley.

A different dilemma, this one with overtly political rather than sexist overtones, faced the Victoria and Albert Museum when in

# THE INCIDENTAL FEMINIST

2015 some 300 items of Margaret Thatcher's clothing were put up for auction by her estate. When a representative from the museum was quoted by the *New York Times* as stating that 'the V&A has politely declined the offer of Baroness Thatcher's clothes, feeling that these records of Britain's political history were best suited to another collection', the outpouring of anger – from the *Daily Mail* to the *FT*, from Boris Johnson to Vivienne Westwood – was palpable. Westwood, who famously loathed MT's politics but admired her style (once convincingly dressing up as her for a 1989 *Tatler* magazine cover), stated: 'She was certainly in her lifetime the best-dressed woman. She had terrific taste. It would be lovely if the V&A showed her clothes.'

The museum, which describes its mission as 'to be recognised as the world's leading museum of art, design and performance, and to enrich people's lives by promoting research, knowledge and enjoyment of the designed world to the widest possible audience', clarified that the conversation had actually taken place some years beforehand (which didn't really add up). Today the story remains much the same. The museum has on display two pieces of clothing owned by the world's first female to lead a G7 and the originator of twentieth-century power dressing. 'If she were someone known for her fashion wardrobe we might collect more,' says curator Oriole Cullen, who says that the museum actually has six articles owned by Margaret Thatcher but that for copyright reasons only two could be displayed. Hardly public service.

If anyone can take credit for the evolution of the Iron Lady into Margaret Thatcher, global style icon, it is Margaret King. In 1987, the then director of Aquascutum (and the only female board member) received a call from her boss saying: 'She's asked for you again.' King – a unique study of poise and elegance herself, now aged ninety-something, and glamorous in chic black pants, a white blouse and Chanel-style jacket – remembers the moments distinctly. 'I said, "I've just come back from Paris – I'm exhausted – please send someone else." I was, I'll admit, rather cross.' The chairman's response – 'No, she is asking for you specifically' – meant that King had to repack a large suit carrier and hotfoot it over to No. 10 Downing Street.

It had been a while. The two had first met when King had designed a silk dress for Thatcher's first trip to Paris in 1979, for her meeting with President Valéry Giscard d'Estaing. King had created quite the impression, telling MT in no uncertain terms that the coat she wished to buy from Aquascutum for the trip did not suit her. But Thatcher did not hold grudges, except where attacks on her family were concerned (and one on her hairy knees, for which, read on). Thus, when Tilney decided to retire, MT's thoughts returned to King.

Margaret King had been watching Tilney and her dressmaker Daphne Scrimgeour's attempts to shoehorn MT into Jaeger, Jean Muir and Mansfield. She'd thought improvements could be made:

> When you are in fashion you can quickly see what works on someone and what doesn't. I thought she's going to be amongst a lot of men, so she needs to both fit in and stand out. So I conceived of business suits, which did not ride up around the waist. This effectively ironed out her silhouette.

# THE INCIDENTAL FEMINIST

King used solely British fabrics, buying tweeds, for example, from Linton Tweeds in Carlisle, also patronised by Coco Chanel (and still in business today). Downing Street sent lists of forthcoming events and trips. King and her secretary meticulously prepared folders for the overseas visits with swatches of fabrics, to ensure the PM knew which outfit to wear and when. Suitcases were packed in the right order of events, to ensure nothing went wrong. Lists were provided, detailing which accessories went with which outfit. For Middle Eastern countries, King switched out the short skirts for ankle-length versions, using the same jacket styles, all in fine wool crêpe. Often there would be several rapid clothing changes in one day.

The initial 1987 call was a request for King to design all of the coats for Thatcher's groundbreaking first official visit to the Soviet Union to meet President Mikhail Gorbachev. King had just four days to create a showstopping wardrobe for a global event. She had a meeting with MT's redoubtable press secretary, Bernard Ingham, formerly a Labourite, and analysed the key moments that she was designing for.

> Bernard told me there was going to be a moment where the world's press would be gathered at the airport for her historic arrival. At which point she'd be expected to exit the aircraft and walk down the steep steps, to greet Gorbachev on one side and the press on the other. I knew it was critical to get this right in fashion terms.

King was given licence by Aquascutum's chairman to have unfettered access to their fabrics and the company's chief pattern cutter.

## AUTISTIC GLAMOUR PUSS?

Her vision was a kind of Julie Christie in *Doctor Zhivago* meets Sigourney Weaver as the boss in *Working Girl*. King had Thatcher rehearse her arrival in Moscow endlessly, using the stairway to MT's private No. 10 exit as a stand-in for the plane steps.

> She needed to lift her head when walking down the steps. Previously, all of the pictures had her scurrying down, looking at her feet. My approach was that she should, like a model, keep her head up, so that the hat did not sink into the coat and so that she was seen to best effect.

Raw ITV footage of MT's Soviet Union trip between 28 March and 1 April 1987 highlighted the beginning of two 'beautiful' friendships. One between two politicians from opposite sides of the political, cultural and geographical divides; the other between two women who instinctively knew to trust one another. King worked on MT's physicality as well as her style choices, persuading her to change her awkward gait. 'I said, don't bend your knees so much and appear in so much of a hurry. Swing your legs from your hips.'

As a result, an extremely chic MT, wearing an immaculately tailored black coat, topped with a Philip Somerville fox-fur hat, was photographed arriving in Russia. Underneath she wore a fitted black skirt suit with a silk pussy-bow blouse (of which, coincidentally, King did not approve as 'they were not really my thing') and her trademark pearls – an outfit she revealed to the flashing cameras as she strode elegantly into the Kremlin, to be officially welcomed by Mikhail and Raisa Gorbachev (accompanied only by an interpreter), their voices echoing around the vast reception hall, hung with golden chandeliers.

# THE INCIDENTAL FEMINIST

On a subsequent day, the footage shows MT visiting an enormous housing project and supermarket in Moscow's Krylatskoye District. This time, thousands of Russian citizens trailed her every move and Kremlin security men protected her from the enthusiastic crowds who flocked in droves to witness this historic female leader, craning out of windows, waving, clapping and cheering wildly. Thatcher, clutching a bouquet of long-stemmed pink roses and wearing her camel cashmere coat with its stranded mink collar and a pair of eye-catching white, high-heeled boots, as directed in a series of written instructions prepared by King, pauses every few minutes to greet people from the crowd. Earlier in the day she'd worn the coat complete with another Somerville confection, seemingly inspired by those worn in the film of *Doctor Zhivago*, to visit St Sergius Monastery in Zagorsk, where she told one reporter that the singing reminded her of a Welsh choir.

On and on the immaculate display of good taste went (although King makes the relevant point that the dresses and suits were MT's choice), each coat detailed in a memo by King. Underneath there was a black lace dress and pearls for *Swan Lake* at the Bolshoi, or a navy suit and green and white blouse for the signing of bilateral agreements with Gorbachev along with Soviet foreign minister Eduard Shevardnadze and his British counterpart Geoffrey Howe. For a farewell photocall with Raisa and Mikhail at the Kremlin, MT appeared in a strikingly feminine purple, pink and blue flower-petal-patterned silk day dress with a long string of pearls, shepherded by a retinue of heavies and saluted by soldiers standing guard at the Kremlin entrance wearing blue and gold. One small, feminine blonde, stalking the red carpet like a runway in her smoky grey tights (a King must-have) and higher than usual

## AUTISTIC GLAMOUR PUSS?

court shoes as she advanced towards the couple, stating, 'I can't thank you enough.' Celebration hung in the air. Together they had pulled off a historic peace mission – and she, for one, had done it in style.

Plaudits followed for both MT and King. 'The PM called me as soon as she landed. "Have you seen the press?"' says King. 'She was very pleased.' It was the beginning of a partnership which would last long after the PM was ousted from office. Were they friends? 'I think so,' says King guardedly, 'but you must understand that I don't think anyone aside from Denis was really able to get close to her.' From then on, she guided MT's fashion choices, and in doing so had a window into the intimate life of Britain's first female PM, which included her ups as well as her down days. 'People speak of her phenomenal energy, but so many times, in the course of dressing her, I saw her completely deflated and exhausted, yet she could dress up and turn it back on again when required,' reports King. MT's ability to isolate herself from what was going on around her in order to think through an issue was legendary. King witnessed the phenomenon many times.

> We'd be talking and suddenly she would look down and cut herself off from everything – she'd be thinking hard about something else or how to deal with a situation. The conversation would stop and you'd wait for a while and then she'd snap right back into the conversation where she left it. It was like a temporary shutter came down. Once you got used to it you'd know it would come back up again.

# THE INCIDENTAL FEMINIST

So successful was MT's makeover, and so noticeable her third-term 'late blooming', that *Vanity Fair*, then the American society and Hollywood bible, led by the renowned British editor, Tina Brown, sent a request for their chief marksman, Gail Sheehy (author of the influential *Passages* in 1976), to interview her for her tenth anniversary in government. Remarkably (and likely flattered by the recognition and attention that America's glossiest magazine wanted to afford her), MT agreed to a sit-down conversation at No. 10 with the journalist and author whose past 'conquests' had included exposing the infidelity of Gary Hart – a potential presidential candidate (but no longer after Sheehy had finished with him). She would later take on Mikhail Gorbachev and Hillary Clinton.

Did Sheehy dig any dirt? Not especially. 'She looks younger and prettier... It's as if she's allowing herself a second girlhood,' she writes, and she counts as MT stands at the despatch box, rocking gently as she makes her points, with 'one slimly shod toe pointed at the floor behind her other foot' – 24 times in fifteen minutes.

Like everyone else, Sheehy wants to know exactly how she does it. That is, maintains the energy to take on the pack of braying, snorting, red-faced and mostly grey-haired men who sit beside, behind and in front of her during Prime Minister's Questions, which she attends on a twice-weekly basis. Not to mention running the nation. We are after all in the pre-gym, post-Jane Fonda era wherein breaking a sweat was still perceived to be unladylike for a woman in Thatcher's position. The most exercise she will have taken will have been bustling along the corridors of power and walking to and from her chauffeur-driven limousine. Even the swimming pool at Chequers (the PM's country residence, a gift from a former British ambassador to the United States) was off limits. MT didn't like to muss her hair and, in any case, she'd had the pool decommissioned the minute she discovered how much it cost to run.

> People are both polarized and mesmerized by the Thatcher phenomenon. Even her most ardent critics, after an hour or so of venting spleen, sit back with a little sigh of awe and say, 'You can't help but admire the energy of this engine, but you can do nothing to change its direction,'

Sheehy writes. And then she offers gossipy details to her readers: MT exists on vitamin C, coffee and royal jelly (she certainly took vitamins sent to her monthly by her friend and admirer, the prolific novelist Barbara Cartland); she has had her teeth capped (an earlier phenomenon and in part the culprit for her elongated vowels), her eyelids lifted (she almost certainly had some of the skin in her upper lids reduced at some point) and her varicose veins removed (in 1982). What captures Sheehy's imagination most is Thatcher's interest in Ayurvedic electric bath and mud treatments, which she says the PM has relied upon 'in recent years'. Sheehy interviews 'Madame', the woman behind the treatments, and her detailing of the PM supposedly disrobing and immersing herself in a floral-oiled hot bath, through which would pass '.3 amps of electricity', naturally captured the imagination of the world's press. News of Thatcher's 'electric baths' quickly crossed the globe from LA to Delhi to Sydney. To say that MT was outraged is an understatement, although the famously terse Bernard Ingham restrained himself with the simple statement that the interview had been 'a waste of time'.

# THE INCIDENTAL FEMINIST

MT regarded the published Sheehy interview as an invasion of her privacy. Throughout her career she had resolutely resisted any attempt to portray her as anything other than perfect and inviolable, where her image was concerned. She was far more affronted by the release of personal details than she ever was by the rough and tumble of politics. And she never forgot a slight by another female, regarding it as a personal betrayal. This is best illustrated by the journalist and editor Vicki Woods, who, as editor in chief of *Harpers & Queen* (and, full disclosure, once my boss), landed a photoshoot with the retired MT for her 'Best of British' issue. The fashion stylist on the shoot had observed close up that MT had not shaved her legs. Woods (another woman not to be trifled with) went on to write an article about the power of our former first female PM, also mentioning her 'unshaven knees'. When the phrase attracted headlines, Woods knew she was in trouble. Years later when Charles Moore — a friend of Woods — ignoring her protestations, attempted to add her to a guest list for a celebratory dinner he was throwing for MT, he received the following response from her private secretary, regarding Woods' attendance: 'There is no persona less grata.'

That Margaret Thatcher was vain and receptive to flattery, there is little doubt. (If she hadn't been she would never have agreed to Sheehy's interview — she certainly didn't need to do it.) Neither was there any question about whether she would have been prepared to suffer for beauty. She suffered agonies over her teeth after having them badly veneered in the early 1980s, and spent valuable time and thousands of pounds trying to have them put right throughout her administration and beyond. Indeed, they altered the way she spoke (again) and from then on she would sound as though she was wearing slightly oversized dentures. This was and is never more apparent than when she is reading the audiobook of her autobiography (during which her famous inability to pronounce particular words, particularly 'foreign' ones, is also evident – she pronounces Buenos Aires 'boones airees'). Later in her retirement she would refer to President Putin as 'President Pewtin'. She disliked watching herself on TV to the point that she would leave the room, or turn off the set if she was scheduled to appear. The intensity of her dislike of seeing pictures of herself in the media intensified, as it does for most of us, with age. 'Phew,' she once said to a guest at a reception, having glanced at her watch, 'I've just finished appearing on TV.' Unlike her friend Nancy Reagan, she resisted having a facelift. 'My face hasn't fallen that far!' she once said in 'outs' from a TV interview (although her jaw, in her seventies, looked suspiciously sculpted). Had she been alive today she almost certainly would have given in to the relentless battering to which women are now subject via social media, and had a 'little work done'. And she would have thought nothing of it – with her binary perspective, she would have viewed it as a simple solution to fix an unavoidable problem.

'Mrs Thatcher expressed in her persona exactly where working women stood in the 1980s: on low-heeled court shoes and in tailored suits that were a carapace of protection in what was still essentially a man's world,' wrote the then journalistic doyenne of fashion, Suzy Menkes, in the *New York Times* a few days after MT's death in 2013. 'Yet she once told me that being elected to the International Best Dressed List in 1988 – as an influential role model "of classic middle-of-the-road elegance" – was "one of the greatest moments of my life".' Menkes adds that she 'didn't dare to ask whether the others were being elected as the first female Prime Minister, having her twins or winning the Falklands War'. It was probably all three.

# 2

# The Mother Complex

> This mother–child bond is the greatest bond in the world.
> MT, quoted in the *Washington Examiner*

Happiness for Margaret Thatcher was Grantham in the rear-view mirror of Denis's sports car. Behind her she left everything she feared and despised: the everyday ordinariness of the small, grey, middle-England town where she grew up, the oppressive patriarchal dominance of her parents' marriage, the suffocating Victorian values of her live-in grandmother, the small-minded, bitchy snobbery of 'the posh girls' in her class at Kesteven and Grantham Girls' School, to which she had won a scholarship just before her eleventh birthday. But above all she rejected the miserable, hopeless dejection of her mother's lot in life, which was, in Margaret's words, to be 'in the kitchen, always in the kitchen'.

Margaret ran from Grantham, and most especially from her mother, Beatrice – known as 'Beaty' – daughter of a railway cloakroom attendant and seamstress, for her entire life. 'She didn't like her mother, I think that is pretty clear if you look at the written evidence, and I think that may have affected her attitude toward women throughout her career,' says Caroline Slocock, a private secretary to MT from 1989 to 1991 and author of *People Like Us* (Biteback 2018). Early in her political career, MT dismissed Beatrice as little more than a 'char', describing her in a 1974 radio interview as 'very much the Martha rather than the Mary', referring to a passage from Luke 10, which emphasises the importance of a listener, Mary, versus a doer, Martha. In 1975, she told the magazine *Woman's Own*: 'I loved my mother dearly, but after the age of 15 we had nothing more to say to each other. It wasn't her fault, she was weighed down by the home, always being in the home.' The implications are clear: those with superior brains and a mission have the capacity, as she did, to go on to great things; those who are intellectually less able – well, they tend to the house and do little more. 'I used to feel, just occasionally,' Margaret Wickstead, an old friend of fifty years' standing, told *Vanity Fair*'s Gail Sheehy, 'that she rather despised her mother and adored her father.'

After Margaret left her parents' home – the flat above their grocer's shop at North Parade on the wrong side of town – for Somerville College, Oxford, in 1943, she rarely returned. To buttress herself against the ridicule and disdain of the class-ridden British society into which she would not only journey but spend the majority of her life, she artfully constructed an 'acceptable' tale about her background, ignoring her mother and mythologising her father. 'She spoke incessantly about "Daddy" – Daddy the Mayor of Grantham rather than Daddy the grocer of Grantham – repeated what Daddy thought of this and that, what Daddy said she should do and how she should behave, and the books that Daddy said she should read,' writes Penny Junor. But after she left home MT cut her father loose – speaking or writing to him only occasionally and visiting him infrequently. And yet, the more senior she became the greater the story she spun about him as an iconic figure in her life, which, as it turns out, was more of a myth than a reality.

Margaret's stubborn refusal to acknowledge her mother was at least in part because she was embarrassed by her. But she also felt guilty. Why? Because she'd abandoned her mother to a fate which the young Margaret Roberts could not herself countenance. The reality was that Beaty, also a seamstress, was trapped in the bone-numbing domesticity of a loveless marriage. It would be thus for the rest of her life. 'The point about Thatcher,' Beatrix Campbell, activist and author of *The Iron Ladies: Why Do Women Vote Tory* (Virago 1987), told Julie Gottlieb, Professor of Modern History at the University of Sheffield in an interview for the *Women's History Review* (June 2019),

> was that she never affirmed powerful women, and she didn't intervene against women's relative powerlessness – she did not connect with women as women. It is routine to locate her political inspiration in her father, a Tory alderman. But I think it is equally important to address what Thatcher might have taken from her mother – the mute, downtrodden, perhaps depressed servant to the Thatcher household, the proverbial doormat. Thatcher was not inspired by her mother. To have connected with women would have taken her to pain and subordination. And perhaps to feminism. That she would not do.

In the social stratum from which Margaret Thatcher originated, there were only two ways out: intellectual success or a good marriage. She achieved both.

Margaret Thatcher was certainly not born to be Prime Minister. In fact, as historian Wendy Webster points out,

> Margaret Thatcher could scarcely have been 'born to be a politician', when in 1925, the year of her birth, British women had been enfranchised for only seven years, women politicians were virtually unknown, there were only eight women in the House of Commons, no woman had ever served in a Cabinet and women had still not won the vote on the same terms as men... A woman prime minister was quite out of the question before 1919, virtually out of the question between the wars, and most unlikely in the 1950s.

Beaty — uncharitably described in one account as 'a right old battleaxe' and by one of Margaret's schoolmates as 'homely' — gave birth to Margaret, her second child, in a bedroom above their grocery shop on 13 October 1925. Life for the Roberts girls, born in 'Britain's most boring town', between the wars was dark, dull and cold. Without an indoor bathroom, with only coal fires to heat their flat and a stern, black-clad Victorian maternal grandmother — Phoebe Stephenson — hovering to ensure their strict Methodist value system was enforced at all times, the two sisters spent their days, when not at school or doing their homework, helping in the grocery store, weighing and brown-bagging items like sugar and tea. Sundays dictated attendance at Finkin Street Methodist Chapel, three times per day if you included Sunday School. On

Sundays, Phoebe decreed there were to be strictly no games, books or entertainment (for which read fun) at any time.

Their father Alfred, a Methodist lay preacher, alderman and later Mayor of Grantham, who had left school at thirteen, was often out of the house, travelling between Lincolnshire villages by horse and cart to preach at local chapels, leaving the girls to the ministry of Beaty and Phoebe, a former below-stairs worker at Belton House, a grand old country pile owned by the Brownlow and Cust families. She died when Margaret was ten. There is no record that any of the girl's friends ever visited the flat. Margaret Thatcher wrote in her autobiography that

> Life wasn't to enjoy yourself – life was to work and do things. I would like some things to have been different. For instance, on Saturday nights some of the girls at my school would go to dances or parties. That sounded very nice, but my sister and I didn't go dancing.

'I know her upbringing: it was humble and mine was not dissimilar,' says Gillian Shephard, MP for South West Norfolk 1987–2005, a junior minister towards the end of MT's period in office and the daughter of a Norfolk cattle dealer. 'Education was definitely a means of advancement for both of us, but I think I probably had more fun than her. But then I don't think fun was ever on her agenda – by all accounts she was pretty serious from the start.'

Margaret told biographer Patricia Murray (*Margaret Thatcher*, W.H. Allen 1980) that her school friends would all do more entertaining things. 'They went out with other people where there was laughter and fun. We always went to serious things, or laughter and fun was at the church social, it wasn't at the village hall where everyone had a dance.'

Music and studies were Margaret's form of escape. She regarded her parents' religion as oppressive. 'I could have done with less church,' she once waspishly said, but for her it was the music which was the saving grace. 'It was, I confess, the musical side of Methodism which I liked best,' she writes, expressing a sadness that at sixteen she gave up music lessons in favour of cramming for Oxford. 'I still regret that I never took up the piano again.'

The signs that Margaret and her mother would never see eye to eye were writ large from early on. The young Margaret was almost certainly as confrontational with Beaty as she was with her headmistress at Kesteven and Grantham Girls' School, Miss Gillies, who, when trying to make clear to the sixteen-year-old Margaret that she thought she was too young to go to Oxford the following year, was met with an obdurate expression of frustration: 'You're thwarting my ambition!' Biographer John Campbell (*Margaret Thatcher* 2 vols, Jonathan Cape 2000/2003) is in no doubt that Margaret had a well-hidden aggressive streak from an early age – much more so, he says, than her father.

> Margaret's temperament was much more combative, more divisive. Both politically and socially she saw the world in black and white and divided people, institutions and countries ruthlessly into sheep and goats: 'us' to be encouraged and rewarded, 'them' to be defeated and destroyed. This crusading quality she did not learn at her father's knee.

# THE MOTHER COMPLEX

The question is, where did the aggressive streak come from? It was likely present from early on, but later it would blossom into a (mostly) beneficial character trait. 'She was in some ways impossible to deal with – you always felt that you were the subject of immediate hostile interrogation, but as you got to know her you understood that this was her only way of getting to the truth,' says Oliver Letwin. Arguing had always marked Margaret out from the crowd.

As a teenager, Margaret's frustration with her parents and the way she lived is palpable, both in her early interviews and in her autobiography, though she tries to conceal her feelings. She speaks, for example, of the frustration she feels over her parents not allowing her to visit the cinema more often, 'which really brightened my life'. Of course it did. In grey Grantham, a town bifurcated by the main London-to-Scotland railway line, which ran almost next to the Robertses' home, blighted by post-war gloom and restrictions, what else was there? The answer was evidently very little. 'My first distinct memory is of traffic,' MT writes in her autobiography. 'I was being pushed in a pram through the town to the park on a sunny day, and I must have encountered the bustle of Grantham on the way.' Soon we learn that her childhood lacked any spontaneity or fun for fun's sake: '[My parents] felt that entertainment that demanded something of you was preferable to being a passive spectator. At times I found this irksome, but I also understood the essential point.'

During a 1985 TV interview with Miriam Stoppard (one of the few lengthy interviews granted to a female journalist by Thatcher), the uncomfortable dynamic which existed between Margaret and Beaty is tangible. When Stoppard asks about the restrictions placed upon her by her mother whilst growing up, Thatcher visibly flinches and tries in vain to force a smile. 'Of course one kicked against it... I would like some things to have been different.' By 'some things', she meant everything that young girls might hope to experience in their early years: playing with friends, attending parties and she and Muriel having the simple freedom to enjoy each other's company.

In the Roberts household there was no time for 'play', which would have been regarded as something indulgent even if they had found a few spare hours: 'I was born into a home which was practical, serious and intensely religious,' she writes. She remembers trying to escape from one of the Sunday services which she and her sister were expected to attend by asking if she could go for a walk with friends. 'Never do things just because other people do them,' her father responded. 'This was one of his favourite expressions – used when I wanted to learn dancing, or sometimes when I wanted to go to the cinema,' she writes. 'Whatever I felt at the time' – which was likely disappointment, twinned quite possibly with unexpressed rage – 'the sentiment stood me in good stead'. In good stead for what? For politics, of course, but ultimately her father's advice would prove fatal. 'Margaret would decide on something and then go full steam ahead without brooking any form of discussion. Ultimately that's what led to her downfall,' one then junior colleague told me.

It is puzzling that Muriel, Margaret's older sister by four and a half years, was not chosen by her father to be groomed for success. The answer is likely to be found in the fact that the sunny Muriel lacked Margaret's singularity of purpose (for which read neurodiversity) and showed far less interest in schoolwork. In 1975,

## THE MOTHER COMPLEX

in a rare interview, she told the *Daily Telegraph* that at school she regarded Margaret as a 'nuisance' because she was always being held up by her teachers as an example. Charles Moore, writing in *The Spectator* on Muriel's death in early December 2004, described the relationship between the sisters as reminiscent of 'those bits in the Sherlock Holmes stories in which Sherlock's brother Mycroft... is even more brilliant than the famous detective, but has no inclination to pursue the thing full-time'. Received history also has it that the sisters were not close, but a glance at any of the letters that they wrote to each other suggests that this is not true. Muriel went to train as a physiotherapy nurse prior to the Second World War and she and Margaret corresponded regularly, although Margaret often played down her relationship with her sister. In 1982 Margaret even spoke of Muriel in the past tense, almost as though she were dead. She tells DJ Pete Murray in a radio interview: 'I had one sister, Muriel, she was older than I was.' 'I think that Muriel definitely felt Margaret had written her mother out of the script and also to some extent that she had written Muriel out too,' says Charles Moore.

Was Margaret, as is so often posited, the son that Alfred Roberts never had? 'Yes,' she told Patricia Murray, 'I think he did try to realise his ambitions in me.' Muriel's fate (or perhaps her lucky escape) was not to be designated by her father as an outlet for his own intellectual pretensions. 'It was all church, church, church,' Muriel told Charles Moore, in an uncharacteristic burst of resentment over her upbringing. 'We had an uncle every Christmas who sent us religious books. Oh God, how we hated it.' Whilst the young Margaret, described by one acquaintance as a 'quite solid, chubby teenager with rich brown hair', was being taken by her father to 'extra' lectures at Nottingham University on a Thursday evening to listen to the learned espouse their theories, or being drilled in the dark arts of debating, or even swotting over her homework late into the night, Muriel's childhood continued seemingly on a much more traditional trajectory.

As a result, she would spend more time at home with her mother, and the two remained close, with Muriel nursing Beaty before she died of cancer in 1960, whilst Margaret was effectively absent. Muriel's warm personality underlined the stark contrast with Margaret, whose precocity was summed up by a fellow pupil at the school:

> [She was] a very clever little girl who was quite unafraid… to ask questions at the end of a public lecture. She could 'use' words correctly at a far earlier age than most of her schoolfriends and she seemed to know more about the world at large and what she wanted to do than most of her contemporaries.

When Muriel left home aged seventeen it marked the beginning of another phase in the already ambitious Margaret's life. In Muriel's absence she would grow closer to her father and increasingly isolated from her mother. 'Perhaps the main interest which my father and I shared… was a thirst for knowledge about politics and public affairs. We read the *Daily Telegraph* every day, *The Methodist Recorder*, *Picture Post* and *John O'London's Weekly*,' she writes.

We know that Margaret Thatcher often claimed to idolise her father. The question is why? Alf might have been clever (although we don't have any proof that he was) but he was certainly not enlightened. Here was a man who had never travelled (he didn't fight in the war for medical reasons), had no interest in art or literature and certainly didn't generally regard women other than his daughter as being up to much. His wife was an entirely subservient, housebound creature, who left the home only to attend chapel or sewing meetings and spent her entire life scraping by, whilst her husband spent freely on buying a sister grocery store at the other end of town and a smart new delivery van in which Margaret would sometimes hitch a ride to school, long before he even considered that his family might benefit from an indoor loo or running hot water.

Margaret told one interviewer that Alf was 'the best-read man she'd ever met'. This seems highly improbable given the luminaries she would meet throughout her career and it suggests an entirely blinkered approach to her six-foot, aloof, shrewd, dominating father, who rarely cracked a smile in female company. Or was her retrospective 'canonisation' of Alf as an intellectual, who could have given any Oxbridge don a run for his or her money, merely a smokescreen, constructed to cloud his humble beginnings and make Margaret a more acceptable parliamentary candidate? Was her underlying message: 'I might not have come from the right class, but at least I hail from clever stock'? After all, her USP was her intellectual capabilities, although some had their doubts. 'She was manifestly a competent equal of the men around her,' says John Gummer (Conservative Party Chairman 1983–5 and appointed Minister of Agriculture, Fisheries and Food under MT in 1989), 'but I don't remember ever thinking, "Gosh, that's a clever woman."' Gummer, who says that 'you couldn't work with Margaret unless you understood that she was challenging and needed handling', will, however, concede that MT had 'an acute mind and strong principles'. Charles Powell says that MT was always ahead of the game: 'one only needed to scrawl across the top of her papers one principal question and she would immediately grasp the essential issue and analyse it – nothing came back without more notes and questions. I think she felt that as a woman she needed always to be one step ahead.'

The Robertses never went on holiday together as a family. Because the store needed to be manned at all times (or at least that was their excuse), Beaty would take the girls to Skegness, where they would stay at a self-catering house which she thought was much better value than a hotel. Alf would take his holiday once they had returned, with every intent of playing bowls every day and smoking up a storm, which was 'very bad for his chest', worried the young Margaret. When they spent any time together Alf focused on his daughter's debating skills rather than his wife's needs. 'We were taught to argue… You never forget. You must make up your own mind. You must learn to examine things. You must learn to think about them,' MT told Stoppard, before emphasising: 'Mummy didn't get involved in the arguments.'

Every Saturday, the young Margaret was sent to the library to collect two books: one, for him, would be about current affairs of the day, and one would have been, according to her, 'perhaps a novel for my mother; and we always read those books, as I got older. We read the books and we always talked about them.' No wonder she took a dim view of most women's abilities with an early role model like Beaty. The relationship between Margaret and her mother happens to fit neatly into one aspect of Swiss psychiatrist and analyst Carl Jung's Negative Mother Complex, whereby a daughter feels compelled to excel in intellectual activities where her mother has no place. 'Its real purpose is to break the mother's power by intellectual criticism and superior knowledge, so as to enumerate to her all her stupidities, mistakes in logic, and educational shortcomings. Intellectual development is often accompanied by the emergence of masculine traits in general' (Jung, *Archetypes of the Collective Unconscious*, 1969). Alternatively, French psychoanalyst and feminist Julia Kristeva theorised that the eternal conundrum for women was that if they identified with their mother they were excluded and marginalised by the patriarchal order, but if they identified with their father or 'made themselves in his image' then they ended up supporting the same patriarchal order that had excluded their mother as a woman. Where MT was concerned, both theories seem equally valid.

Throughout Thatcher's career and even after her death there was speculation that Alf was not as upstanding as his smitten daughter made out. Rumours about his treatment of other women swirled when a satirical novel called *Rotten Borough*, based in Grantham and written by local author Oliver Anderson under the pen name Julian Pine, first appeared in 1937 (it was republished in paperback in 1989 by Fourth Estate). Featuring a 'naughty' councillor, 'a Grocer in a Big Way of Business', who one evening 'thought he would have a Bit of Fun with one of the Young Ladies who Served behind the counter', only to forget to 'draw the Shop Blind' and expose his 'Unusual Business' to several of the townsfolk, the book was a satire on small-town life with particular focus on the council and the upper echelons of Grantham society (if such things existed). The implication would be preposterous, were it not for the fact that, as biographer, amateur Freudian analyst and politician Leo Abse points out, the book was swiftly withdrawn from the market under threat of legal action from many of the town's most prominent people including an MP and an earl. In 1997, the rumours resurfaced when satirical magazine *Punch* ran a story by Professor Bernard Crick, who alleged that Alf was a serial abuser of young women who worked in his shop. 'We're not saying this has been established in a court of law. We thought we should check it out further,' said editor Paul Spike, adding: 'People have been talking about this but no one has been willing to run this until now. Crick has been talking about it for decades – he's a known, responsible figure.' Indeed Crick, a biographer of Orwell, was at the time Emeritus Professor of Politics at Birkbeck College, University of London. *The Independent* followed up the story with quotes from Grantham locals including a 74-year-old woman who told them she had been molested on frequent occasions by Alderman Roberts when she worked at his shop, aged fifteen. Another elderly resident confirmed that two of her cousins who had worked for Roberts at the shop had also suffered similarly. 'He was forever pinching their bums when they bent over – and looking up their skirts.' In 2007 Carol Thatcher condemned a suggestion that had been made in *The Guardian* in 1988, at the time of the book's republication, that the grocer in *Rotten Borough* might have been a caricature of Alderman Roberts, 'my grandfather', calling it 'another false narrative'. But in 2013, Moore also drew attention to the rumours in the first part of his official biography, featuring quotes from Grantham locals including Mary, the sister of Kenneth Wallace, a friend of Margaret's from her teen years, who stated that Alf Roberts 'touched women in a way completely uncalled for'.

# THE MOTHER COMPLEX

For Abse, Margaret Thatcher's domineering, hectoring approach was likely a direct response to the severe, emotionally barren parenting mostly executed by Beaty and her black-clad Victorian live-in grandmother, Phoebe Stephenson. Whilst Abse's book, *Margaret, Daughter of Beatrice* (Jonathan Cape 1989), was aptly reviewed by the *London Review of Books* editor, Mary-Kay Wilmers, as 'slander by psychoanalysis', within the 250 pages of cod Freudian analysis there are some relevant points to be made. For example, Abse posits that MT 'brutally repudiates her mother by suppressing her very existence… she simply describes herself as the daughter of *Alfred*'. Indeed, MT traces her parentage through the patriarchal line twice in print: once in *Who's Who* and also in the *Sunday Times Magazine* in 1973. 'She fantasises herself,' says Abse, an author never happy to use simple vocabulary when tortuous psychological terms were at hand, 'as an autochthonous Adam.' This is, of course, all grist to the popular theory that MT was effectively a man in a skirt, which would be offensive were it not so binary.

There's little doubt that MT was in search of a different and 'bigger' life than that of her mother. She was not alone. The lot of most 1950s women of Thatcher's era and class was that they were trapped by their marriages, and by their lack of education and societal expectations. As *The Guardian* aptly put it in its summing up of feminist Betty Friedan's bestselling book, *The Feminine Mystique*: 'The core message in [her] landmark work is this: being a housewife sucks.' Few would disagree. Despite the fact that she often stated that 'the job of a mother is the most important in the world', Thatcher never walked the walk. By the time her twins were out of nappies, she was out of the door and back in the workplace. And by the time Friedan's groundbreaking feminist treatise was published in 1963, Margaret Thatcher had already made her escape permanent. She'd been an MP – representing Finchley in North London – for four years. It was a position she would hold for 33 in total. Would Beaty have approved? She died in 1960, just one year after her daughter became an MP. Margaret never wrote about nor even mentioned her mother's response to her daughter's elevation. Perhaps there wasn't one?

'Thatcher has never brought to bear her own experience as a critique of the patriarchal family and of the conditions of most women's existence. She hasn't taken her own mother's side and she hasn't taken other women's side,' writes Beatrix Campbell. It's a sentiment which is hard to argue with, but that's certainly not how MT would have seen it. The role of 'mother' is not one she wanted to undertake exclusively. In *The Path to Power* she wrote that 'to be a mother and a housewife is a vocation of a very high kind. But I simply felt that it was not the whole of my vocation. I knew that I also wanted a career.' Then she cited a much-loved quote from Irene Ward, MP for Tynemouth: 'While the home must always be the centre of one's life, it should not be the boundary of one's ambitions.'

Margaret Thatcher's approach to women in the workplace was clear: do as I say, not as I do. 'She has reworked the story of her life, remoulding it to fit an "ism" that bears her name but which she does not fit herself... Within Thatcherism there is no room for a woman like her,' writes Wendy Webster. Bringing up her own children was left to nannies and housekeepers most of the time, and both went to boarding school – Mark aged eight to Belmont

School and Carol aged nine to Mymwood, the prep school for Queenswood Boarding School in Hertfordshire (she would later move up to Queenswood and then on to St Paul's Girls' School in London). Thanks to Denis's salary and her own, the Thatchers were able to afford it. 'I was very fortunate that everything bounced right,' she acknowledged on more than one occasion. On a 1981 ITV Judith Chalmers show, a female audience member asked the question: 'Some of your senior colleagues have expressed... or seem to be expressing some doubts about the value of wives working outside the home. Surely you can't actually agree with this?' She was referring to Thatcher's Social Security Minister George Young, who had stated, presumably with her approval: 'In general I do not accept that it is the state's job to provide day care to enable parents of young children to go out to work.'

Thatcher tried to defend the statement by saying that the Conservative Party didn't want 'some women feeling guilty if they don't have a job as well as running a home'. Perhaps she'd forgotten that in 1972, as Education Secretary, she'd pledged that 'within ten years, nursery education should become available without charge to children of three or four whose parents [wish] them to have it'? Although, even in embracing the concept of nursery education, she had also been at pains to add that the purpose was 'to enable children to learn and not to provide a day-care service', thereby reinforcing the Tory view that women were 100 per cent responsible for the family's domestic life and, worse still, refusing to acknowledge the direct link between childcare, education and a woman's right to return to work. 'It's easy for a professional woman who's earning quite well to pay for extra help in the house, and that of course does not apply to most women,' she agreed in the ITV interview, before suggesting patronisingly that women who had been out of work for a while and wanted to return could 'make arrangements with other women who also want to go out and do a little bit so that you can keep in touch for half a day a week… if you've been a doctor do some voluntary work.' She finished with a plea which, given her own particular situation, was pure hypocrisy: 'I beg, I beg, I beg, never put the children second.'

The Conservatives were not the first party to focus on early education – it had been on the agenda since the Wilson government published the Plowden Report in the 1960s calling for universal nursery education. A 2017 report written by the Labour MPs Caroline Flint and Sharon Hodgson for the Fabian Society entitled 'Childcare: Ensuring a Good Start in Life', which analysed two decades under the Thatcher and Major governments, stated that

> at the tail end of their 18 years in office, the Conservatives had few coherent policies aimed at tackling disadvantage or poverty. They failed to see patterns of intergenerational poverty. They knew that more women wanted to work, but failed to see the lack of affordable childcare as a barrier to women's aspirations, or as a mechanism to achieve equality in the workplace. By the mid-1990s, less than two thirds of women had entered the workforce, and growth had plateaued.

To judge her by her own standards and those of the 1970s Tory Party, Margaret Thatcher was neither a 'good mother' nor an advocate for childcare, allowing women to enter the workforce. It seemed she had learned little from the lessons of her own mother's style of parenting. Some said she rejected them entirely, by indulging her children in an attempt to compensate for being absent. 'My mother, who had grown up in a frugal and very purposeful household, told me when I was grown up that she had wanted her children to have the opportunities she hadn't had,' writes Carol Thatcher (*A Swim-on Part in the Goldfish Bowl*, Headline 2008), describing how MT had allowed her children the luxury of riding lessons, choosing the wallpaper for their bedrooms and making Sunday church optional.

Margaret did not, in the manner of most modern-day politicians, seek to judiciously shield her children from publicity. In fact, she often encouraged it, allowing pictures to be taken of them with her from an early age – eager to show the media that she was a 'present' mother. Later she would help them in other ways which would be frowned upon today – for example, allowing Carol to accompany her on official foreign trips and, it was said, 'smoothing' Mark's passage into various business deals and working environments. But she was not a 'warm' mother. 'The Robertses are not very good at feelings,' her niece, Jane Cullen, told Charles Moore. 'They deal with facts and reality.' But MT worried about her children nonetheless: 'Things which were said about her never bothered her, but she used to get very upset if something negative appeared in the press about her family, particularly about Mark,' says Stephen Sherbourne, her political secretary from 1983 to 1988. In 1995, she told MP Michael Spicer, 'If I had my time again, I wouldn't go into politics because of what it does to your family.'

The paradox, of course, is that whilst MT acknowledged what her mother 'lacked' and then repeated the pattern, she was also only too happy to embody Beaty's non-threatening traditional 'stereotype' when it was required for political gain. 'Any woman who understands the problems of running a home will be nearer to understanding the problems of running a country,' she would proclaim with relish, implying that matters of state were in some way tantamount to a visit to the butcher's, or that balancing the housekeeping and an economic summit were tangentially related. Being the daughter of a housewife, then, allowed Margaret Thatcher a non-threatening edge unavailable to those of the opposite sex – in the early days of her political career at least. And whenever she needed it, she would slip back into domestic mode and dialogue. 'Pennies do not come from heaven, they have to be earned here on earth,' she told London Weekend Television in 1980, as if preaching to her children before handing out their pocket money.

There is plenty of evidence that the experience of growing up as the child of Margaret Thatcher was not easy. In the 2019 BBC documentary *Thatcher: A Very British Revolution*, Robin Butler, her Principal Private Secretary from 1982 to 1985, revealed that, such was her emphasis on 'looking right', MT had once made the teenage Carol hide in a closet to avoid him seeing her wearing jeans. Charles Powell was direct in his assessment, telling the documentary makers that 'the challenges of being a mother and Prime Minister were considerable and, to be perfectly frank, she rather failed. She didn't have time enough for her children. She rather overindulged Mark when she perhaps underindulged Carol.'

'Look, she was a great PM and a terrible mother,' states one No. 10 advisor; 'there isn't another way to put it.' Jonathan Aitken witnessed the situation first-hand when he began dating Carol in 1976. The relationship lasted for approximately three years.

'I think, as a result of her own parenting, she [MT] longed to be a good mother herself and… she overdid it for Mark and underdid it for Carol – she was much more critical of Carol, who was very hurt by that,' he says. 'But then, it simply wasn't possible for her to be around all the time – she was far too busy, all of those late nights at the House, writing speeches or attending dinners.'

However guilty she might have felt privately, publicly MT presented a much more pragmatic view of motherhood to the world. 'Look, you can't have everything,' she told *Saga* magazine.

> It has been the greatest privilege, being Prime Minister of my country… Yes, I wish I saw more of my children. We don't have Sunday lunch together; we don't go on holiday skiing any more. But I can't regret. And I haven't lost my children. They have their lives. I took a different life.

Her children rarely, if ever, complained. As Carol writes,

> Having both parents working was the exception in the 1950s and '60s, but it was the norm in the Thatcher family. It was a thoroughly modern partnership and way ahead of its time. Looking back, I am in awe of how they did it. They left the nitty-gritty of running a household and caring for twins to our redoubtable nanny. Neither of my parents was hands-on in in the way that successive generations have become.

Her father Denis, who spent most of his spare time refereeing rugby or playing golf, famously resisted undertaking any form of childcare, other than bowling cricket balls to Mark in the garden.

'For God's sake, teach them some manners,' he once barked at the nanny, after a particularly difficult road trip with the children. Both Carol and Mark declined to be interviewed for this book. 'I think they are over it,' says a friend. 'There's just been too much exposure and they never think it ends well.' Days later, Carol appeared on Times Radio for a full hour being interviewed by journalist Matt Chorley, during which she happily regaled him with tales of being the child of Britain's first female PM. Mark Thatcher called me at the behest of a mutual friend. 'We don't need the publicity,' he said, before adding: 'But I was close to my mother. Very close. There were special things that I would do or say to make her feel better if I thought she was feeling down – of course I'm not going to tell you what they were.' A source from inside No. 10 at the time confirms this:

> Yes, he was her favourite and yes, he was always a support to her – he could cheer her almost like no one else. He was very helpful to her. I know she felt that, especially during times of crisis like the Falklands. But he was also her Achilles heel. She was blind to his faults.

Robin Butler says: 'Later, I think she felt very guilty about being a neglectful mother.' Anne Hamilton, wife of PPS Archie, who became a friend of MT during her latter years, says:

> The moral of the story is that you can't have a sensational career like Lady Thatcher had and have an amazing family life – the two are not complementary, if you work and travel all the hours that she did. I know it's an unfashionable thing to say but when

you are raising children to a certain degree it's got to be you doing it.

'Carol became a great friend. She and Denis were very close and they both had a tremendous sense of fun. They were always sneaking out without the security detail. Mark was quite another matter,' says Charles Powell, possibly referring either to Mark's reputation for creating trouble or to his grandiosity. Others have been less oblique. 'Carol was a very nice lady. I won't say the same for the son. He treated us, the advisors and speechwriters into whose meetings he would occasionally wander, as if we were inferior beings, like something bought in by the cat, not worth bothering with,' says one advisor. 'He was the type of bloke who used to insist on an extensive security detail every time he landed in the UK – and for what? All it did was to take up police time and cost the taxpayer money. It was his mother who mattered, not him,' says another. 'There were some difficulties relating to Mark which made it impossible for him to be involved in every aspect of her day-to-day life,' says one source close to the family tactfully.

This could, of course, refer to any number of Mark Thatcher's exploits – from getting lost in the Sahara Desert during the Paris–Dakar Rally (during which time his mother, according to Carol, writing in her autobiography, 'fell apart' and was 'completely unable to function') to various media accusations that his business deals were benefiting from his mother's stellar worldwide reputation.

In 2004, after numerous questionable business deals had been reported by the press over preceding decades, Mark Thatcher appeared to have involved himself in another 'problematic' enterprise. This time he was really at the sharp end. He was arrested at his then home in South Africa for allegedly helping to finance a coup in Equatorial Guinea. A year later, he pleaded guilty to charges related to the coup attempt. He was not charged but received a four-year suspended jail term. It was said (although never officially confirmed) that his mother had paid his bail and that she also later paid the fine which he received in lieu of a jail sentence and in return for a plea bargain.

When she went public about the end of their marriage in 2006, Mark Thatcher's first wife, Diane, who divorced him on the grounds of irreconcilable differences, spoke at length to the *Daily Mail* and the *Evening Standard* about Mark's relationship with his mother.

> His mother doted on him. Soon after we married, we visited Downing Street and Lady T handwashed all of Mark's shirts, pressed them and folded them neatly in little plastic bags for travelling. Mark used to refer to moments like that as 'little spurts of mothering'. He would say to me: 'Oh, she had a spurt of mothering today.'

In the articles, Diane effected a 'demolition job' on her ex-husband, which in fairness to her she claims to have resisted for twenty years. She relented, she said, in the interests of closure and to show him 'that Christian humility does not include being his personal doormat'. She doesn't hold back, attacking what she claims was his 'infidelity, his controlling behaviour'. She states he determined the appearance of both the interior and the exterior of their houses – he would replant the flower beds before his mother came to stay. She digs the dirt on his offshore accounts, his secrecy, his 'repressed anger', his rudeness, his hatred for cats ('he just couldn't understand pets') and his need for an English butler, which was, she said, 'totally pretentious. [The butler] hung out at the house and served at dinner parties, which we always had catered, but the rest of the time I didn't know what to do with him so I would have him go grocery shopping.'

Fatherhood, she says, did not come naturally to Mark. 'Having grown up with nannies, Mark had a favourite expression he'd use about children, which was: "Those things come with nannies."' It was a statement redolent of the tones of his father, Denis. Above all, Diane makes clear that, where her son was concerned, Margaret Thatcher had a monumental mothering blind spot: 'I think Mark had been in awe of his mother since he was a child and he obviously ran the women in his life past his mother to get the prime ministerial approval. If she hadn't approved of me, I think he would have dropped me.' Lady T, she says, would never use the word 'divorce'. 'She never talked about Mark's infidelity… we both knew what had happened. He was still her "blue-eyed boy". We spent family gatherings with her but it was a formal relationship. The Thatchers are a very articulate family, all wonderful conversationalists, but as far as emotions go, it's that stiff upper lip.'

Carol, who was always thought to be closer to her father, was never particularly overt about feeling any resentment over her mother's preferential treatment of her brother – at least during her mother's time in office. 'Mark had hung an "Occupied" sign on the family's Embarrassing Relative slot,' she writes in her autobiography. She cheerfully details that her mother was often so preoccupied that she 'fell to calling me by her secretaries' names, working her way through them until she reached "Carol"... I was never the Chelsea teenager whose mother waited for her to come home before the decreed curfew. In fact, it was the other way around,' she continues, explaining that her mother would return home at breakfast time, if the House had been sitting through the night. 'You can't be as nervous as me,' chided her mother, when the two met at the breakfast table before one of Carol's final exams and Margaret's leadership election, as though it was a mother/daughter contest. Amongst the other details Carol shares are that her mother was permanently distracted. 'When my mother wasn't reading legal briefs [during her time as a barrister], she pored over bulb catalogues.' MT paid little attention to culinary niceties for the family. Once at No. 10 she narrowly escaped setting the place on fire by forgetting she had a boil-in-the-bag meal on the gas stove top. For the record, though, why should she have been invested in mealtimes? It's stating the obvious, but this would never have been a criticism levelled at male leaders.

In later years Carol admitted life had been tough at University College London, where she was studying law. 'They'd say, Carol, we're just going off to demonstrate against your mum. Can you tell us where her office is?' It was no coincidence that, as soon as she could, Carol escaped Britain for Australia, where she lived a life of relative and welcome obscurity for four years, working at the *Sydney Morning Herald*.

Later, she returned to London and had a successful career as a journalist with the Conservative Party paper of record, the *Daily Telegraph*, where her surname can't have hurt her career. 'Everyone thought she was very nice, fun and easy to deal with,' says a fellow *Telegraph* journalist and editor at the time, adding as an afterthought, 'though her copy did always need a bit of an edit.' But what did editing matter when Carol had such unfettered access? She parlayed her maternal and paternal connections into two books: one about her famous father, *Below the Parapet* (HarperCollins 1996), and the other, which she freely admits she dreamed up herself, an account of following her mother on the campaign trail, called *Diary of an Election* (Sidgwick & Jackson 1983). There were rumours that MT disapproved of Carol living 'in sin'. 'She had never felt that her mother accepted either her choice of a career or lifestyle,' said Diane Thatcher. 'Lady T definitely is a moral woman, a Christian. She has never approved of Carol living with the Swiss ski instructor Marco Grass.' In 2023, Carol married Grass. Her mother would have been delighted.

Carol's personal media victory came later in life when, aged 52, she participated in the reality TV show *I'm a Celebrity… Get Me Out of Here!* At the close of the show, watched by 12 million people, she was voted 'Queen of the Jungle 2005'. She had eaten grubs and a fish eye and swum amongst biting snakes and poisonous cane toads, and worn a large Perspex ark on her head containing rats, beetles and cockroaches. 'Nothing prepared me for the public outpouring of goodwill,' she wrote, as though in shock over her positive publicity. Her mother, writes Robin Harris, was immensely proud. 'She did not watch every episode, and friends ensured that she avoided some of the less tasteful bits, but she was glued to the screen for the final and was ecstatic at Carol's triumph. She was equally proud of the way in which she turned her success to financial advantage.'

As Harris also reports, the rapprochement between daughter and mother which had been brought about by Carol's 'adventure' was short-lived. In Carol's autobiography in 2008, she had written about her mother's declining mental condition and had used the word 'dementia', which prompted headlines around the globe. The result was that MT received even fewer invitations to private functions, and questions were raised about her competency to sit in the House of Lords. Her staff, who had initially kept the serialisation of Carol's book in the *Daily Mail* from her, eventually gave the newspaper to her to read. As Harris tells it, she was 'shocked at seeing in print facts about her condition which she only half acknowledged, but above all wounded by the thought that her own daughter could behave in such a fashion'.

In 2009 Carol admitted to Bryony Gordon of the *Telegraph*, 'I always felt I came second of the two. Unloved is not the right word but I never felt that I made the grade… I've written books. I won *I'm a Celebrity*. But nobody will ever know me for being anything other than Margaret Thatcher's daughter so at the end of the day, whatever I did was never good enough.'

The supreme irony, of course, is that whilst Margaret Thatcher rejected her own mother and to some extent her own daughter, her unstoppable rise to the top was predicated on her initial ability to appear (at first glance) to be a non-threatening, domesticated, hat-and-glove-wearing Tory wife and mother, upholding essential Conservative values and reinforcing the same stereotype she was seeking to escape. 'What people don't realise about me is that I am a very ordinary person who leads a very normal life. I enjoy it – seeing that the family have a good breakfast. And shopping keeps me in touch,' she told the *Daily Mirror* in 1975. 'The role from which Mrs Thatcher fled, the role of her mother, whom she has obliterated from her story, is exactly the role which

Mrs Thatcher envisages for most other women,' wrote Wendy Webster.

The truth is that Margaret Thatcher didn't think other women could or should be like her. Whilst she chose not to admit it, she considered herself 'outside' the realms of normal womanhood, perhaps even superior to it, all the while eulogising the benefits of it for others. Leo Absé wrote that

> on the doorstep I have met so many women who fiercely react against Thatcher... These are women who resent being lectured to by a woman who constantly tells them of the importance of the housewife, that the family is the centre of the universe, and the home the centre of the woman's life, when they sense or know that her whole life belies her declared commitment.

But there was perhaps an even greater advantage to MT's domesticated, non-threatening, capable, 1970s 'Nice Mrs T' persona – and that was where her male cabinet members were concerned. She'd realised early on – possibly whilst at Oxford and also probably later by witnessing Denis's relationship with his own mother – that upper-class men idolised, some might say canonised, their mothers, but by the same token they feared and respected them too. Being raised by nannies and sent away to all-boys schools, sometimes as early as the age of five, will do that to a man. This guaranteed the sort of obeisance that Britain's first female PM would require in order to get things done. 'Certainly, she knew how to exploit that public-school resistance to fight with a lady,' says Charles Powell. 'She did think the sexes were different but she thought women had a more realistic world view,' says Charles

Moore. 'And to that end her message was very powerful. She could do things the men wouldn't do — she wasn't above holding up shopping baskets and framing things within the domestic sphere, which is of course where the untapped female voter lived, and she used this to her advantage.' David Howell thinks that, on top of this, her timing was critical:

> We were in this era where a general feeling of defeatism prevailed and along comes this very clear, decisive woman who seems to know what's what and gives out the general feeling that all the men around her were useless and has an aura that's she's going to take the whole lot on: the cabinet, the Labour Party, the trade unions — of course, the country loved that.

Once in power, MT would play the maternal card when circumstances required. It was a winner because it conveyed that most humane of political sensibilities and the one she most famously lacked — empathy. Oftentimes, friends say that she was sincere and compassionate, especially in private. And that when tears finally fell, they were genuine. She sobbed over the loss of 'our boys', as she called the British forces during the Falklands crisis.

'I know for a fact that she was up all night in tears at the 321 deaths,' wrote Tim Bell, of the controversial sinking of the Argentine cruiser *General Belgrano*, outside the agreed exclusion zone. The tragedy, spun by the tabloids into a 'victory', gave rise to *The Sun*'s infamously crass front-page headline of 4 May 1982: 'GOTCHA – Our lads sink gunboat and hole cruiser', which ran together with a picture of the sinking ship. The newspaper's proprietor, Rupert Murdoch, had purportedly sanctioned it with the phrase 'it seems like a bloody good headline to me'.

Rather less significantly, but possibly more tellingly, Howell remembers MT sobbing uncharacteristically in the early days of campaigning for the 1979 general election (which she would go on to win).

> We were in the Crest Hotel in Bolton – all of us, her advisors, were gathered round. We had to tell her that the *Evening Standard* had published a poll saying we were five points behind. We were telling her things really didn't look so good and, to our surprise, she began to cry, saying, 'Oh, I thought I was doing rather well.' Carol, who was with her, put her arm around her and said to us all, 'Look what you have done to Mummy.' The evening ended very badly and the tigress who emerged later was not visible then at all.

Caroline Slocock writes of her experience in August 1989 accompanying MT on an informal visit to Mildmay Mission Hospital in the East End of London – the first AIDS hospice in Europe. Some 800 people per year were dying of the disease, and the number would rise to 1,800 a year at its peak in the mid 1990s. The intention was for the visit to take place without photographers or reporters, and MT and Slocock met two AIDS patients who were introduced with the most cursory of medical briefings. What shocked the young Slocock was not only the tragic plight of the patients – 'I have never been at the bedside of a dying person before' – but also MT's response: 'She comes across as more of a mother than a prime minister... she is above all, kind – loving even.' Both patients were in the advanced stages of the disease – one was delusional because the virus had attacked his brain. 'Margaret Thatcher is unfazed and behaves as if she has all the time in the world... It is simple human stuff, but I am in awe of it.' Slocock later learned that one of the patients had died alone (neither had had the courage to tell their families that they were gay or that they had the disease) so she left MT a note with the news. The PM did not respond with her customary underlining or swift jottings across the top of the note. Instead, she remained silent. Slocock posits that 'she just did not know what to say'. (MT's files reveal that she had sent a handwritten note and a cheque for £1,000 from her personal bank account to the hospital.)

Her mothering skills, however, were in evidence amongst her staff at No. 10. 'We adored her. We all cried when she left. We just couldn't believe it,' one permanent member of staff confided to me in 1991, much to my astonishment, as she served me tea whilst, as a young journalist, I waited in the White Drawing Room to interview Norma Major. Our conversation, during which the tea lady detailed MT's solicitousness to her staff, stayed with me because it was so at odds with the former PM's public persona and my own perception of the woman I had resisted voting for. 'The less senior you were, the kinder and more motherly she was towards you,' says one aide. 'She absolutely loved the Garden Room Girls [the group of secretaries who supported the No. 10 staff, so named because of the proximity of their office to the Downing Street garden].' 'I remember very well bumping into a secretary in the corridor of No. 10,' says Stephen Sherbourne. 'She was new and we'd hired her from the Palace. When I asked her how she was getting on, her eyes widened. "The PM," she declared, "talks to me! I still can't believe it. At the Palace NOBODY talks to you!"

During the IRA bombing of the Grand Hotel in Brighton on 12 October 1984, where the Conservative Party were staying before the party conference, Oliver Letwin recounts that he was awoken by what he describes as a 'loud noise', to sleepily discover that his bedroom no longer had a window and that most of the front of the building was missing. 'That was when I thought I should probably get out.' He made his escape down the fire exit, following Keith Joseph 'in his paisley dressing gown and carrying his boxes'. A few hours later, as he was wandering, dazed, back to the conference hall in borrowed clothing, a member of the PM's staff rushed over to Letwin. 'Thank goodness I've found you; the PM has been very concerned,' he said. 'I was very struck by this,' says Letwin.

> It showed her for the person she really was. Somebody had tried to blow her up, she'd been taken miles away to a safe house for the night where she hadn't slept, she'd had to completely rewrite her speech, find some clothes and then return to the conference again to give the speech. And yet she found time to worry about me.

'She could of course,' he adds as an afterthought, 'be utterly maddening.'

Being both a successful mother and an impressive PM was and, in our patriarchal society, seemingly remains an impossible quest, given the strictures and expectations placed upon the conflicting ideals of 'good motherhood' and 'great leadership'. Post-Thatcher, this theory has, of course, yet to be tested. Our subsequent two female PMs have been Theresa May, who served for three years and has no children, and Liz Truss, the mother of two teenage girls, who served for only 49 days. It is also partially true that it was only by harnessing the vocabulary of maternal domesticity that Margaret Thatcher was initially able to succeed, by winning over that most vital of voters, the C2 female (and her counterpart the C2 man). Her genius, though, was that in presenting herself as a 'very ordinary woman' she flattered to deceive. 'I'll freely admit,' says Robin Butler, 'that when I saw her standing on the steps of No. 10 quoting from St Francis of Assisi I remarked to my wife, "That woman won't last three months."'

# 3
# Breaking the Class Ceiling

Class is a Communist concept. It groups people as bundles and sets them against one another... Underclass? Socialist claptrap!

MT, *Newsweek*, 1992

'Mrs Thatcher,' the academic John Vincent told Charles Moore,

> is the point at which all snobberies meet: intellectual snobbery, social snobbery, the snobbery of Brooks's [the whiggish London club], the snobbery about scientists among those educated in the arts, the snobbery of the metropolis about the provincial, the snobbery of the south about the north and the snobbery of men about career women.

And yet... Margaret Thatcher liked posh people. She would probably have disagreed with that statement, and she certainly wasn't one herself, to which her much maligned, overly elocuted vowels testified. She despaired of the languidly passive entitlement of her first, inherited 1979 cabinet, most of whom she famously christened as 'wet', with a knowing wink to the language of the boarding-school dormitories, where, including her one woman minister, Baroness Young, all but three had spent their formative years. And yet she loved nothing more than the attentions of a dashing, charming, tall, 'upright', besuited (or better still uniformed) posh bloke. To Margaret Thatcher, these types of men (many of whom – like Peter Carington, Christopher Soames, Francis Pym and Jim Prior – she famously fought and ultimately demoted or sacked from the cabinet) resonated with the values and standards of her revered 'old Britain', a place where men proved they were men by oppressing or killing other men and animals, large and small, where the Empire was more than just the villain from a media franchise and Mr Kipling made poems, not cakes. But it would be the combination of 'old posh Britain' – represented by Geoffrey Howe (Winchester and Trinity Hall, Cambridge) – and 'nouveau' Britain – represented by Michael Heseltine (Shrewsbury and Pembroke, Oxford), the grandson of a dock worker, and famously maligned by Tory grandee Michael Jopling as 'a man who bought all his own furniture' – which would hold the key to her downfall.

Perhaps the greatest irony of the Thatcher class paradox was that bestriding the apex of this aristocratic house of cards was a female monarch, Queen Elizabeth II, one of the few women of whom Margaret Thatcher was, if not scared, then at least wary. MT revered the Crown as she revered tradition and religion: 'Thatcher was a respecter of the rituals and strictures of monarchy and at the same time a kind of working-class rebel,' says one former advisor.

'For example, she wouldn't allow privatisation of the Post Office simply because she couldn't bear the idea of privatising anything with the Queen's head on it.' Charles Powell says Thatcher was socially insecure: 'She was instinctively uncomfortable with the class system and acutely uncomfortable around the royal family. She felt this wasn't her world.' MT stayed scrupulously schtum on her audiences with the Queen, which according to tradition and protocol are required, regular fare for the sovereign and his or her PM. Robin Butler, Principal Private Secretary 1982–5, says he and the Queen's Private Secretary would often supply cards with topics which might come up.

> She simply couldn't be herself with the Queen. I think their meetings were very tricky. Mrs T would revert to her very nervous and uneasy self – she was never relaxed and was totally in awe of the Queen. She was suspicious of some of the Queen's attitudes and they went head-to-head over sanctions in South Africa. But MT knew she needed to stay on her right side, otherwise it would be very damaging to her politically. She certainly made no friends amongst the courtiers.

And then there was MT's greatest challenge, her visits to Balmoral, the royal family's privately owned Scottish home since the nineteenth century and Queen Elizabeth's summer residence, which PMs would traditionally be invited to visit whilst the monarch was on vacation. For MT it was not a holiday – it was everything she despised. For starters, it was deep in the Scottish countryside (her trademark heels were out and wellies, which she famously only wore once a year at Balmoral, were de rigueur), it was often cold and wet, the emphasis would be on outdoor activities like stalking, walking or barbecuing, and to top it all off there would be a plethora of the three things in life she most distrusted: over-excitable dogs, horses and aristocrats. 'She would hate going up to Balmoral with the associated aristocracy who would be invited,' says Charles Powell. 'Mrs Thatcher's idea of a good time was certainly not a bothy in Scotland, let's put it like that,' laughs Caroline Slocock.

Stephen Sherbourne is more circumspect about his former boss's relationship with the monarch. 'It strikes me that the truth is to be found somewhere in the reality of the fact that the Queen went to Margaret Thatcher's seventieth and eightieth birthday parties and she also attended her funeral. Absolutely none of these attendances was mandatory for the monarch.' Sherbourne also points out that the Queen awarded Thatcher the Order of Merit just one month after she stepped down. The order is held exclusively by only 24 people at one time and is at the discretion of the monarch. Alumni include Florence Nightingale, T.S. Eliot and Winston Churchill. Harold Brooks-Baker, publishing director of Burke's Peerage, told the *Baltimore Sun* at the time that the honour 'exposes the talk that Mrs Thatcher and the Queen did not get on as rubbish'. Perhaps even more convincing was the fact that five years later MT was made a Lady Companion of the Order of the Garter, the highest order of chivalry in the country. 'I actually think that they had great respect for each other,' says Sherbourne, whose insight is borne out by the diarist and insatiable gossip Woodrow Wyatt, who records a conversation with the Queen Mother in his *Journals* (Volume II, Macmillan 1998).

# BREAKING THE CLASS CEILING

Thursday 23 February 1989: We talked about Mrs Thatcher. She feels that people simply don't understand how compassionate and kind she is. I said, when she dashes off to scenes of disaster, she does it because she feels she must, because she feels so sorry for everybody. She said, 'I know. We think she's wonderful.' I said how difficult it had been for her as a woman and a grocer's daughter becoming leader of the Tory Party with so many people who were both snobs and didn't like being run by a woman. She said, 'She has done it marvellously.' She recognizes, as obviously the Queen does, the terrific things she has done for the country.

As Clive James once said: 'The essence of a class system is not that the privileged are conscious of their privileges, but that the deprived are conscious of their deprivations.' Margaret Thatcher's class roots are meaningful. This is because she spent the early part of her political career as a member of the lower middle class, trying to assimilate into a party which revered upper-class values, only then to set about destroying those upper-class boundaries and values in an attempt to create a property-owning, meritocratic democracy.

She always said she hated class politics and refused to use the word 'class'. Instead, she used the term 'ordinary working people'. As a disciple of Alfred Sherman at the Centre for Policy Studies (CPS), she envisaged an entirely new class reflecting her own roots: those of 'middle Britain', united by what Jon Lawrence and Florence Sutcliffe-Braithwaite (writing in *Making Thatcher's Britain*, ed. Ben Jackson and Robert Saunders, Cambridge University Press 2012) describe as 'common-sense social and political values'. She underlined this in 1972 when she said: 'I had a very ordinary background – probably a lot more ordinary than many of their own [Labour's] front bench.'

For a woman who would later tell the 1979 Young Conservative Conference in Eastbourne, 'I believe we should judge people on merit and not on background,' MT was fascinated from a young age by the privileges and ease which being a member of the upper classes and aristocracy bestowed. At school, Margaret gravitated towards the 'well-to-do' girls, the principal amongst these being Caroline Cust, the daughter of landowner Lord Brownlow, who was a close friend of the future King Edward VIII. (As the King's equerry, Brownlow accompanied Wallis Simpson on a plane to France to escape the media publicity surrounding the abdication crisis, an action which led to his being summarily and permanently dismissed from the new court of King George VI.) The family home, Belton House, visited by Margaret at Caroline Cust's invitation, was a grand pile, built with the proceeds of the Industrial Revolution, standing in 1,300 acres of ancient deer park, with formal Dutch and Italian gardens, just outside Grantham. Later, when she became PM, Margaret would borrow the Cust family silver in the form of cutlery and a dinner service to be used at No. 10 for formal dining.

Muriel, Margaret's sister, told Moore that Caroline Cust used to 'rave' about Margaret. Perhaps both girls were aware of the infamous rumour that Margaret was in fact the granddaughter of Harry Cust, who had supposedly seduced Margaret's grandmother Phoebe whilst she was in service as a maid at Belton. Most biographers of MT refute this theory, although Woodrow Wyatt would write in his diaries that 'John Julius [Viscount Norwich] has great vigour… he himself acknowledged that his grandfather was not the Duke of Rutland but Harry Cust… [he] is absolutely convinced that he and Mrs Thatcher are cousins.' As unlikely as this might seem, Wyatt pronounces that he himself now believes the story is true. 'How lucky for England there were no contraceptives for women and no abortions when Harry Cust was seducing Margaret's grandmother. We would never have halted our national decline.' Indeed, he riffs on this story with another friend – Queen Elizabeth the Queen Mother: 'We speculated a little on the jolly possibility of Margaret Thatcher's grandmother… as some kind of a servant being seduced in the house by Harry Cust.'

'I did not grow up with the sense of division and conflict between classes,' writes Margaret Thatcher in her autobiography. Even if this were true, which it patently is not, there is no way that the young Margaret was not acutely aware of the limiting concept of coming from 'the wrong class', when it came to succeeding in class-ridden Britain. Certainly, her father Alf knew all about the advantages of the young upper classes. The son of a Northamptonshire bootmaker, he had left school at thirteen to go out to work. His first job was as an assistant at the tuck shop at Oundle, one of England's oldest and toniest public schools (founded 1556), where on a daily basis he would witness the children of the upper classes spending likely more than his week's wages on bars of chocolate and bags of boiled sweets. If Margaret had failed to comprehend the benefits and peculiarities of British privilege on her visits to the Custs, then her father unwittingly underlined them when he took his young daughters to watch the setting-off of the Belvoir Hunt – the Duke of Rutland's foxhound pack – which met in Grantham every Boxing Day. He told the girls he approved of the hunt, under the spurious premise that 'foxes stole babies from their prams'.

Is being posh the same as being clever and cool? Not these days, but during the 1930s and 1940s, whilst MT was growing up, the concepts were closely aligned. In other words, one could not be cool (modern might have been a better word for the times) without first being posh. MT's first brush with 'cool mean posh girls' was likely at Kesteven and Grantham Girls' School or KGGS, when, in 1941, Camden School for Girls (CSG) was evacuated from war-torn London, to share KGGS's classrooms for five terms.

If ever there was a school which defined edgy intellectual cool it was (and still is) the non-fee-paying CSG. The pioneering girls' school, founded by the suffragist Frances Mary Buss in 1871, attracted the daughters of what we might now call the liberal elite. Today's alumni include Julia Donaldson, Emma Thompson, Geri Horner, Sarah Brown, Fiona Millar, Jodhi May, Lily Donaldson – the list is endless. Boys were admitted to the sixth form in 1990. Whilst the Camden girls attended the school in the afternoons and the KGGS pupils in the mornings, the idea that girls too could be intellectually superior (and not just boys and men) will have made its mark on MT. What the sophisticated Camden girls made of the ugly navy blue serge tunics and blue felt hats worn by the middle-England Kesteven girls is only to be imagined. Sartorial matters were made worse by the fact that if the girls were to play hockey, they were forced to take off their tunics and play in their blue blouses, big black knickers and black stockings.

The stay of the CSG girls was short-lived. After it became obvious to the powers that be that Grantham was high-risk as far as bombing raids were concerned (the town was home to a munitions factory and located at the junction of the Great North Road and the East Coast Main Line), the girls were moved on to the safer location of Stamford High School.

The girls from CSG were alluring for more than just their intellectual 'cool' – they came from the place MT had already earmarked as her own: London. An early encounter with the city aged twelve had entranced her. She had been invited to stay with family friends – the Revd Skinner and his wife, who lived in Parliament Hill Fields, Hampstead. 'I was given a life of enjoyment and entertainment that I had never seen!' she told Patricia Murray. The ultimate highlight, though, was not the sights which she drank in – the Houses of Parliament, the Changing of the Guard, the Tower of London and London Zoo – but 'my first visit to the Catford Theatre in Lewisham where we saw Sigmund Romberg's famous musical *The Desert Song*', she wrote in her autobiography. She would remember that the Skinners' 'kindness had given me a glimpse of, in Talleyrand's words, "*la douceur de la vie*" [the sweetness of living]'. She would never forget the experience and was never happier than when she was in central London (preferably at No. 10 Downing Street) – as Charles Moore says: 'Except in political allegiance the centre was always where she wanted to be.'

When Muriel left home to study physiotherapy at Birmingham Orthopaedic Hospital MT, who was just thirteen, effectively became Alf and Beaty's 'only child', which might have accounted for some of her precociousness. In her autobiography she references two books she read with her father. One was Bruce Lockhart's story of travelling through Nazi-controlled Austria to Germany: *Guns or Butter*. Its title would appear indirectly in one of MT's most significant early speeches, delivered at Kensington Town Hall on 19 January 1976, which warned of the Soviet threat: 'The men in the Soviet Politburo don't have to worry about the ebb and flow of public opinion. They put guns before butter, while we put just about everything before guns.'

The second, more controversially, is Douglas Reed's *Insanity Fair*, written on the eve of the *Anschluss* and examining Hitler's megalomania. 'He analysed and blisteringly denounced that policy of appeasement by Britain and France which paved the way for Hitler's successes,' MT writes in her autobiography. This may have been so, but when *The Times* ran Reed's obituary in 1976, they described him as a 'virulent anti-Semite', referring in particular to his belief in a Zionist conspiracy seeking to enslave humanity and impose a world government.

If things were not a barrel of laughs at home (and quite clearly they were not), it was from other classmates, particularly Jean Farmer, a fellow scholarship girl, that MT learned about the concept of fun. 'When I went to stay with my great friend Jean Farmer, they all went to tennis together. They all went to dances together. They would all do far more of those things – out with other people where there was laughter and fun,' MT wistfully told journalist Patricia Murray. Another friend was Margaret Goodrich, daughter of the vicar of Corby Glen, who came from a comfortable, intellectual home and was a year older than Margaret. Canon Goodrich became one of Margaret's early intellectual mentors, who later coached her for the Oxford entrance exam, and the two girls would stay in touch long into adulthood.

According to Margaret Goodrich, MT exhibited both intellectual superiority and courage from an early age. At the end of any public lectures at KGGS, Thatcher made her mark, likely using the experiences and terminology she gained from the Nottingham University extra lectures she'd attended with her father on a Thursday evening.

> She used to stand up and put her question in a very parliamentary fashion, starting with 'Does this speaker think this or that?'... I always had the impression that Margaret was interested in politics and in retrospect it is interesting to contemplate that she may have felt even then that she was ultimately destined to go into Parliament,

said one friend, quoted by Patricia Murray. Other girls were not so kind: 'We used to roll our eyes and think, here she goes again,' said another classmate.

Unlike the boys (and some girls) from public schools for whom entry to Oxbridge was practically a shoo-in, children from lower classes, particularly women, struggled to get a place. This was not for want of intellectual abilities; rather it was because the type of state schooling prevalent during the forties and fifties (and beyond) in the UK failed to prepare children to sit the Oxbridge entrance exams. The few state-educated children who did make it were mostly male and from the grammar schools. Even fewer from the old-fashioned secondary modern schools and the early comprehensives would even have considered trying. It was a blunt but effective form of educational segregation, in a Britain where everyone still 'knew their place', to borrow from the famous 1966 *Frost Report* sketch. By the late 1930s only 24 per cent of students at Oxford and 19 per cent at Cambridge had begun their education in state schools. In 1948 Oxford lifted its quota on women from the original 840 to 970; there were far fewer places available to women because there were only five colleges open to them. Cambridge University did not even grant degrees to women until April 1948. Shamefully, it was the last university in England to do so. Before 1974 only 16 per cent of Oxford's graduates were women. Has the trend reversed? It did so, if only momentarily. At the time of writing (2024) Cambridge announced that it had accepted fewer state school applicants for the first time in a decade.

For the record, when Margaret Thatcher became Education Secretary in 1970 she said she would fight the sweeping tide of comprehensive education, set in train by the Labour government, to preserve some of the 'old-style' grammar schools. She didn't try particularly hard. On her first day of office, there were 1,137 comprehensives. By the time she left, she had approved 3,286 comprehensive schemes; only 326 had been rejected and she had saved just 94 grammar schools.

Margaret's university journey did not begin smoothly and nobody seems clear – least of all her – why she chose Somerville College, Oxford. The fact that it was wartime (1943) made entry easier for her and hundreds of other women who were applying, but still she did not have Latin, a prerequisite for Oxbridge entry, neither did she have the backing of her school headmistress Miss Gillies, a Scot with a backbone almost as unyielding as Margaret's. 'Too young' is how she dismissed the seventeen-year-old Margaret Roberts' plea to study for the Oxbridge exams. No matter, because Alderman Roberts was once again there for his daughter, paying for her private Latin tuition from a classics master at the nearby

King's School, of which he was a governor. His daughter mastered five years' worth of Latin in as many months.

By now Margaret Goodrich had gone up to Lady Margaret Hall in Oxford and her father, the canon who had a soft spot for the grocer's daughter, lent her books to read and coached her for the general paper. To her mortification, she was only put on the waiting list. As Penny Junor puts it: 'She was forced to swallow her pride and return to school for a third year in the sixth form.' Her humiliation was short-lived. After two weeks of serving as joint head girl, she received a telegram offering her the place of another student who had dropped out. Throughout her life, until her final few weeks in office, Margaret Thatcher was possessed of the enviable kind of luck normally attributed to the Hibernians.

'Oxford does not set out to please,' writes Margaret Thatcher in her autobiography. Thomas Arnold would have disagreed. But then he wasn't a seventeen-year-old lower-middle-class 'mousey' girl going up to the city of dreaming spires, which she had visited only once before during the application process. MT paints a picture of a gloomy 1943 blacked-out Oxford that very few would recognise: 'Stained-glass windows were boarded up. Large static water tanks stood ready for use in case of fire.' For reasons which were surely down to luck more than judgement, Oxford miraculously avoided being bombed during the war, despite being the location of a munitions factory. The food was 'unexciting' (and still rationed). As for bathing: 'There were tight controls over the use of hot water. For example, there must be no more than five inches of water in the bath and of course I rigidly observed this, though coming from a family where the relationship between cleanliness and Godliness was no laughing matter,' she writes in her autobiography.

Margaret's social awkwardness made her first term difficult. When Margaret Goodrich and her father visited her in her rooms on the ground floor of Penrose, one of the halls of residence at Somerville, she found her 'sitting, toasting crumpets and feeling very homesick'.

Margaret did not find friendship or 'meaning' at Oxford until she joined the Bach Choir and, more importantly, the Oxford University Conservative Association (OUCA), of which she became president in her third year, only the second woman to do so. It quickly seems to have become clear to the young Margaret that politics at this level was a remarkable leveller and that her background was not a complete hindrance to progression, within the cloistered walls of Oxford at least. (Later, as a young woman in search of a parliamentary seat, she would swiftly be disabused of this notion.) 'OUCA provided a further network of acquaintance and friendship,' she wrote. 'It was, indeed, an effective forum for matchmaking, as a number of my OUCA colleagues demonstrated.' Through OUCA she would meet people like Edward Boyle, the son of a Liberal MP from whom she would absorb much ('he moved easily in a sophisticated social and political world which I had only glimpsed'), William Rees-Mogg, a future editor of *The Times*, and Robin Day, whose 'pioneering television interviewing', she writes, would mean that he and MT would cross swords on several occasions.

It was at Oxford, specifically at Somerville, where Margaret got her first taste of the unique combination of intellectual snobbery, sexism and classism perpetrated by women rather than men.

At that time, and perhaps even now – although it's more subtle – one's social class was immediately pinpointed by the answer to the inevitable, tiresomely loaded question: where did you go to school? Rather than dismissing the question, Margaret was perpetually embarrassed by her answer, which she instinctively knew would create judgement and prejudice: 'Don't you wish,' she once asked Margaret Goodrich, 'you could say you had been to Cheltenham or somewhere instead of KGGS?'

Female sexism would dog Margaret Thatcher for the rest of her life, in perhaps a less binary but far more subtle fashion than plain common-or-garden male misogyny or class bias. At OUCA, when she first joined, the men would initially dismiss Margaret as a helpful 'administration assistant' willing to do the dogsbody work, whilst at Somerville the snobbery was more finessed. In hall, where meals were taken, the all-female social stratum was dictated by which tables you sat at. The top three tables nearest the 'high' table where the principal sat were filled with what Penny Junor terms the 'more exotic element'. The bottom three – furthest away from the principal and effectively the back rows of the classroom, where loud laughter and 'less appropriate' conversation could not be heard – were dominated by the 'posh girls': rich, aristocratic and often from schools like Cheltenham Ladies' College or 'The Marys' – Calne, Ascot or Benenden (the last later made famous by Princess Anne's attendance) – St Paul's, London, and Wycombe Abbey. Both sets of women looked askance at the middle tables, where sat 'girls from grammar schools with scholarships, good middle-class ethics and every accent from Yorkshire to Somerset', according to Junor.

Margaret, who was definitely 'in the middle', was acutely uncomfortable and awkward amongst this gaggle of women, none of whom particularly warmed to her. They teased her about her accent and about her male 'crushes', when 'she would blush red to her roots'. Author Nina Bawden was a fellow state school-educated scholarship girl. In her autobiography *In My Own Time* (Virago 1994), she writes of trying to persuade Margaret that they should be trying to build a new and better world, not joining the ranks of the privileged. MT's biographer John Campbell describes the reply Bawden reports as 'the sort of shrewd opportunism which Mrs Thatcher displayed throughout her career'.

> Margaret smiled her pretty, china doll's smile. Of course, she admitted the Labour Club was, just at the moment, more *fashionable*... but that, in a way, unintentionally suited her purposes. Unlike me, she was not 'playing' at politics. She meant to get into Parliament and there was more chance of being 'noticed' in the Conservative Club just because some of the members were a bit stodgy.

Charles Moore, who spent considerable time interviewing both classmates and university contemporaries of MT, found that her schoolfriends were much more friendly and positive about her than the 'Oxford women'. 'The Grantham girls were all saying, "Splendid, well done her!" and her Oxford contemporaries were clearly wondering "why did she of all of our intake get to be so powerful – why not us?"' Rachel Willink, the first female president of OUCA, told Moore that she remembered MT as 'rather a brown girl', a 'humourless mouse'; someone who 'hadn't got the style' to 'make up' for her background. Fellow student Ann Dally told John Campbell,

# BREAKING THE CLASS CEILING

If I had been told that the first woman Prime Minister would be one of us, I would not have put Margaret among my first six guesses. This was because most of us found her boring and I think it did not occur to any of us in those heady days that anyone who was boring could possibly reach high places.

Janet Vaughan, later who would become principal of Somerville in 1945, felt uniquely threatened by Margaret. 'Nobody thought anything of her... She was a beta chemist,' she said. Moore describes Vaughan as 'one of those progressives who regard being a Conservative as a sort of mental defect'. Vaughan told journalists Nicholas Wapshott and George Brock (*Thatcher*, Futura 1983): 'She stood out, Somerville had always been a radical establishment and there weren't many Conservatives about then... We used to entertain a good deal at weekends, but she didn't get invited. She had nothing to contribute, you see.'

Upper-class women would, in the main, never take to Thatcher (with some notable exceptions). She was too nouveau and far too ambitious for their liking. The perfect example of an MT adversary was Mary (later Baroness) Warnock, author, headmistress of Oxford High School for Girls and later chair of a committee of inquiry (1974–8) into the rights of education for disabled children and author of the 1984 report on human fertilisation and embryology. Despite having been appointed to the last of these roles by MT, Warnock took up a personal vendetta against her. She specifically disliked her for her education cuts of the early 1980s, but more broadly she simply didn't like the way she looked, nor what she stood for. Mrs Thatcher, Mary Warnock told one interviewer, 'epitomised the worst of the lower middle class'. Her neat, well-groomed clothes and hair were 'packaged in a way that's not exactly vulgar, just low'. She felt, she said, 'a kind of rage' whenever she thought about Mrs Thatcher's 'odious suburban gentility'.

If Oxford brought Margaret's upbringing and her lack of social skills sharply to the fore, it also gave her some indication of the battles ahead. She could not, as many past and future PMs had, test her debating skills and develop her Conservative ethos at the Oxford Union, because women were still banned from the 120-year-old debating society. She had to rely at first on the John Wesley Society, where she found discussion and friendship and developed her preaching skills. The society used to send out its members to nearby villages to preach sermons, and the young MT was amongst them. 'Never forget,' says Gillian Shephard, 'that Margaret Thatcher was a preacher first and a politician second.' Whilst Margaret kept her politics separate from her faith, she maintained her connection to the Wesleyans throughout her four years at Oxford, although her time was increasingly taken up by OUCA. Her own account of the moment she decided to go into politics underlines the fact that, as she grew in stature, she 'embroidered' her life story to smooth down the sharp edges and create a compelling storyline. Her story changed over time, beginning with an epiphany at a birthday party. 'At the end of the evening we all finished up in the kitchen and somebody who happened to be talking to me said, "I feel that what you would really like to do is to be a member of Parliament," and that was the very first time that it had occurred to me that perhaps one day I could, if the chance ever came,' MT told Patricia Murray. The story was later embellished into a scenario which involved a village hop, complete with dashing RAF pilots. But even as (and if) she made the bold statement 'I want to be an MP', Margaret Roberts would have been aware that the possibility of this happening was extremely slim – at least until 1946, when Labour increased the pay of MPs from £600 to £1,000. 'With no private income of my own, there was no way I could have afforded to be an MP on the salary available,' she admits in her autobiography.

As a chemist, MT had to put in far more work than those studying humanities. That and a lack of funds limited her social life and her acceptability to others, as she reflects.

> I might have had a more glittering Oxford career, but I had little money to spare and would have been hard put to make ends meet if it had not been for a number of modest grants secured for me from the college at the insistence of my ever-helpful tutor, the chemist Dorothy Hodgkin.

Indeed, Dr Hodgkin – later a Nobel Prize winner and the only other woman Thatcher was scared of, according to Charles Powell – came to respect MT as 'someone who could write a decent essay', but she seems, at the same time, to have been somewhat underwhelmed by her student.

If the women at Oxford gave her a taste of what she could expect in the wider world (and possibly fostered her distrust of women in general), the men left her in no doubt of the limitations of her class where relationships were concerned. From 1944 she writes that the feeling of Oxford changed 'as older men, invalided out, started coming back from the services either to complete a shortened wartime degree or to begin a full degree course... By the time I left I found myself dealing with friends and colleagues who had seen much more of the world than I had.' It was during her fourth year, whilst living 'out' at 18 Walton Street with two fellow students, Mary Mallinson and May Foss, that she summoned up the courage to let herself go – at least by her standards. 'I first went out to dances and even on occasion drank a little wine,' she admits. She tried smoking but did not like it: 'I spent my money on *The Times* instead.'

It was in the world of politics that MT would feel most engaged and accepted – even amongst those Tories who clearly did not approve of her on the basis of what would turn out to be her two most winning assets: her class origins and the fact that she was a woman. 'She had a very lively sense of the conditions that people were living in. She'd grown up in circumstances which meant that people's problems were not that distant. This was not, after all, a woman who'd lived a life in palaces,' says Oliver Letwin.

Her first real sponsor, the Tory backbencher Alfred Bossom, *had* known a life of privilege. A 'starchitect' before there ever were such things, he'd designed buildings in New York, Dallas and Houston before returning to London to buy a large house with the tony address of 5 Carlton Gardens. A few years later this grand Nash white stucco home with its chandeliers and sweeping staircase would be the venue for the Thatchers' wedding reception. Bossom's progressive attitude led to his most famous pronouncement: 'We've got to find successors to Lady Astor!' When he heard young Margaret Thatcher speak he was smitten and tucked her firmly under his wing, helping with her expenses, throwing lunches for her and introducing her to the great and the good. Her nomination to stand in the safe Labour seat of Dartford in Kent was indirectly thanks to the exposure Bossom had supplied.

# BREAKING THE CLASS CEILING

'A grand young candidate. Speaks Well. Good-looking. Keen, knows her subjects. Watch and encourage,' wrote one of her referees, Lord Balfour of Inchrye. 'She is without exception the best woman candidate I have ever known,' the Dartford election agent reported.

Anthony Kershaw MC, MT's opponent, was a perfect example of the kind of 'old Tory' she was going to come up against for her entire career: ex-Eton, Balliol, 16th/5th Lancers and a barrister, he hunted with the Beaufort and the Berkeley and played rugby for Harlequins. Unfortunately, for someone with such a privileged background, Kershaw was not very smart. But when did that ever hold a man back? Margaret Thatcher eventually won the nomination by a meaningful majority, with a convincingly passionate fifteen-minute speech. The Central Office deputy area agent who attended the final interviews described MT's speaking ability and political knowledge as 'far above those of other candidates'. Naturally, Kershaw was unfazed. He had all of the right Tory qualifications and he knew that for him it was only a matter of time. He became MP for Stroud in 1955 and a junior minister in the Heath government. Margaret Thatcher knighted him in the 1981 New Year Honours 'for political and public service'.

On 13 December 1951 Margaret Roberts became Mrs Denis Thatcher at Wesley's Chapel in the City of London. Her choice was both wise and pragmatic. In one short ceremony, she had elevated her status and acceptability within 1950s society, in true Austenesque fashion, by marrying 'the Major', as Denis was later to be nicknamed, a man with a certain raffish charm, the Second World War honour of an MC, and if not enough cash to challenge *Pride and Prejudice*'s Mr Darcy, then certainly sufficient to give his friend

Mr Bingley a run for his money. Within twelve months, Margaret Thatcher would be pregnant. Was it love? Reader, see Chapter 10.

Despite her reservations (at one point she asked for her name to be removed from the potential candidates list), the young Mrs Thatcher kept up her relentless attack on the portals of male Conservative power. She tried and failed five times to find a seat. At Maidstone she was asked about her ability to cope as a Member of Parliament, 'having in mind the fact that she had a husband and a small family', in the words of the area agent. No similar questions were asked of the Old Etonian fruit farmer John Wells, who won the nomination. She did not even make the shortlist in Canterbury, and when she did in Orpington, Beckenham and Hemel Hempstead she could not make it past the post. When she decided to try for the safe seat of Finchley, North London, Sir John Crowder, the incumbent, was apoplectic. His response mirrored that of the majority of male Conservative MPs of the time, accusing Conservative Central Office of trying to rig the selection in order to give Finchley a choice between 'a bloody Jew and a bloody woman'. What he really meant, of course, was 'a bloody *bourgeois* woman' elevated only by marriage. The same issues were only too prevalent at the Bar: specialising in tax law, she struggled during her pupillage to find a seat. 'It was still a Dickensian milieu,' writes Jonathan Aitken, 'at best only half open to women of talent.'

In April 1958, MT was finally adopted as the Conservative parliamentary candidate for Finchley. The press were positive, if a little taken aback. The *Evening Standard* trumpeted: 'The woman many Tories reckon their most beautiful member has been chosen as candidate for Finchley.' At the time, politics was tough going for a woman (not much has changed) and, a few weeks after her selection, Thatcher confessed to the party's Central Office: 'I am learning the hard way that an anti-woman prejudice among certain Association members can persist even after a successful adoption meeting, but I hope it will subside.' In Charles Moore's official biography, Haden Blatch, the son of the then Chairman of the Finchley Conservative Association, Bertie Blatch, said his father had confided that Margaret Thatcher 'didn't actually win. The man [Thomas Langton] did, but I thought, "He's got a silver spoon in his mouth. He'll get another seat." So, I "lost" two of his votes and gave them to her.' However: 'Vote-rigging,' concludes Jonathan Aitken, 'was highly unlikely.'

On Friday, 9 October 1959, four days before her thirty-fourth birthday, MT won her seat in the general election. In finding Finchley – then a slightly rough-around-the-edges, north-east London suburb in the Borough of Barnet and a place where she never spent a single night, although she was a loyal, attentive and effective representative for 33 years – MT also found a community which both reflected her values and underscored her mission. Made up of a mix of white British, immigrants and a strong Jewish community, the predominant beliefs were that it didn't matter where you came from, but it was what you did, how you did it and what you gave back to your community that mattered. Margaret came to love Finchley, and in return its people loved her back. But still, it wasn't plain sailing. After all, a woman standing in a north London seat in the 1950s was the sort of extraordinary anomaly, which invited comment. To paraphrase one voter: 'I wasn't going to vote for a woman because it wasn't the done thing. And then I heard her speak and changed my mind.'

'Thatcher was one of only 25 women MPs when elected to Parliament in 1959,' wrote historian Amanda Foreman in the *Daily Mail* (2012).

> Despite the presence of women MPs since 1919, the extent of their integration into Westminster was a separate tearoom for 'Lady Members'. The gesture served to highlight their exclusion since the majority of daily business took place in the Members' Bar, a place only marginally less out-of-bounds to women than the male lavatories.

It is a common theme amongst political historians to say that it was Edward Heath who broke the class ceiling, as far as the Tories were concerned, with his 1965 election to lead the Conservative Party and his subsequent 1970 election to PM. This is only partially true. The son of a carpenter and a lady's maid, Heath certainly changed what Michael Heseltine politely terms 'the class balance'. 'Ted, Margaret, John Major; these people changed the balance of the party totally,' is how he puts it. The difference between Heath and Thatcher was quite obviously their sex, the implications of which were meaningful in terms of party politics, regardless of their birth. Notably, both had elocution lessons as part of their transformation, which resulted in Heath's strangely plodding, patronising tones with his infamously elongated vowel sounds. Margaret Thatcher, whose father had paid for elocution lessons to rid her of her Lincolnshire twang (which some writers have benevolently described as more of a lisp), had embellished her accent whilst at Oxford and made it worse: 'She'd taught herself the cod-RP whilst she was at Oxford and done a rotten job,' writes Tim Bell. But for both, the way they sounded was probably less important than their access to the power players within the party. And here, Heath held the major advantage. He could join any of the all-male London clubs, where informal but influential schmoozing was the order of the day. 'Ted was infinitely club-bable,' says one insider, 'which is just another way of saying that he could join all the right men's clubs and smooth his path to power by meeting all of the right people there. In that way he was admitted to the inner circles of the Tory Party.'

'It was definitely more difficult for Mrs Thatcher,' reflects Stephen Sherbourne.

> When she became leader she couldn't easily embed herself into the Conservative Party like a man would — a man would have the right friends and join the right clubs; she couldn't do that. Margaret Thatcher always felt that she had to prove herself by merit — to simply be more competent than the men. She did not have anything like a 'man's club' or even a 'kitchen cabinet', there was no one she was especially friendly or pally with in the political world.

In 1973, the *Sunday Times* published a study of fourteen of the eighteen members of the cabinet in a guide to their 'domestic style'. Included was a question concerning which clubs they belonged to. Ten of MT's thirteen colleagues who participated belonged to the Carlton Club (founded in 1832, it was described by Disraeli as the 'social citadel of Toryism'). Between them, the cabinet could claim membership of no fewer than 48 clubs. Willie Whitelaw's total was thirteen. Margaret Thatcher's entry read 'nil'. 'Of course, she did suffer from both extreme misogyny and snobbery in the House but I think her view was always that we just have to put up with this madness and not let it distract us,' says Robin Butler.

The other issue for MT, which is hard to comprehend these days, was that she had not served in the Second World War. It's easy to forget that the male camaraderie engendered by the war swiftly turned to heavy-handed patriarchal sexism the minute the conflict ended. Women who had been liberated into male occupations during the war – from munitions to engineering, intelligence and farm labour – were swiftly 'demobilised' and redirected back to the home in order that returning soldiers could have 'their jobs' back. But the genie of female domestic subjugation could never be entirely squeezed back into the bottle, and the post-war forties and fifties marked the beginning of female working independence and emancipation. Still, the resistance to women in the workplace and in politics remained palpable when MT first took up her seat in the Commons. If anything, her meteoric rise to party leader in 1975 exacerbated both the sexism and the snobbery in the House.

David Howell, the only minister to have served in Ted Heath's, Margaret Thatcher's and David Cameron's governments, remembers Thatcher as a young, ingénue minister working for Heath.

> Heath was a great entertainer and he was always having parties down at his home in Broadstairs. Margaret would be asked along and, as ridiculous as this sounds now, one always felt sorry for her. She was a loner, not very good at chatting and inclined to lecture people. She wasn't really in the swim and most of us saw her as over-obsessed with ideas.

# BREAKING THE CLASS CEILING

Faint praise indeed. When I ask the gentlemanly Howell, who is buying me tea in the Lord's tea room (burned teacake, PG Tips and full-fat milk), whether he has anything to add, he pauses. 'Well, she had a nice husband, who didn't say much.' He laughs gently, startling the two mice who are hovering expectantly beside our table. 'Of course,' he says, 'times change. I must say that I was surprised when she started to move up the ranks.'

The election of October 1974 was the second general election fought in the space of eight months. In February, Edward Heath's Conservative government had proved unable to take control of a hung parliament, leaving the Labour Party to form the first minority government since 1929. Prime Minister Harold Wilson returned to the country in October to gain the majority. Within a few months, the Tories were plunged into a leadership crisis, having lost confidence in Ted Heath, and Ladbrokes, the betting agents, opened a book on the new leader. When the then young MP Ken Clarke took a call from a prominent Sunday newspaper asking for a quote, he pointed out that Ladbrokes had omitted one name from the running order: Margaret Thatcher. 'The journalist laughed heartily. I said I thought she would get backing, at which the journalist offered me very long odds against her himself!' Clarke says he regrets not accepting the bet (he voted for Heath in the first round out of loyalty and for Geoffrey Howe in the second) because within three weeks MT was leader of the Conservative Party. (Clarke would go on to hold myriad Tory cabinet posts including Secretary of State for Health under MT from 1988 to 1990.) 'My God! The bitch has won!' exclaimed a vice-chairman of the party when the news of Thatcher's victory reached Tory Central Office.

# THE INCIDENTAL FEMINIST

Charles Moore thinks that MT was able to take hold of the Conservative Party because of circumstance as much as ability. 'I really think she managed to pull it off because the Tories were in such low water, they were ready for the shock of the new.' He also says that MT's sex and the fact that she was attractive helped overcome what would have been a 'class resistance'. 'If there's one thing upper-class men appreciate it's pluck. They would say things like, "I don't care what you say – she's a brave girl – a very brave girl." Had it been a male equivalent with a slightly lower-class voice there would have been many more rumblings. It would have been: who is this grocer's boy from Grantham?'

'When Thatcher chaired her first Shadow Cabinet meeting on February 18, 1975, she did so in the knowledge that almost every man around the table had voted for one of her opponents. Those who weren't in awe of her were openly condescending,' writes Amanda Foreman. Almost all of the shadow cabinet of 24 had attended public schools – and approximately a third had been to Eton. The exception was Norman Fowler, Shadow Secretary of State for Social Services, who had attended a grammar school, King Edward VI in Chelmsford. The only woman, Sally Oppenheim, had attended Lowther College, then a public school for girls. Snobbery was rife. Famously, at a shadow cabinet meeting in 1976, Thatcher mused out loud whether Jimmy Carter would make a good President, adding that 'sometimes the job could make the man'. 'Yes,' replied Reginald Maudling, her Shadow Foreign Secretary (Merchant Taylors' and Oxford – both scholarships). 'I remember Winston [Churchill]'s remark – "if you feed a grub on royal jelly it will grow into a Queen Bee."' MT was only too aware of their disdain. The feeling was mutual: 'Success is not an attractive thing to many people… and, of course, some of them are snobs. They can never forgive me for coming from a very ordinary background,' she told journalist Brian Walden in a later TV interview. On sacking the imperious Christopher Soames in her 1981 reshuffle, she would write with glee: 'Christopher Soames was equally angry – but in a grander way. I got the distinct impression that he felt… he was, in effect, being dismissed by his housemaid.'

'Margaret pretty much had to keep Ted Heath's old cabinet,' says former Conservative Party Chairman Norman Tebbit when I ask about the logic of MT maintaining a cabinet seething with hostility. 'Those chaps would have been pretty miffed if she'd bought in other people – she needed to keep them onside.' 'Look, there was definitely a class thing from the beginning,' says Gillian Shephard. 'She trusted who she trusted, and that included Airey Neave and Ian Gow, both upper-class gents. She particularly respected their war records.' Her mainstay, says Shephard, was the bluff Bernard Ingham. 'He wasn't a smooth Oxford grad, he didn't waste her time, she trusted him completely.' Paradoxically it was Willie Whitelaw, who had stood against Margaret in the leadership election, who was to prove a conduit between her and the cliquey patrician cabinet she inherited after she was elected PM. 'They were terribly snobby about her behind her back,' says David Howell. 'They would say "Isn't she ghastly?" and Willie [Whitelaw], who was the bridge between the sneering aristos and zealots, would say, "Well, you may not like her but she is PM and we must back her."' The irony, says Gillian Shephard, was that Whitelaw, the son of Scottish landed gentry himself, was 'seriously posh and that's how he kept them all onside'.

Howell agrees. 'There'd be a lot of grumbling – "Of course, she's never had to sack a gamekeeper" – and Willie would say, "You can grumble as much as you like BUT..."' Ironically, it would be Whitelaw who would offer one of the most damningly snobbish indictments of Thatcher after she left office. 'Willie's words, which were reported in the newspapers, struck me as particularly unpleasant,' says Archie Hamilton, PPS 1987–8 and Armed Forces Minister 1988–93. 'They were something to the effect of "I admired her as PM but she is not the sort of person one would have to stay for the weekend."' He adds: 'At which point my wife Anne promptly said, "Well, we'll have her to stay every year," and from then on that's exactly what we did.'

If class was at the heart of MT's struggle for control over the grandees of the Conservative Party, it was also at the centre of her plan to remake Britain on her own terms and in her own image. Polls published in the mid 1970s reveal that two thirds of Britons thought the class struggle in Britain was real. Jon Lawrence and Florence Sutcliffe-Braithwaite point out that this was double the level recorded at the beginning of the decade. 'Thatcher's hatred of class politics ran deep, but it was the need to play down her own class image that most urgently pressed her to minimise this theme in favour of a more positive vision of a new popular constituency that bridged the fault lines of class.'

If one of Thatcherism's main goals (aside from free-market economics) was to redefine the British middle class and blur the distinctions between the working and middle classes, she had both Keith Joseph and the academic (and ex-communist) Alfred Sherman to thank for providing the impetus. The former, who had missed his own chance at the No. 1 spot by giving a disastrous speech illustrating his eugenicist tendencies (which in turn gave rise to the infamous declaration from MT: 'If you're not going to stand, Keith, then I will'), set up the Centre for Policy Studies (CPS) in 1974, with the radical thinker Sherman as chief fire starter. The two men created what MT described as 'the powerhouse of alternative Conservative thinking on economic and social matters', helping her crystallise her vision. It quickly became *the* Tory think tank. Bruce Anderson, in his obituary of Sherman in *The Times*, wrote:

> She knew that there had to be drastic change, and at that critical moment she was fortified in her conviction by a small group of men including Keith Joseph – and Alfred Sherman. They helped to persuade her that far from being a banal suburbanite, she was at the frontline of economic thinking, alongside Hayek, Friedman and [Ludwig] von Mises.

'Behind the scenes, Thatcherites were clear that they hoped to explode once and for all the Marxist/socialist model of class,' write Lawrence and Sutcliffe-Braithwaite. The clue was in the language that Margaret Thatcher employed, speaking of 'hard-working' or 'honest, loyal, decent' people sharing 'decent common-sense values'. In other words, people like her, who came from a similar background to her own. She despised the term 'class': 'I hate these labels, I really hate them. I simply don't understand why you can't look at a person quite apart from their social background for what they are, for what they can do, for what contributions they can make,' she said in a 1975 TV interview. 'Whilst Margaret Thatcher remodelled herself on the way up and she was clearly determined to remove any trace of a Midlands accent to fit in, she later rebelled against the backdrop of the way Britain "normally did things",' says William Waldegrave, junior minister and Secretary of State for Health 1990–2. 'She was a classic disrupter, and she turned being bourgeois into a positive.'

According to Lawrence and Sutcliffe-Braithwaite, 'In many respects [the Thatcherites] embraced a much bolder, more genuinely transformative political vision than Blair, Brown and company in the 1990s: the Thatcherite project meant recasting the dominant social discourses of British public politics.' Clearly, during her early years both at Oxford and as a young MP, Margaret had worked hard to rub off her lower-middle-class edges, but, as early as the mid seventies (and with the help of the CPS), she re-embraced her roots in what some might claim was a cynical, vote-winning strategy.

In fact, Margaret Thatcher never really forgot where she came from. The Thatcher 'project' – the disruption that Waldegrave speaks of – revolved around the concept of creating or embracing a different way of looking at class in Britain. Margaret Thatcher was as ambitious for the previously Labour-voting C1 and C2s – and for all those who wanted to get on in life and better themselves – as she was for herself. These were the new property owners, the deregulated Big Bang 'city boys', the successful immigrants, the young graduates and new business founders from the sixties and the 'plate-glass' universities (built in deeply unfashionable places like Lancaster, Warwick and Norwich). These were the unashamedly hard-working 'children' of the Thatcher revolution, and precisely the type of people who would vote for Margaret Thatcher, making her the longest serving British Prime

Minister of the twentieth century. They were also exactly the sort of people the upper classes despised and felt threatened by. Why? Because, until what some still like to call the 'Thatcherite Revolution' of the 1980s, success in Great Britain had always been predicated upon what family you were born into and not what you managed to do for yourself, your family or your wider community.

# 4

# The Incidental Feminist

> At the height of the Suffragette movement women chained themselves to the railings outside Number Ten Downing Street. Today, women are not content to be outside Number Ten looking in.
>
> MT, speech celebrating the fiftieth anniversary of<br>equal female suffrage, Westminster Hall, 3 July 1978

'I hate feminism – it is poison' might be the most inflammatory thing Margaret Thatcher never said. After all, the only person to report her saying it was her advisor, speechwriter and former member of the left-wing political elite Paul Johnson, in an article he wrote for *The Spectator* in 2011, entitled 'Failure of the Feminists'. Despite the fact that it has never been corroborated, this quote has been used millions of times by respected news organisations (back when there were such things) and seized upon by feminist groups as explicit proof that Margaret Thatcher was anti-feminist.

Was she? 'We got here, not by saying "you've got to have more women doing so and so" but saying "look, we've got the qualifications, why shouldn't we have just as much a chance as a man?"' she told the children's TV show *CBTV* in 1982, in an off-the-cuff remark with which many women will have sympathy and which was, as near as dammit, Thatcher's real view on how feminism should work. 'She told me that she thought the feminist thing was a diversion to hold her and other women back,' says Charles Moore.

Talking about Thatcher and feminism in the same breath has always been controversial. On 27 August 1979 – just a few months after she became Britain's first female Prime Minister (and the first woman to run a G7 country) – the *New York Times* ran an article with the headline: 'Mrs Thatcher Divides Feminists: A Woman in Power, but Not "a Sister"'. The 'not a sister' part is probably the second most lifted quote about MT with regards to her feminism in history, but at least this one's verifiable. It was uttered by Eileen Fairweather, an editor at the feminist magazine *Spare Rib*, which, the *NYT* piece tells us, 'has sharply criticized the conservative new course that she is charting for Britain'. In the same article, bestselling author Fay Weldon says that, in her household, Thatcher's name is never mentioned, before begrudgingly acknowledging that 'it is certainly true that every little girl in school knows now – as she did not know a year ago – that she can aspire to being the Prime Minister, that to be a woman is not necessarily to be second rate, and that's wonderful'.

It's hard to argue with the latter sentiment, especially since the *New York Times* also takes the opportunity in the same article to point out the parlous state of Britain's antiquated, male-dominated system by alluding to its tax laws. During the first decade that

## THE INCIDENTAL FEMINIST

Margaret Thatcher ran the country, British tax law prohibited our first female PM – like every other married woman in the country – from submitting her own tax returns. Instead, they had to be submitted by her husband, Denis. As improbable as it sounds now, it was not until 1990 that independent taxation, a law passed under Thatcher (but advocated for by her Chancellor, Nigel Lawson, it should be noted, and not the PM herself), allowed a married woman to submit her own returns and benefit from her own personal allowances. This marked the culmination of the fight for equality (at least where taxes were concerned) initiated by the Married Women's Property Act of 1870. The *NYT* also acknowledges that MT hasn't said much about feminism herself, except to respond when asked about it on the campaign trail: 'I reckon if you get anywhere, it's because of your ability as a person and not because of your sex.' Thatcher was notoriously chary of her overall focus being immersed in and overcome by the 'woman's debate'. Throughout her career she would constantly swerve the roadblock of being typecast and marginalised by her gender.

The fact that MT achieved her astonishing victories, to which no other woman had come remotely close, was seemingly not enough for her female critics – for some it still isn't. (Arguably Barbara Castle, the glamorous red-headed firebrand of the Labour administrations of 1964–70 could have given her a run for her money had her own party been less yoked to the patriarchy.) One of the first letters of congratulation which Margaret Thatcher received on her election as Conservative Party leader in February 1975 was from Castle. 'I happened to be with her when she wrote it, as soon as the news came in,' wrote Jack Straw, her then advisor and later to serve as a cabinet minister under Tony Blair. 'I can't help feeling a thrill,' Barbara recorded in her diary. 'She is so clearly the best man among them.'

Other women were not so generous. Glenda Jackson said in 2022 that it was Margaret Thatcher who was responsible for her decision to give up acting and go into politics. 'That was the extremity of everything I thought was the worst way for the country to go forward,' she said of MT's policies. Jackson did recognise, however, that 'of course the House of Commons wasn't welcoming for women, but in my generation we're so used to that.'

Why are so many women uncomfortable with acknowledging Margaret Thatcher's success as a supreme victory for women globally? Men never suffered from a similar lack of restraint. When MT died, President Barack Obama said, 'She stands as an example to our daughters that there is no glass ceiling that can't be shattered.' Regardless of your political leanings, Margaret Thatcher's journey represented a remarkable achievement. Only 76 women MPs sat in Parliament in the 45 years after 1919. 'In 1979 there were more MPs called John than women MPs, so of course she broke the glass ceiling,' said Cherie Blair KC.

Thatcher acknowledged the 'woman problem' herself when she wrote of her early endeavours to find a seat and the prejudices against her as a woman and mother. 'Perhaps some of the men at selection committees entertained this prejudice, but I found then and later it was the women who came nearest to expressing it openly.' When she became Prime Minister in 1979, her constituency office in Finchley was picketed by a vociferous feminist group who complained: 'We want women's right's – not a right-wing woman.'

# THE INCIDENTAL FEMINIST

> Margaret Thatcher presented the perfect argument for what it meant for women to see another woman achieving and running a G7 country – and a woman not from a privileged family dynasty, unlike the very few female leaders who had managed it before her or were in office when she came to power: Indira Gandhi and Sirimavo Bandaranaike of Sri Lanka,

says Virginia Bottomley, a junior minister for Thatcher in 1988–9. Interestingly, Golda Meir, Prime Minister of Israel 1969–74 – another of the cadre of female leaders to precede Margaret Thatcher, who died five months before MT became PM – was also the daughter of a shopkeeper. When Meir's family immigrated to the US from present-day Belarus, her mother ran a grocery store on Milwaukee's north side. Like the young Margaret Thatcher, Meir, known then as Goldie Mabovitch, worked in the store during her childhood.

> It's really simple when it comes to Margaret Thatcher and the so-called 'feminism' of today. She was born outside feminism and certainly before the current wave and its vocabulary. If you look at what she says about women, that they are the ones who make decisions, they decide on the household budget, everything about her implies an enormous respect for women and their ability,

says Gillian Shephard. Indeed, Thatcher's early views on women and work allude to the feminist cause – even if she never said the 'F' word. A series of newspaper articles and publications make clear her position. In a 1952 article for the *Sunday Graphic* headlined

'Wake up, Women', she wrote at length about females entering the workforce. 'I hope we shall see more and more women combining marriage and a career. Prejudice against this dual role is not confined to men. Far too often I regret to say it comes from our own sex.' She ended with a shot across the bows of male politicians, which they would have done well to heed: 'Should a woman arise equal to the task, I say let her have an equal chance with the men for the leading Cabinet posts. Why not a woman Chancellor – or Foreign Secretary?' In a 1954 article for *Onward*, a magazine published by Conservative Central Office for Young Conservatives, she continues her theme: 'Some men I know are far too ready with the phrase "a woman's place is in the home" – forgetting that their own daughters will almost certainly have to earn their living outside the home, at any rate for a time.'

Journalist and commentator Julie Burchill, a woman only too familiar with the Thatcher years, during which she was (she arguably still is) one of Britain's leading female opinion writers, says:

> No one ever spoke about feminism in her formative years, so it would have been rather odd if she'd come to power spouting feminist slogans – and rather opportunistic. Her contribution to feminism was to inspire, to show that it could be done. I'm always amused when that saying 'you've got to see it to be it' is applied to every other disadvantaged group – but when it comes to women, doing a thing first is seen as some kind of betrayal of one's less able sisters.

One of the few political women brave enough to put her head above the parapet, where Thatcher was concerned, was Oona King, now

Baroness King of Bow and only the second black woman to become an MP. In 1998, just seven years after the end of MT's final term, she wrote: 'I don't care if Margaret Thatcher was the devil, it meant so much to me that I was growing up when two women – she and the Queen – were running the country.'

King's quote appeared in Natasha Walter's book *The New Feminism* (Little, Brown 1998). In it, Walter evaluated feminism's successes, failures and future. She examined female role models, stating: 'No one can ever question whether women are capable of single-minded vigour, of efficient leadership, after Margaret Thatcher. She is the great unsung heroine of British feminism.' The response was nothing short of an avalanche of vituperation. In 2012, she told *The Guardian* that 'nothing I have ever written before or since has brought so much fury on my head. It was unacceptable then, as it seems to be now, for feminists to do anything but denounce Thatcher. Obviously, Thatcher was no feminist,' Walter continued.

> She had no interest in social equality, she knew nothing of female solidarity. I knew that then as I know it now… We should never forget her destructive policies or sanitise her corrosive legacy. But nor should we deny the fact that as the outsider who pushed her way inside, as the woman in a man's world, she was a towering rebuke to those who believe women are unsuited to the pursuit and enjoyment of power. Girls who grew up when she was running the country were able to imagine leadership as a female quality in a way that girls today struggle to do. And for that reason she is still a figure that feminists would be unwise to dismiss.

Looking back now, Walter says the response underlined one of the fundamental issues with modern-day feminism:

> As feminists, let's not romanticise women. I can't stand that kind of 'if women ruled the world there'd be no more war' kind of shit, which is patently nonsense. I mean, look at women leaders today – May, Truss, Patel, Badenoch et al. They are evidence that women who get into power are often not that different from men. I think one of the things that Thatcher definitely suffered from then still remains a challenge today: that women succeeding to that degree are still such a minority.

Gillian Shephard contends that a number of today's journalists, particularly a couple of prominent female columnists, wilfully interpret some of Thatcher's policies, like mine closures or the Falklands War, as 'anti-women'. She also suggests that the term 'feminist' has been sanctified. 'Of course, you can be a feminist and a bad person. Why does the term "feminist" now mean you are beyond reproach? This is intellectually lazy and rather stupid thinking.'

Historian Amanda Foreman adeptly summed up the problem: 'Her brand of women's rights – the right to compete, fight and succeed on equal terms with men – did not fit the fashionable orthodoxies of left-wing feminism. She wasn't interested in banning, separating, promoting or defining: she was interested in winning.'

The 'feminist' issue has long posed difficulties for those females who spent time around MT. 'I felt very nervous about whether writing a book about my experiences of working with Margaret Thatcher would destroy my reputation as a feminist,' says Caroline

Slocock. In her memoir, Slocock details her relationship (not always positive) with Thatcher as No. 10's first-ever female private secretary. Slocock's quandary also nails the 'Thatcher dilemma' when it comes to socialism and feminism – firstly, that no one on the left under any circumstance should be able to say anything positive about Thatcher. Concomitant with this is the subsequent belief that, to be a feminist, one must be left-wing. Amongst the many problems with this theory is the fact that feminism is then directly associated with the very fabric of the Labour Party's heritage: the trade unions, organisations whose link with the industrial past is by its nature predominantly male and patriarchal. 'Trade unions are as much in denial about the "woman problem" as they were about antisemitism because they refuse to see it as a structural problem that emanates from hard left politics,' wrote *Telegraph* columnist Suzanne Moore, coining the term 'Brocialism'. 'For them, equal representation for women is something that can wait till after the revolution – it's only Waitrose shoppers who care about that kind of thing.'

Julie Burchill is clear on the problems with feminism's entwinement with the left wing.

> Ever since Mrs Pankhurst was refused membership of Manchester Labour Party for the crime of not being a man, the relationship between women and the Left has been an abusive one. I would actually go so far as to say that it's not possible to be left-wing and a feminist any more. A left-wing woman has to sign up to so many misogynistic belief systems, from 'trans rights' to the alliance with Islamism. Why is Labour the only British political party which has never had a female leader?

# THE INCIDENTAL FEMINIST

Anyone who says you have to be left-wing to be a feminist needs to be able to answer this very simple question.

Harriet Harman (who declined to be interviewed for this book as 'it sounds like you are looking for the sort of commentary which I would not be comfortable giving') began an interview with UK magazine *Harper's Bazaar* in 2019 with an apology. Why, the magazine wanted to know, has there not been a female leader of the Labour Party? 'The first thing to say is that there should have been,' she responded. 'It's embarrassing and wrong that the party that regards itself as the party of equality, the party that has had more women MPs than all the other parties put together, has nonetheless never had a woman leader and the Conservative Party has had two.' (The figure is now four.)

She goes on to say that 'challeng[ing] the structures of the party' and being 'a subversive, critical force' don't 'win you any friends because the men think the women are taking the places that they could have had. This means we're seen as criticising the party hierarchy rather than being part of it.' Somebody like Thatcher, she says, was not seen as subversive within her own party. 'She wasn't saying, "It's been a party of men, I'm going to make it a party where women and men share power on equal terms."'

In criticising Margaret Thatcher and refusing to accept and acclaim her historical role as a powerful role model who cleared the path for other women, 'Thatcher haters' en masse do two things. Firstly, and perhaps most glaringly, they ignore the historical context of Thatcher's rise to power. Secondly, they undermine what is perhaps the greatest tenet of feminism: that women should support other women, no matter what – the very thing they criticise

Margaret Thatcher for not doing. In 2013, just after Thatcher's death, the Radio 4 *Today* programme presenter, Emma Barnett, then women's editor of the *Daily Telegraph*, argued that 'just because the Iron Lady did not consider herself to be a feminist... doesn't mean she cannot be an icon to all those women who do'.

The failure to embrace other women's views or achievements, regardless of whether they chime with our own beliefs, represents feminism's greatest and most dangerous blind spot. In their book *Hardball for Women* (Plume 1993), Pat Heim, Tammy Hughes and Susan K. Gollant discuss the concept of the 'power dead-even rule', which they say shapes women's interactions with each other as a result of centuries of misogyny. The principle of the rule is that power and self-esteem must be equal between women – in other words, 'dead-even'. They suggest that when this power balance is upset in situations such as promotion or elevated status, via whatever means, women who are left behind may ostracise the successful woman or belittle her.

Harman and thousands like her clearly did not get the memo. In 2009, the Government Equalities Office, led by Harman, then Labour's Deputy Leader, produced a 'Women in Power' fact sheet, designed as a reference document for schools. It listed sixteen women politicians who had 'shaped British history'. Margaret Thatcher's name was not on the list. She was in good company. Harman's department had also omitted to mention Britain's first female cabinet minister, trade unionist Margaret Bondfield (Minister of Labour 1929–31), Shirley Williams, former Education Secretary (1976–9), and Britain's first-ever female Secretary of State, Barbara Castle. These three women were from her own party. (Although perhaps Labour never forgave Shirley Williams for defecting to form the Social Democratic Party in 1981.) At a recent reopening of the National Portrait Gallery, complete with new wing and portico, funded in part by a £9.4 million National Lottery grant, attention was drawn to a new seven-panel mural entitled *Work in Progress* depicting 133 'Great British Women'. The panel included such luminaries as Margot Fonteyn, Mary Quant, Florence Nightingale, Dawn French and Queen Elizabeth I. But of Britain's first woman Prime Minister and the globe's first-ever female leader of a G7 country? No sign.

It's easy to see why and how in this world of vague school curriculums (the only thing mandated to be taught on the history curriculum is the Holocaust), five-second memes and logo-ridden merchandise, the two most common tropes about MT – 'milk snatcher' and 'mine closer' – have taken hold. 'I was giving an interview the other day and the interviewer was maybe 30 years old,' says Stephen Sherbourne.

> I was explaining about the pre-Thatcher Britain of the 1970s with the strikes, the power cuts, the inability to even get a telephone landline in less than eight weeks. When we were done she expressed absolute incredulity over what I was saying. She simply had no idea. And that's a problem.

'I was in a shop recently,' says Julie Burchill. 'It was the sort of place that sold all sorts of "cool" bits and pieces and prominently displayed was a row of mugs which said "Thatcher is still dead", and I thought, "Really – we're still doing this?"'

Author Lionel Shriver, writing for the website Slate in 2013, said:

# THE INCIDENTAL FEMINIST

If we had more feminists like Thatcher, we'd have vastly more women in Parliament and the US Senate, as well as more trees and fewer tedious television talk shows. More 'feminists' like Thatcher, the first woman to lead a major Western democracy, and young women would be clamoring to be called one, too.

Admire her or not, the facts are that when Margaret Thatcher was born women had only been enfranchised for seven years (and they wouldn't be able to vote on a par with men until 1928, when there were only eight women in the House of Commons). British women had spent decades looking to their counterparts in the USA for inspiration. American women were already way ahead of the game. Inspired by both Mary Wollstonecraft's *A Vindication of the Rights of Woman* (1792) and their post-revolutionary French counterparts, they had been advocating for women's rights in various forms using movements like Temperance and Abolition since the early 1800s. In Britain, post-Wollstonecraft, the control of the burgeoning feminist movement was very much in the hands of white upper-middle-class women like Millicent Fawcett and the Pankhursts, who achieved the Representation of the People Act in 1918, allowing women who were 30 or over, owned property or were married to someone who owned property, to vote. In 1919 it took an American, Nancy Witcher Langhorne Astor, who became Viscountess Astor, and thus British by marriage, to become the first woman to take a seat in Parliament, serving from 1919 until 1945.

As improbable as it sounds now, it is quite plausible to suggest that with Margaret Thatcher's strict Methodist upbringing and her conservative schooling, the construct of 'being a feminist' would have seemed entirely irrelevant to the path she was taking.

## THE INCIDENTAL FEMINIST

At Oxford, whilst Thatcher was studying at a woman's college, Somerville, from 1943 to 1947, feminism was the preserve of the left-leaning, privileged and upper-class 'bluestockings'. To be a feminist at this particular seat of learning meant to be both wealthy and a radical, and that was certainly not how the young MT, soon to be chair of the Oxford University Conservative Association (though she could not debate at the Oxford Union, where women were only admitted in 1963), could be described.

She was much more influenced by the right-wing Christian writings of Oxford alumnus C.S. Lewis than she was by feminist Simone de Beauvoir, whose treatise *The Second Sex* was published in 1949, just after MT left Oxford. And feminism was certainly not the kind of movement that her father or mother would have validated, or even discussed. It is likely, though, that the Robertses' grocery stores would have benefited from the campaigning of female MPs like Barbara Castle, Peggy Herbison and Jean Mann, all of whom argued for the reduction of rationing. All in all, the post-war 1940s were a relatively quiet time for feminism and women's campaigning – notwithstanding victories like the 1948 British Nationality Act, which allowed women who married a foreigner to retain their nationality, equal compensation for war injuries in 1943, the abolition of the marriage bar in teaching and the civil service in 1944 and 1946 and the passage of the Family Allowances Act in 1945.

In his book *Women and the Women's Movement in Britain* (Macmillan Education 1992), Martin Pugh asks whether 1945–59 was the 'nadir of British feminism'. Labour had been defeated by the Conservatives in 1951 on a ticket to 'set the people free', and a bombed-out, financially exhausted Britain was struggling with a 'reset', coming to terms with its denuded post-war global status. Pugh points out that there was a sense of historical detachment from the women's liberation movement because, for the younger generation of the 1950s (which would have included MT), the combination of welfare reform with their economic opportunities and political rights seemed to deprive the women of the movement of any real significant targets at which to aim. In other words, early British feminism had accomplished what it had set out to achieve: enfranchisement for all women.

It was not uncommon for women at this time to think that feminism was a redundant label – on both sides of the House. Take Barbara Castle, for example, who told Melanie Phillips (*The Divided House*, 1980): 'I had never had any conscious determination not to take up women's issues – I have just not been particularly interested in them... I always thought of myself as an MP, not as a woman MP.' In April 1960, Shirley Williams told the *Daily Telegraph* that being a feminist was a 'matter of generations'. 'Rights for women, so far as my generation is concerned, is a dead issue,' declared Marghanita Laski, the prominent author, journalist and critic in 1952. In 1978 MT underscored Laski's perspective, telling the *Hornsey Journal*:

> Each person is different. Each has their own talents and abilities, and these are the things you want to draw and bring out. You don't say: 'I must get on because I'm a woman,' or that 'I must get on because I'm a man.' You should say that you should get on because you have the combination of talents which are right for the job. The moment you exaggerate the question, you defeat your case.

# THE INCIDENTAL FEMINIST

It almost goes without saying that, if publicly declaring one was a feminist was seen as unnecessary for two notorious left-wingers like Castle and Williams, it was hardly surprising that MT might view it as a roadblock on the motorway to success. According to Caroline Slocock, 'There was just no way she would ever have been elected an MP, let alone PM, on a feminist ticket, nor would she have wanted to, given her political beliefs. She did not see herself as a feminist but the fact is, misogyny in politics was rife. It still is.'

Charles Powell says that MT was not, as many believe, opposed to putting her weight behind women's issues, rather she was acutely aware of how it would look.

> She definitely enjoyed the uniqueness of her position, but she wasn't blind to women's issues. She spoke to women's organisations and took their views on board, but I think she didn't want to be characterised by feminism, because she thought it would undermine what she ultimately wanted to achieve if all she was known for was 'women's issues'. She was scared that she wouldn't be taken seriously with all of the other issues.

This says more about the patriarchal dominance within society than it does about Margaret Thatcher. In his article in *The Spectator* in 2011, Paul Johnson wrote:

> What has often struck me is that all the successful women I have known in politics have been anti-feminist, though some have not dared to say so publicly. Barbara Castle, though stalwart Labour all her long life, and fairly far to the left, too, used

to say: 'The feminists have done absolutely nothing for me. I have had to do it all myself.' She thought feminism, with its insistence on 'Chairs', etc., was often counterproductive. So did Violet Bonham Carter, the best woman speaker I have ever heard. Indira Gandhi believed she owed everything to her family and nothing to the women's movement.

During the seventies, both political parties regarded the idea of feminism and women working 'outside the home' as a dangerous threat to the stability of society. 'Our aim is straightforward,' wrote James Callaghan, the then Labour Prime Minister, in 1977. 'It is to strengthen the stability and quality of family life in Britain.' The *Socialist Register*, which published a paper on Thatcherism in 1987 ('Thatcherism and Women: After Seven Years' by Elizabeth Wilson), pointed out that both major parties clung to an ideology of familism 'because it articulates a number of different and sometimes disparate hopes and fears: of crime and a breakdown in law and order; of sexual unruliness and deviance and, most important but least explicit, men's determination to hang on to the privileges of their gender'.

It was perhaps Thatcher's solution to the feminist dilemma that would prove more problematic to women in the long run than her failure to embrace old-fashioned 'feminism'. 'I say a wife can do two jobs,' she told the *Evening News* in 1960. And therein lay the problem. In July 1982, MT gave the inaugural Dame Margery Corbett-Ashby Memorial Lecture, arguing for what we, as women, might justifiably (and angrily) define as the 'two-role solution'. 'What are these special talents and experiences which women have to bring to public life? Are they any different in kind from those of men? Yes... because we women bear the children and run the home. It is noticeable... that many of the suffragettes were very womanly.' (For which we might substitute 'wealthy', as that enabled many of the leaders of the moment to have extensive domestic help so that they could get out and campaign).

As MT saw it at the time (unfortunately for the rest of us), a wife *could* do two jobs – she could leave the house and run a country, but not before she'd cooked Denis his breakfast and checked the twins' homework. By yoking (or was it guilting?) women into the twin role of matriarch and working mother, she offered an almost unobtainable ideal for any woman without enough funds to pay for help (and an uphill, unwinnable battle for those who could). She also ignored the concept of male responsibility within the family unit for child-raising and child-care.

Is it enough to excuse her that she was a woman 'of her time'? The early signs are that she understood at least the frustration of women feeling trapped in the home. She advocated only a 'short leave of absence at the mother's discretion' after giving birth. But later, in an unfortunate 1970 interview, she spoke of the need to employ an English nanny. 'I wouldn't have been quite sure if the au pair could speak English... so I always had a good English nanny.' Although she claimed that she never thought of her sex as an obstacle, MT's anxiety about her gender, and its place within the political arena, was writ large early on. When writing about being shortlisted for Dartford in 1949, her first stab at finding a seat, 'It was the questions which were more likely to cause me trouble. There was a good deal of suspicion of women candidates, particularly in what was regarded as a tough industrial seat like Dartford. This was quite definitely a man's world into which not just angels fear to tread.'

By taking the enormous step to stand as a female candidate, Thatcher was making her mark for women, whether she (or we) acknowledged it or not.

> In her, we saw a woman who did not shy away from showing how much she loved power, and in turn she made it legitimate for us to love it too... [she] gave us a road map, a route to follow, a vantage point from which to strike out in a new direction,

wrote Helen Wilkinson in *On the Move*, edited by Natasha Walter (Virago 1999).

Once she became an MP, Margaret knew that she would routinely have to run the gauntlet of misogynist abuse. Nothing can have prepared her, though, for the onslaught she would face once in Parliament, where misogyny and overt sexism were endemic, with female MPs, particularly those who were identified as feminists, treated as domestics at best and sexual playthings or objects of ridicule as standard. '"Ditch the Bitch" was one of the milder insults Margaret Thatcher had to bear,' confesses a former male colleague. 'A great deal was unrepeatable, but she heard it all right.'

In her book *Women of Westminster* (I.B. Tauris, 2019), Rachel Reeves details some of the earliest and most outrageous behaviour directed at Bessie Braddock and Leah Manning, MPs during the forties, 'both of whom were on the large side... with a habit of going everywhere together, arm-in-arm', and who were referred to by one MP as 'a couple of tanks' and by others as 'United Dairies' – a reference to their 'ample bosoms'. As Parliamentary Secretary to the Ministry of Food, Edith Summerskill often had to answer questions about rationing after the Second World War. She recalled how 'the jeers and the counter-jeers drowned my voice time after time'. It was precisely the sort of abuse which would have informed, daunted and dismayed a young, naive, sexually awkward Methodist and burgeoning MP like Margaret Thatcher and persuaded her that, were she ever to consider it, sitting on the front or back benches as a feminist was not a career-furthering profile.

There's no doubt that Margaret Thatcher ardently and openly rejected the domestic drudgery to which so many 1950s women were still subject. She says so in her autobiography:

> Of course, to be a mother and a housewife is a vocation of a very high kind. But I simply felt that it was not the whole of my vocation. I knew that I also wanted a career… And not just any career. I wanted one which would keep me mentally active and prepare me for the political future for which I believed I was well suited.

Just a week after delivering twins, six weeks early by C-section in August 1953, she sent off the application form for her Bar finals,

> knowing that this little psychological trick I was playing on myself would ensure that I plunged into legal studies on my return to Swan Court with the twins, and that I would have to organize our lives so as to allow me to be both a mother and a professional woman.

## THE INCIDENTAL FEMINIST

In this, she was on her own. Denis's response to his first sight of the twins (after missing the birth because he was watching cricket at the Oval) was 'My God, they look like rabbits. Put them back.' His solution to his own childcare crisis was to rent the apartment next door to their own, thereafter shutting the evidence of his new responsibilities out of sight, leaving them to be raised by a nanny – and by Margaret when she arrived home.

She explained in her autobiography what selection committees would subject her to:

> I would be short-listed, would make what was generally acknowledged to be a good speech – and then the questions, most of them having the same purpose, would begin. With my family commitments, would I have time enough for the constituency? Did I realize how much being a Member of Parliament would keep me away from home? And sometimes more bluntly still: did I really think that I could fulfil my duties as a mother with young children to look after and as an MP?

Whilst she acknowledges that the selection committees 'had every right' to ask her those questions, she admits that she resented the 'feeling that the House of Commons was not really the right place for a woman anyway'.

As Wendy Webster observes,

> A great deal of what Mrs Thatcher has to say about women can be read as an attempt to resolve the contradictions between the role she assigns to other women and what she herself has done.

The combination of career and family she envisaged was possible only for middle-class women who could afford to employ the magic figure of a housekeeper–nanny.

When MT finally gained her Finchley seat in 1959 she joined just 24 other female MPs in the House. Conservative victories in 1951, 1955 and 1959 had been achieved in the wake of increasing prosperity, fuller employment and rising real wages. Meanwhile, a young monarch in her twenties, described earlier in the decade by MT in a newspaper article as 'the loveliest ever to reign over us', was learning the ropes. Gradually, wages and disposable incomes rose, leading Harold Macmillan to utter the phrase: 'most of our people have never had it so good.'

By 'our people' he must have meant 'our men'. For women, if anything, the lauded 'time-saving' technological developments of the consumer age of the 1950s – the TV, the washing machine, the vacuum cleaner – served only to reinforce female status as housewives, whilst returned servicemen bedded back into their roles as heads of the family and dominant members of the workforce. It is only with hindsight that the fifties can also be viewed as the decade which ultimately heralded the birth of a new movement – the rise of the working mother.

Could the so-called 'second wave' of feminism led by young, glamorous magazine journalist Gloria Steinem and writer and campaigner Betty Friedan, which emerged in the USA during the 1960s in reaction to the post-war backlash against women and was soon nicknamed 'Women's Lib', really have passed MT by? The answer is no. As a young female MP, living and working at the epicentre of the drug-soaked, miniskirt-toting, pro-hirsute 'youthquake' which was occurring on both sides of the Atlantic, she cannot have failed to notice or hear 'Swinging London'. And as the daughter of a Methodist lay minister and the mother of a young daughter, it's easy to see why she probably didn't like it very much. She certainly would not have approved of Friedan's attack on the family in her revolutionary book *The Feminine Mystique*, written in 1962, which took direct aim at the 'happy housewife' myth and what she described as 'the comfortable concentration camp' of the family unit.

One thing MT did appreciate about the counterculture of the sixties was the single medical advancement that did more than anything else to free women from the burden of inevitable maternal responsibilities: the pill. As MP Teresa Gorman recounts in her book *No, Prime Minister!* (Blake 2001), the Thatchers had together agreed that they would take no 'chances' where a further career-limiting pregnancy was concerned. She began taking the pill (which became available in the UK on the NHS in 1961) soon after giving birth to the twins. In the *Socialist Register* report of 1987, the author points out that whilst there is little if any evidence to support the idea of a 'moral backlash against the so-called "permissive society" of the 1960s', politicians like Margaret Thatcher, Norman Tebbit and MT's greatest early influence, Sir Keith Joseph, all tended to locate the origins of many of their era's problems in the sixties.

Certainly, it was during the 1960s and 1970s, when MT was already an MP (her first government post was as Parliamentary Under-secretary at the Ministry of Pensions in 1961), that working-class women and so-called 'lesser-educated females' became entwined with the modern-day feminist movement. Their

# THE INCIDENTAL FEMINIST

bible might have been Germaine Greer's groundbreaking book *The Female Eunuch*, published in 1970, which argued for revolution not evolution of the women's movement, but in fact working-class women had long been engaged with the socialist Co-operative movement and its Women's Guild (founded in 1883). These organisations were already working towards educational economic and social improvement, and women's enfranchisement. But it was during the 1950s that socialism and feminism really engaged with their involvement in protests such as the Ford machinists' strike and the Trawler Safety Code protests of 1968.

In 1970, a Women's Liberation conference on feminism at Ruskin College in Oxford attracted over 500 women, from mainly working-class and lower-middle-class backgrounds, whose lives had been changed by the growth of further education in the UK, drawn together by a common mission: to make a difference to those of their background whom they felt were under-represented in the feminist fight for equality. In 1979 the first Black and Asian Women's Conference was held by OWAAD (Organisation of Women of African and Asian Descent), 'recognising Black Women's fight for liberation from the triple oppression of male-dominated black groups, white-dominated women's groups and middle-class-dominated left groups' (according to the radical feminist journal *Off Our Backs*, January 1980).

It was MT's actions as Ted Heath's Education Secretary (1970–4) over the so-called 'school milk scandal' that enabled her critics to label her as 'anti-woman'. The war of words also created a benchmark in her controversial progress towards the top job, one by which she would always be judged. Shakespeare or Freud could not have scripted it better: a female minister effectively banning milk – with all of its nurturing mother and breast associations – from the mouths of 7–13-year-old schoolchildren. Never mind that most children despised the hideous stuff, delivered to schools, rattling in blue or green crates, only to sit by classroom radiators or in the sun, congealing into rancidity before break. Cue headlines, including 'Is Mrs Thatcher Human?' from *The Sun*. Other newspapers made allusions to Lady Macbeth, and the furore dominated front pages and TV news for days. Worse still was MT's serene appearance, in a prim lemon tea dress, on a Thames TV morning show, battling with a militant mother in a leopard-skin-print blouse. 'How would Mrs Thatcher like to go all day without a drink… never again will I vote Conservative. Hurting children is absolutely the end.' 'I'm either the witch or the Lady Macbeth of English politics,' Thatcher once joked (or was it a joke?). 'I think she regarded cutting school milk as little more than a box-ticking, money-saving exercise,' says one ex-cabinet minister. 'She didn't think it through.' She had no reason to – after all, the withdrawal of school milk wasn't a new policy: Harold Wilson's Labour government had already put a stop to the provision of milk to 11–18-year-olds in 1968 without so much as a whimper. The removal of milk from younger children was a modest reduction in an otherwise positive education budget, from which the *Daily Mail* had initially pronounced that MT emerged a 'new heroine'. As she says in her autobiography: 'It was pleasant while it lasted.'

The publicity over school milk got a whole lot worse before it got better. In November 1971, *The Sun* voted her 'the most unpopular woman in Britain'. Even more damaging was the fact that the phrase 'milk snatcher' simply would not die – although the jury is out on who coined it. In her autobiography, MT says it was a Labour MP. In her book *Difficult Women: A History of Feminism in 11 Fights* (Jonathan Cape 2020), journalist Helen Lewis details an interview with domestic abuse campaigner Erin Pizzey in her home: 'When I made it up the stairs to Pizzey's flat, the first thing which greeted me was a poster reading: "Margaret Thatcher, milk snatcher". (She claims to have coined the phrase.)' Whoever came up with it, the school milk scandal taught Margaret Thatcher a valuable lesson, as she later admitted in her autobiography.

> I and my colleagues were caught up in battles with local authorities for months, during which we suffered constant sniping in the media, all for a saving of £9 million which could have been cut from the capital budget with scarcely a ripple. In future if I were to be hanged, it would be for a sheep, not a lamb, still less a cow.

What she does not mention (because she would have thought it merited little attention) is the type of misogynist abuse she received from polytechnic students from Coventry to Liverpool, documented by her speechwriter and advisor Robin Harris: 'Thatcher out, Tories out, fascist pig, get her fucking knickers off!' Although she denied it, in the early days the abuse stung. But then, perhaps it always did? She was depressed for weeks afterwards. 'Despite her tough public persona, the criticism rankled, especially when she thought it was downright unfair. Dad was brilliant at rallying her spirits,' writes Carol Thatcher.

Years later the school milk saga re-emerged and Thatcher's response illustrated just how scarred she had been. When her then Education Secretary Ken Clarke suggested that they finally end all school milk for junior school children, her note back to him in response says it all: 'No – this will cause a terrible row – all for £4m. I know – I went through it 19 years ago.' A veil was never entirely drawn over school milk for MT, as it most certainly would have been had she been a male minister of education. When she died in 2013, almost every major obituary made reference to it. In David Cannadine's book *Margaret Thatcher: A Life and Legacy* (OUP 2017), he claims that Ted Heath considered sacking her and she briefly thought of leaving politics altogether over the matter. Who could have blamed her? As John Redwood, who joined Thatcher's front bench in 1989 as Parliamentary Under-secretary in the Department of Trade and Industry, pointed out, the headline 'Edward Heath, milk thief' (which might have been more apposite given that it was under his auspices as PM that the milk was withdrawn) was never and would never have been used.

The abuse that she received over school milk did not persuade MT that she should play the feminist card. In fact, it seemed to harden her resolve against it. Despite the advice given to her by her advisor and speechwriter, former journalist Patrick Cosgrave, that polling during the 1970s suggested that she should use her gender to connect with those women interested in, or increasingly influenced by, the re-emerging feminist movement, she ignored him. She did, however, take the advice of her Svengali, the 'polished and amusing former TV producer' Gordon Reece, in her words, who persuaded her not to debate the then PM James Callaghan in her prime ministerial campaign because men (and possibly women too) wouldn't like to see a woman effectively 'duffing up' a male leader on TV. Instead, he persuaded her to take on softer daytime TV appearances to appeal to the women's vote.

'Perhaps the most striking and successful response of the women's movement to the Thatcher era lay in the return to issues of war and peace,' writes Martin Pugh. The Falklands War of 1982 notwithstanding (see Chapter 6), two protests uniquely marked and marred MT's time as PM, where left-wing women were concerned, fuelling the fire of the feminist movement against her. You could see their point. Her actions, or rather her reactions, to both went straight to the heart of the preservation of the family unit and underlined the need for effective feminist resistance to 'Big Government'.

The Greenham Common protests began innocently enough. In 1981, a group of Welsh women walked the 100 miles from their homes in Cardiff, arriving at RAF Greenham Common in Berkshire, England. They were protesting against the government's approval for the United States to store their cruise missiles on the site, and made their views known by attaching themselves to the chain-link perimeter fence. It blossomed into one of the largest, longest and most impressive all-female peacetime protest movements, with some women living on site for the full 19 years of its existence. Marching under the banner 'Women for Life on Earth', the protesters succeeded in uniting the anti-nuclear campaign, anti-militarists and feminists. In 1982, the decision to make the protest 'all female' only served to highlight the stark contrast between, on the one hand, Thatcher, the patriarchal army camp, the soldiers and police who were responsible for protecting the base and, on the other, the women themselves, who camped outside in the most basic of conditions, routinely decorating the wire perimeter fence with genderised totems including nappies, children's clothes, flowers and teddy bears. 'From my point of view, it was the best way to live under Margaret Thatcher – to work for peace and live off the meagre dole money. I was about 36 when I arrived and I didn't leave until eight years later, in May 1990,' wrote one peace camper in *The Guardian* in 2017.

An inspired 'action' organised in April 1983, when 70,000 women formed a 14-mile human chain from Greenham to Aldermaston, where the UK's Atomic Weapons Establishment (AWE – yes, really) was based, attracted global press attention. Other international peace camps followed. Above all, this long-running 'feminine' resistance and suffragette-like surge of protests, summarily broken up by heavy-handed, often aggressive police, who routinely evicted or arrested groups of encamped women, served to highlight the difference between British 'women' and their Prime Minister, who waspishly dismissed the protests as 'an eccentricity inflamed by the media'. Then Defence Secretary Michael Heseltine says that, rather than being effective, the women protesters merely served to reinforce the idea that they were a 'hindrance'. 'When I arrived on the site in 1983, the women did me a huge favour by behaving like banshees. This enabled me to say "I don't debate the mob"; they were then shown to be out of control and were eventually overwhelmed by the police.'

The Greenham women were undoubtedly an impressively bonded, proactive force for protest for almost twenty years in the UK. Furthermore, they represented a united female voice, moving as one against their female Prime Minister, who never seemed to be able to pluck up the courage (or was it the heart?) to have them evicted, fearing a national and international backlash. They also served to illustrate the blatantly misogynistic narrative which existed within the media towards women (in general) but most especially towards women who refused to accept the status quo. A brief look at the press cuttings from the time tells the story, with the Greenham women described by *The Sun* as 'burly lesbians' and by *The Spectator* as 'hefty ladies... a fairly gruesome bunch'. Acres of (male-generated) coverage was devoted to the on-site hygiene. Commentator Auberon Waugh launched his own 'offensive' offensive, stating that the Greenham women smelt of 'fish paste and bad oysters'.

The second female uprising came from a far more unexpected and almost incidental source. The miners' strike of 1984–5 shone a new light on the traditional narrative of patriarchal mining towns and villages, with women as simply supporting domestic players, their lives revolving around the stove and the kitchen sink. Instead, women emerged as the heroes of the conflict, becoming an effective anti-Thatcher pressure group: organising, mobilising and picketing against pit closures, and challenging the government in a bid to preserve their existing way of life. That these women were initially not motivated by the concept of female empowerment is not in doubt. But it was their emergence from the domestic sphere and into wider society as an effective protest movement that led ultimately to a fundamental life change for many of them. 'The strike would never have lasted as long without the women. Thatcher put the arm of the state between her and the miners and we stood with them,' Heather Wood told Beverley Trounce for her book *From a Rock to a Hard Place: Memories of the 1984/85 Miners' Strike* (The History Press 2015).

Many of the mining women admitted that their own forays into supporting the strikes, alongside their partners, husbands and sons, were the first time they had stepped out of the sphere of 'the home', and once out, few wanted to go back. 'We organised trips for women… some of them probably hadn't been out of the village before,' Anne Scargill, wife of the striking miners' leader Arthur, told Radio 5 Live's *Eye of the Storm* (26 July 2018). 'We were fighting for our future… even though the miners were chauvinists and had to have their dinner on the table.' For many women, this taste of freedom outside the home, albeit in desperate circumstances, was empowering. 'It changed a lot of women,' remembers Anne Scargill, who tells of one young miner complaining of his newly emboldened wife post-strike: 'I don't want her I've got now, I want her I had before!' 'The strike made women think for ourselves. I always say Maggie Thatcher educated us for free,' miner's wife turned activist Aggie Currie told Trounce.

'She made the lives of a great mass of working women a whole lot worse,' says Frances O'Grady, now a Labour peer. It's a statement I have heard time and again from left-wing women. In O'Grady's case, her views are both personal and political – she was the sister of a striking miner and her disdain for Thatcher is visceral: 'The Thatcher government's policies – from attacking single mothers' welfare to mass unemployment – devastated the lives of millions of working-class families, and we are still living with the consequences.' Over the course of the 1960s and 70s (before Thatcher's premiership), 300,000 mining jobs disappeared. Around one million disappeared between 1920 and 1980. And Britain was not the first to deindustrialise. The reality is that in the 23 most advanced global economies, employment in manufacturing declined from about 28 per cent of the workforce in 1970 to about 18 per cent in 1994.

From MT's perspective, her battle with the trade unions was for 'freedom', against strong-arm, male-dominated organisations, who had long held a metaphorical gun to the heads of the government and the British public. Would Thatcher have presented less of a 'hate figure' had she been a man? Almost certainly. In part, the miners' own leader, the intransigent Marxist Arthur Scargill, presented the perfect foil in Thatcher's fight: 'Scargill was a pain in the arse at sixteen and he remained a pain in the arse,' says Neil Kinnock, the former Labour leader (1983–92). 'He never had any intention of negotiating. He wanted to bring her down, he wanted to bring the government down. For him, it was personal.'

In the bigger picture, feminism's response to Margaret Thatcher was a whole lot more surprising than that of the patriarchy. But was this more about her persona than her policies? Could it be her outward appearance, demeanour and – as so many have commented on – voice that so many women found equally disturbing? Was the problem that she didn't manifest as a 'woman's woman' in her two-piece business suit, her shoulder pads and her string of pearls? Could it really be that some women (and men, but particularly women) didn't like what she wore and the way she looked? Author Beatrix Campbell makes the distinction: 'feminine, not feminist'. 'She gave the feminine face to a thoroughly patriarchal political project.' Historian Mary Beard writes in her book *Women & Power* (Profile 2017) that, historically, women who claim a public voice get treated as 'freakish androgynes'. 'We have no template for what a powerful woman looks like,' she writes, 'except that she looks rather like a man.' Does she? As evidence, Beard points to the regulation trouser suits of Angela Merkel and Hillary Clinton (she might now have added Kamala Harris and Melania Trump). This is flimsy theory. One only need look at other past and present female leaders in business, the media and politics – from Jacinda Ardern to Melinda French Gates to Oprah – for examples of 'women in dresses'. In an ironic wink to the patriarchy, international icon Taylor Swift dons a Thatcher-style big-shouldered suit jacket over her sparkly leotard to sing one of her biggest hits, 'The Man', in which she ponders the fact that women have to metaphorically run much faster than men to get ahead.

Margaret Thatcher, of course, never 'wore the trousers' either. 'My impression of her was as an immaculate woman. She literally never had a hair out of place. She dressed to kill, every single day,' says Virginia Bottomley. MT thought, albeit in a rather quaint, old-fashioned way, that she should always 'look her best' for the electorate she served and for the political leaders she was meeting. And, in any case, isn't marking out a woman by dint of her appearance objectifying and anti-feminist? Do we really need a template for women in power? Did we ever?

> Her stiff serge tailoring, boxy croc handbags, patent court shoes, pussycat bow blouses and set hair have been fetishised by a moronic, apolitical fashion industry. But feminist iconhood has nothing to do with looks, because it is sexist to rate women by our appearance rather than our words and actions, as we are not objects,

wrote Bidisha in *The Guardian*, successfully managing to do the very thing she derided.

'Certainly, it was the belligerence of Margaret Thatcher that I found so anti-feminist and her assault on every value that feminism held to be important,' says author and psychotherapist Susie Orbach, who concedes that her leadership must have come at great cost.

Given what we know about the misogyny and the patriarchal power balance within society and Parliament, is it any wonder that MT felt she needed to create a starchy, deflective avatar to get the job done and invite as little sexist abuse and gender-based subordination in the ranks as was humanly possible?

Wendy Webster says that Thatcherism was a 'profoundly gendered view of society' and that MT viewed herself as 'different' to other women (and men for that matter). 'She saw herself as a unique individual who had made it through her own talent and her own determination.' This is a commonly held view of Margaret Thatcher in the UK, and it is an indictment of British society that we should regard her singular approach as something negative. In America, it would get you a standing ovation.

But Thatcherism, whilst promulgated by a woman, was most certainly not a female-focused ideology. Amongst the uncomfortable truths which prevail around any study of Margaret Thatcher is the fact that she failed to promote women to her cabinets. In total, she appointed precisely two – one an 'old friend', Baroness Janet Young, who served in the cabinet in 1981–2 as Chancellor of the Duchy of Lancaster. She lasted just fourteen months. She was also Leader of the House of Lords from 1981 to 1983 and Lord Keeper of the Privy Seal between 1982 and 1983. 'She turned out not to have the presence to lead the Lords effectively,' said MT of her dismissal in 1983, without even the hint of faint praise. Then, Sally Oppenheim served as Minister of State for Consumer Affairs from 1979 to 1982 before also 'graduating' to the Lords. Later, Edwina Currie, Gillian Shephard and Virginia Bottomley were all appointed as junior ministers by Thatcher, with Shephard and Bottomley both going on to become cabinet ministers under John Major. There seems to be little excuse for MT's anti-female stance – if it was that. 'She was Prime Minister for eleven years. She could have promoted whoever she liked, but she did not promote any women MPs into the cabinet, even though Lynda Chalker, Janet Fookes and others would have made it in any other environment,' says Edwina Currie, adding: 'Part of the problem was an all-male Whips' Office, often the entry point for high ministerial office. She could have put in female whips but she chose not to.'

When I ask a former cabinet minister of Thatcher's whether Currie's theory holds water, he concurs. 'Everything was so, so male. They were already struggling with her. I don't think she thought it was in her interest to try to promote women – it would have been yet another obstacle in keeping the cabinet and the backbenchers onside.' Beatrix Campbell put it differently to Julie Gottlieb in 2019:

> Femininity was what Thatcher performed, it was the frock she wore; but she eschewed any concessions to equality, to the world of women except to invoke patriarchal rhetoric of home and hearth. She didn't extend solidarity to women colleagues. I think she associated female experience – and feminism – with sacrifice, subordination and defeat, and she disparaged feminism for drawing attention to that.

So, what did Thatcherism do for women in the eighties – or rather do *to* women in the eighties? 'The 1980s are generally seen as a difficult decade for feminism in terms of popular representations as well as inner divisions,' write Stéphanie Genz and Benjamin A. Brabon in *Postfeminism: Cultural Texts and Theories* (Edinburgh University Press 2009). In her book *Backlash* (Chatto & Windus 1992), Susan Faludi says that the 1980s represented 'a powerful counter assault on women's rights, a backlash, an attempt to retract the handful of small and hard-won victories that the feminist movement did manage to win for women'. She locates the backlash in the emergence of 'the hard right' in 1980s Reaganite America and a hostile mass media, which proclaimed the death of feminism and the emergence of a generation of post-feminists who were underlining the female predicament of childlessness and singledom. Radical feminist Andrea Dworkin's book *Right-Wing Women* (Macmillan 1983) suggested that the patriarchal right exploited women's vulnerability by offering them a level of security (in part against the violence of men) in return for the suppression of their newly won rights and a return to right-wing values. Both books had and still have relevance on this side of the pond too.

Brought to its natural (and admittedly much more lightweight) conclusion, 1990s feminism on this side of the Atlantic witnessed a volte-face in popular/populist form in the extraordinary success of Helen Fielding's hapless Bridget Jones and the emergence of 'chick lit', wherein the holy grail for a young, educated, modern woman returned to the Victorian ideal of marriage and children. And, once again, the unreconstructed male stamped his boots all over society in the form of the testosterone-fuelled, sweary, lairy, lads' mag culture.

# THE INCIDENTAL FEMINIST

Where women were concerned, the Tory government of Margaret Thatcher was neither explicit in its attacks, nor were they targeted. As Robin Harris writes, MT never 'achieved any great coherence on the questions of how to balance a woman's right to fulfil her talents with her duties as a mother'. It is certainly true that her 1972 promise of nursery education 'without charge to children of three or four whose parents wished them to have it' was abandoned. The *Socialist Register* report states that it was not Margaret Thatcher's government which initiated a policy of monetarism and abandoned the commitment to full employment (to include women); rather it was the Labour government of the second half of the 1970s under James Callaghan. According to research by the Newcomb College Institute, of the seventeen major legislative decisions made during Margaret Thatcher's tenure as PM, eleven were favourable and five unfavourable to women.

What is certain is that some sectors of women did worse under Thatcher than others, with middle-class women working in non-manual jobs being better paid and having better conditions of employment than most female workers. It is also true that the feminist uprising against Thatcher never really took off. Amongst the many reasons for this, the most salient seems to be that the movement was divided and fragmented along the lines of race, class and sexual orientation, for which the feminist movement itself must bear some responsibility.

Any form of female praise for Thatcher (other than from her own party) is inevitably tempered. Even when it's in a book entitled *Women of Westminster: The MPs Who Changed Politics*. At least the book's author, at the time of writing our first female

Chancellor, Rachel Reeves, a woman who sprinkles her own rhetoric with Thatcher-style references such as 'My mum showed me how to balance the books at the kitchen table', acknowledges that Margaret Thatcher showed her what was possible. 'I never doubted that a woman could lead and be Prime Minister. Thatcher fundamentally challenged assumptions about women and power.' MT could not have found much strength in female solidarity in Parliament even if she had chosen to look for it, concedes Reeves: 'Excluded from many of the parliamentary clubs in which male MPs socialised and networked, female MPs did not form a woman's caucus to add strength to their numbers.'

Instead, women were forced to find solidarity where they could – and in small gestures. Reeves mentions the famous incident when Labour MP Shirley Williams robustly took an hour of parliamentary questions as Secretary of State for Prices and Consumer Protection in October 1973, and then retired exhausted to the Lady Members' Room – a tiny space where women members could hang their clothes and compose themselves. Here she found Margaret Thatcher MP, who had been in the chamber observing Williams' performance, now intently ironing a dress: 'You did well,' she said to Williams, pausing for a moment from her task to look up. 'After all, we can't let them get the better of us.'

# 5

# The Three Marketeers

## *Anatomy of an Icon*

> The trouble with you is that you think I'm Anna Neagle.
> MT to special advisor Ronald Millar

For a woman who allegedly didn't like other women, Margaret Thatcher surrounded herself with a surprising number of them. And together, they all served to create a barrier between their boss and the outside world, protecting her from the perpetual threat of intrusion and guiding those who were permitted – at the right moment – to intrude. Omnipresent at government meetings (this was after all the pre-digital age, where someone had to be there at all times to take notes), her secretaries' (diary, parliamentary and otherwise) names appear with regularity on government briefings, personal notes, fact-finding documentation and simple scheduling requests: Tessa Jardine Paterson, Joy Robilliard, Alison Ward (later Lady Wakeham), Caroline Stephens (later Lady Ryder), Amanda Ponsonby... In fact, MT's coterie of secretaries, designers, beauty experts and assistants were some of the people closest to her throughout her career. As confidantes and co-conspirators within the inner circle, they were an iron ring of the keepers of her secrets. So much so that she exacted a promise from almost all of them that they would not talk, even after her death. 'I think her closest relationships during her time at No. 10 were almost certainly with the women who supported her – like Crawfie and Joy Robilliard [previously Airey Neave's secretary],' says Robin Butler. 'She trusted them to be her gatekeepers.' These were the women who organised not only the PM's diary but also her meals and often her clothes. 'One of the girls – often Joy Robilliard – would do the cooking, shepherd's pie or something with chicken; Margaret loved bloody chicken,' says one insider, who would often eat in the flat above No. 10 if they were working late. 'We ate a ridiculous amount of chicken.'

It was Cynthia Crawford – Crawfie – who would organise and buy Margaret's 'personals', everything from headache pills to M&S underwear. A perfect example of the cordon which surrounded MT (and inevitably involved Denis) appears in the archives in the form of a minute sent by Joy to Denis and copied to Sally Dickson, her appointments secretary, on 4 March 1980: 'Mrs Zerney phoned. She says she knows the PM. She wants the PM to stay when she is in Yorkshire. She sounds a nut, but I thought I would just check to see if you had heard of her.' Denis's response: 'Yes she _is_ a NUT and there is nothing the PM would like LESS...' Archie Hamilton testifies that the most gossip and chat he would ever hear issuing from the mouth of the PM was during the time that she was having her hair washed and set in the mornings:

# THE THREE MARKETEERS

> As her PPS I used to think it was my duty to sit and wait for her to get ready in the mornings in case she needed something. As I waited, I could hear her happily chatting away about nothing really. This was very out of character, but it was also when she was at her most relaxed.

One wag wrote that the most powerful person in the land was Margaret Thatcher's dentist. In fact, it was probably Crawfie, who came to No. 10 with the blessing of Great Universal Stores tycoon and special advisor David Wolfson in 1979, when MT assumed the premiership. Crawfie, who had previously been Wolfson's secretary, came on a secondment for two years and overstayed by several decades. She was one of the people closest to MT until her death in 2013. It was Crawfie – and later Margaret King from Aquascutum – who knew where the bodies were buried, when it came to the secrets and lies of the Thatcher years. They have proved worthy of her trust. But that doesn't mean there haven't been some 'acceptable' secrets to share. Margaret King, for example, refuses to name MT's perfume because it would be 'too intimate'. (For the record it was said that she wore two: Penhaligon's Bluebell and Guerlain's Mitsouko.) What she will allow is that MT could easily have been an actress.

> Oh my goodness, she could be very dramatic – and not only that, she was good at it. She needed to be – many times I've seen her get dressed and square her shoulders for a 'performance' – a meeting or something at the Commons – from which she would return, drop her guise and look utterly exhausted. Sometimes she was barely able to speak afterwards.

Crawfie has told of her closeness to MT during some difficult moments – of her tearful distress at the loss of lives during the Falklands crisis, their near miss in the Brighton bombing, after which she put the following day's speech into the PM's black Launer handbag for safety before accompanying her to the Police College in Lewes. They shared a room that night (complete with avocado bathroom suite), praying and talking intermittently throughout the few remaining hours before the conference began.

But if women were Margaret Thatcher's gatekeepers and confidantes, three men (well, perhaps five if you count the Saatchi brothers) were Margaret's 'makers'. Without them, it is almost certainly the case that Margaret Thatcher would not have been elected Prime Minister, nor could she have sustained her leadership over a period of eleven years. As the first truly televisual PM, she needed, demanded and received a lot of marketing. It was to her credit that she was willing to listen to the experts. 'She was a sponge,' says one former advisor. 'She listened, learned then cast out.' In fact, she did not take this approach with her 'laughing boys', as she liked to call them, keeping them close until the last days of her premiership.

Thatcher's pet name for the triad of former TV producer Gordon Reece, playwright Ronald Millar and adman Tim Bell was born of the trio's arrival at the Thatcher's rented country flat in Scotney Castle in July 1978, where, according to Bell, they enlivened a tense, dull, Thatcher family photoshoot and lunch party having already sunk two bottles of champagne between them at a local pub. But the three marketeers were no ordinary court jesters. Alongside their jokes and japes (which succeeded

# THE THREE MARKETEERS

where no one else could in making MT laugh) they were seasoned professionals, all from different backgrounds, who, between them, helped to create one of the most enduring and iconic media personalities of the twentieth century.

Margaret met Gordon Reece first. A freelance TV producer and son of a car salesman, Reece was a diminutive Ronnie Corbett lookalike with a penchant for cigars, expensive champagne and Range Rovers. (When Lady Young, who was in charge of Conservative Party finances, complained about Reece's expenses, Alistair McAlpine, the treasurer, responded: 'As you have to run your car on petrol, so you have to run Gordon on champagne.') Reece had read law at Cambridge, before deciding rather implausibly that journalism paid better (perhaps it did in the 1970s?). He had previously directed religious broadcasts and the soap opera *Emergency Ward 10* and worked with talk-show hosts and comedians, including Eamonn Andrews, Dave Allen and Bruce Forsyth. Reece was already working for Ted Heath when he and Margaret met on the set of her very first party political broadcast. Reece, then a freelance producer, charmed her, and they stayed in touch.

After Ted Heath's 1974 defeat at the polls, Reece let it be known that he thought there was a 'unique opportunity for a woman leader'. She demurred. He flirted with her respectfully and she, always a sucker for a clever, charming man, flirted back. There was no intent on either side.

> [Gordon] was a very devout Catholic – sometimes he would go to Mass several times in one day because he liked it so much – and had six children... His wife was an Anglican... He would

say, 'We don't spend all night fucking; we spend all night arguing about the difference between Catholicism and Anglicanism,'

writes Tim Bell in his autobiography.

Four months after MT's victory in the leadership election in 1975, Reece joined her staff on a full-time basis and three years later became Director of Publicity at Conservative Central Office. It was Reece who famously moulded Thatcher's outward appearance into what journalist Simon Hoggart, quoted by Wendy Webster, described as 'a softly spoken, intimate, woman-next-door, a political Avon lady.' 'It was an extraordinary image to choose,' writes Webster. 'Domestic arts have not usually been regarded as a qualification for any public office... Nor is housewifery associated with ideas of intelligence, skill or status.'

But Reece, from whom it would not be too bold to suggest that the Labour supremo spinner, Alastair Campbell, might have garnered a few pointers, had a cunning plan, which he outlined for Central Office in a memo dated 24 March 1978 and entitled 'Some Guidelines on the Media in a General Election'. He leads with the principal purpose of the Tories' use of the media, which he saliently describes as 'to influence those voters who might conceivably change their vote in our favour'. Amongst his strategy points is the key to MT's victory, which is to influence the so-called 'floating voter' (although he never uses the term). He suggests that the one thing common to this group is 'a low interest in politics' and the fact that they do not watch news programmes, read broadsheets or listen to national radio. The only national paper which he suggests might have any cut through or influence on this group is *The Sun* (circulation then 4.5 million). His suggestion is

# THE THREE MARKETEERS

that the party target these voters in their own territory via local newspapers, magazine-style radio shows between 10am and noon, and, most importantly (and revolutionary at the time), television, stating that it 'is the principal occupation after sleeping and working of our primary target. The average viewing time is around 4 hours daily.'

> The television audience needs to see a relaxed woman in 'soft' situations, recognisable surroundings – supermarkets, factories, streets – out in the country. Press conferences, however well they might go in the hall, are seen on television to be strident, defensive, angry occasions where one hostile questioner after another puts 'objections'. A one-to-one interview is far better for Mrs Thatcher.

Reece outlined his simple but effective strategy later for Charles Moore, which was based upon MT's own observation that the middle-class divide was breaking down:

> Mrs Thatcher was advised by me that the majority of the electorate in the late 70s voted for what they perceived to be their own best interests, the party that would do best for them and their families... she decided to concentrate upon the voters who had the greatest need or ambition to improve their lives. Priority was given to women in Labour-voting households, the people who actually spent the family budget, the people most at risk from economic mismanagement. Secondly, priority was given to skilled and semi-skilled workers, those who had the best opportunity to benefit from increasing prosperity. And

thirdly, to first-time voters, people who would not just hope for a better life but vote for one.

It's a sexist statement to make, but it's also hard to avoid the notion that this strategy had a uniquely female perspective.

That Reece saw the potential for Thatcher to become one of the globe's first political TV sensations is not in doubt. He'd spent time in America studying US campaigning styles including Carter vs Ford in 1976, the first time TV debates has been used since Nixon and Kennedy in 1960. And he applied the principle of using (or rather manipulating) the fast-expanding medium of TV to persuade the British public, not only of Thatcher's suitability, but also that it was plausible that a woman could lead Britain, without falling into the sexist tropes of harridan, hag or harpy. All of those would follow later.

Reece's plan to get MT elected in 1979 was a stroke of genius (even if he'd stolen the TV bit from across the Atlantic). For not only did her informal TV and press appearances encourage the patriarchal male and sexist female 1970s voter not to be 'scared' of her, they also created the illusion amongst the Tory grandees that 'housewifely Margaret' would be a one-hit wonder: a single-term PM. So desperate were the grandees of the party for change and any level of success that they held their noses and jumped in line behind her, thinking that they would quickly be able to dispense with her services. Perhaps they should have heeded Willie Whitelaw's response to Ted Heath's initial suggestion that Margaret join his cabinet: 'Once she is there, we'll never get rid of her.'

Pictures of MT sweeping garden paths, baking cakes, washing up, decorating with Denis, shopping for groceries, trailed by a pack of cameramen and journalists, flooded the media. 'Television is an intimate medium, is better for interpretations than messages. Interviews in real locations will always score,' continues Reece's memo: cue MT visiting farms, factories, markets and offices all across Britain. In summation, Reece made it clear he thought that London-centric campaigning was a waste of time: 'The key is television. Whatever our opponents do, it will be no advantage to us if the leader of our party is isolated in central London during all campaigning hours.'

Was it kismet that Reece's strategy played to MT's secret desire to be a 'thesp'? He'd marked her out as a winner from the start when, having watched clips of unused party political broadcasts from the 1970 election, he noticed how she 'dominated the screen when she was on it', as quoted by Charles Moore. 'Gordon Reece taught me that television is a conversation, not a lecture,' she said. It was Reece who calmed her nerves too, encouraging her to be 'normal' and to get up close to the microphone for a more intimate conversation with the viewer. Charles Moore thought it was also MT's keen sense of injustice which worked:

> She had an instinct for placing herself on the side of the person without power, rather than the official or the union boss. The actress side to her character made her extremely effective in walkabouts and factory visits... she found that they energized her. And she well understood how to play to the huge interest in her, which resulted from the fact of her sex.

For a small man, Reece packed a punch. Few would disagree with him; not other staffers, not press secretary Bernard Ingham, or even, most importantly, Margaret Thatcher herself. She might grumble and push back — she was at first awkward around the camera and dubious about his methods — but she listened to Gordon's media mantra, which might have been summed up in two words: simplicity and seduction. No hats, suits in block colours in jewel tones (or black for important formal occasions), all softened by flattering blouses — some with pussy bows and some without. Where Reece partially failed was in his request to her not to wear too much jewellery. She was rarely parted from her pearls, which she set off with gobstopper pearl earrings and a brooch pinned to her left lapel (never the right). Pearls, she proclaimed in 1986 to Angela Ruth of the BBC, 'have been the thing for an Englishwoman for years, but they have a sort of luminescence about them, and particularly pearl earrings, and they do just give your face a little lift'.

'There are moments in life when something goes "click" in what one assumes to be the brain and you find yourself without warning on the same wavelength as a total stranger. This turned out to be that moment.' So wrote Ronald Millar of his first meeting with MT. She had been casting about for what she liked to call a 'wordsmith', someone who could craft her speeches into showstoppers. 'Margaret definitely had a thing about people who could write. She would always say to me: "Oh but you're so clever, you can write,"' says David Howell. 'Whether she meant it or not was another matter.'

As far as Millar was concerned, at least, the admiration was both genuine and mutual. Millar, who read English at Cambridge for a year before joining the Royal Navy in 1940, had been a close friend of Noël Coward and a successful Hollywood actor and screenwriter, having starred in or written a series of successful movies, musicals and West End plays, including *The Affair*, *The Masters* and *Abelard and Heloise*. He lived with his mother on Sheffield Terrace in Kensington and was openly homosexual, at a time when to be so was still considered outré. (The Sexual Offences Act decriminalised private homosexual acts between men over 21 in 1967.) MT was famously non-judgemental about people's private lives (with the sole and unforgiveable exception of the egregiously oppressive Section 28). Millar had first come to her attention as Heath's speechwriter, and once she'd become Leader of the Opposition she summoned him to her office in an attempt to persuade him to help her with a five-minute party political broadcast, which she had inherited from Heath. Millar, who was still understandably feeling resistant and loyal towards his former boss, described the moment he saw her 'in daylight for the first time'; they'd met previously and briefly at a candlelit dinner (thanks to the Heath-era power cuts) in the Disraeli Room at the Carlton Club when she'd been Secretary of State for Education. 'There was a kind of senior girl-scout freshness about her that was rather appealing, as though she had stepped straight out of *The Sound of Music*, though I doubt if "soft woollen mittens and whiskers on kittens" were ever her favourite things.'

Millar's other great advantage, aside from his writing abilities, was that he, unlike most other people in the Margaret Thatcher firmament, was fearless, perhaps because he refused any form of payment. His description of her before her first conference speech is laced with the unbridled admiration of a theatre impresario.

> The Leader came out of her bedroom, looking as though she'd come straight from a health farm. She was wearing a Conservative-blue dress with a wide skirt that was very becoming and her hair had been set by someone who actually knew about these things. She was three days short of fifty but she suddenly looked young and vulnerable and pretty and scared... She was like a star on a first night.

Other than Denis, Millar was the only person to call MT 'darling', or occasionally 'love', which he got away with because of his theatrical props. She, in turn, called him 'Ronnie dear'. She was protective of him: 'You must be kind to Ronnie,' she would tell Tim Bell. 'He's very delicate.' After Millar had written her speeches, she'd sit and listen to him reading them with her hands shading her eyes, as though the sun was bothering her: 'it helps me concentrate.' In the tense countdown to the general election of 1979, Millar was detailed to distract Britain's potential new PM and generally keep her out of trouble by taking her to the theatre, where, during a performance of *The Two Ronnies*, she leaned into Millar and confided into his ear, whilst watching the colourful opening number with girls in sequinned gowns and feathered headdresses, 'I love this sort of thing. So pretty.' On another occasion he took her to see Tim Rice and Andrew Lloyd Webber's *Evita*. In her thank-you note afterwards she wrote to Millar: 'I was thinking, if a woman like that [Eva Peron] can get to the top without any morals, how high could someone get who has one or two?'

Between them, Reece and Millar reached the conclusion that Margaret Thatcher's voice, 'a kind of high-pitched alto in the early days', would be an impediment to her reaching No. 10. Listening to old recordings of MT, it is hard to see the 'voice problem' as little more than a 'man problem'. With so few women in the House, MT's voice would have sounded higher and shriller, because, biologically, it was. Research from the University of South Australia revealed that the 'fundamental frequency' of women's voices dropped by 23 Hz between the 1940s and the 1990s – from an average of 229 Hz (roughly an A# below middle C) to 206 Hz (roughly a G#) – a fact they linked to the increasing empowerment of women. 'One of the problems about being a woman in politics is that a man can shout, but if a woman increases the volume of her voice, she tends to squawk,' Norman Tebbit told *The Guardian* in 2013, underscoring the prejudice that MT and all female MPs would have encountered (and still do). It was Millar who took advice from his friend Laurence Olivier, who met with MT himself before advising voice coaching from the National Theatre instructor, Kate Fleming. MT dutifully took lessons peripatetically for the next four years. By the time she became PM she had lowered her public voice by nearly half an octave and, as Millar notes, she would go further – extending her range to 'an impressive baritone which if you weren't expecting it could be quite alarming'.

For all her appreciation of both Millar and Reece, MT was careful to protect her own evolving image, presenting it as something that was happening spontaneously, without guidance or interference. When asked by a TV interviewer if she took advice from Reece, she looked disingenuously askance. 'Do you know…' she said, shifting uneasily in her tweed suit and pearls, looking for all the world like a Chipping Norton lady who had cycled to the studio on her upright Pashley complete with basket. 'Do you know, I think he's consulted me, not I him. I think it's always been that way round.' And what of the rumour that she'd taken up humming to improve her voice? At this her voice probably did raise an octave as she responded indignantly: '*Humming lessons!* I'm not a very good hummer!'

It was Millar too who, without complaint (until he wrote his autobiography at least), would bear the brunt of the infamous 'speechwriting sessions'. Working as part of the team (which normally included the Party Chairman and a handful of others who were considered 'wordsmiths') on an important speech meant writing into the early hours and often right up until she left the room to give the speech itself.

> We, the writers… sort of debouched, usually just before lunch on THE DAY, some of us haggard and ghostly pale, some of us in need of a bath and a shave, all more or less semiconscious, semi-triumphant and a little wiser or a little less… anyone who participated in Mrs Thatcher's annual Party Conference speech, which was a killer, was hooked for life or what remained of it. There was something compulsive about the agony… The lady was the driving force behind the speech, its coronary artery was hers. Her views, her opinions, her kind of language and her guidance were behind every contentious syllable.

He was aware, too, of the prejudices which would be visited upon him regularly once he attached his star to Margaret's wagon. 'Does she think she's the Queen or something?' one society airhead asked him. But perhaps no one was subject to a greater one-line put-down than the then head of the Policy Unit, John Hoskyns, who, as Millar tells it, once informed a former fellow officer that he now worked for Mrs Thatcher, to which he received the following blistering reply: 'I say, you must be the most frightful shit!'

Some of Millar's key phrases and lines have gone down in history. His inspiration was the great Peggy Noonan – or 'La Noonan', as he called her – who had written for both Ronald Reagan and George H.W. Bush; Noonan is currently a columnist for the *Wall Street Journal*. Hers was Reagan's moving *Challenger* disaster speech, into which she worked the magical John Gillespie Magee Jr phrase: 'slipped the surly bonds of Earth... and touched the face of God'. For Bush, she wrote the punchy and memorable 'Read my lips, no new taxes'. Millar was fond of quoting Noonan's aphorism that 'All great soundbites happen by accident'. Amongst Millar's top zingers: 'This is no time to put party before country. I start from there'; and 'Help me to help you', a line to which Tom Cruise's character Jerry Maguire, from the eponymous movie, is almost certainly indebted. Millar's greatest line was the 'U turn' as in 'You turn if you want to. The lady's not for turning.' The line, which went down in the annals of speechwriting history, became known within the party simply as TLNFT. It was a twist on the title of Christopher Fry's romantic comedy set in the Middle Ages: *The Lady's Not for Burning*. 'TLNFT has stood the test of time precisely because it's not a one-liner,' writes Millar. His suggestion that MT quote St Francis of Assisi on the steps of No. 10 in 1979, as she arrived to assume the premiership, was, however, met with greater scepticism. Not least because, after the event, it was revealed that it had not actually been written by the Italian friar, rather it had first appeared anonymously in an early twentieth-century French clerical magazine called *La Clochette*.

---

Like all good TV producers, Gordon Reece was a calculated risk-taker. Perhaps his greatest risk, which in turn reaped the greatest rewards, was the hiring of a little-known, hungry and creative advertising agency run by two young brothers of Iraqi–Jewish descent, Charles and Maurice Saatchi, to create advertising for the run-up to the 1979 election. 'While no one would claim that it was the Conservative account that made them rich, Mrs Thatcher's election success certainly made their reputation,' wrote *The Guardian*'s senior political commentator Hugo Young. According to Young, when the Conservatives took on Saatchi & Saatchi in 1978, their annual profit was £1.8 million. A decade later, S&S would have 150 offices worldwide, over 60 of the world's largest advertisers on their books, and profits in excess of £50 million.

The brothers were an uncomfortable, spiky mix of the inscrutable, eccentric genius of Charles, who never attended client meetings but would often hide in the projection room to watch the performance of his socially ambitious, smooth-talking brother and 'front man', Maurice. Alongside their groundbreaking campaigns, they brought something else with them which would endure far longer than their account with the Conservative Party, at least where Margaret was concerned. That something was the shiny, flashy, ebullient (some might say obnoxious), fast-car-driving, chain-smoking adman and later PR supremo, Tim Bell. Bell, who was head of accounts at Saatchi's, was on holiday in Barbados when Maurice and members of his team met with Reece and were duly offered the account. After the meeting, they called Bell to get his blessing, which he immediately refused to grant, believing that the account would pay little and had the potential to disrupt the entire agency. 'Over my dead body do we take this account on,' he told the Saatchis with an air of finality. 'We'd like it very much,' Maurice immediately told Gordon Reece. As Bell recalls: 'By the time I came home they had just ignored me – as they often did – and had signed the account.'

Two things, or rather two people, soon changed Bell's mind: Gordon Reece, with whom he shared a passion for the sybaritic; and MT, for whom he would harbour something akin to love. The appreciation was, by all accounts, mutual. The *House of Cards* author Michael Dobbs is said to have described their relationship as 'one of the great love stories of the twentieth century'. History does not relate whether Dobbs' tongue was firmly in his cheek. It seems likely. By his own admission, Bell treated MT 'like a woman'. He bought her gifts of chocolates and flowers, flattered her with positive comments about her appearance and, above all, made her smile, something which none of her cabinet managed to do. 'They were all too baffled or too frightened,' writes Bell. 'One of them once said it was like leaving home and finding that Nanny was at the office.'

Bell remembered his first meeting with Margaret Thatcher, in the Leader of the Opposition's room in the House of Commons, for two things. The first was that one of her secretaries – either Alison Ward or Caroline Stephens – identified him as 'the man from *Starsky and Hutch*', a popular American cop show of the seventies featuring a couple of lovable if dodgy detectives who drove a red Ford Gran Torino. The second was the edict MT issued at the close of the meeting:

> I want you to understand three things. First, politicians have very, very large toes and very large fingers and it's easy to tread

on them. I have neither. You will always tell me the truth, however painful you may think it might be to me. Secondly, if you have any tricks that will get me elected, don't use them. Because if the people don't want me, it won't work. And finally, you will get a lot of abuse working for me. I hope you're a big boy.

Was it purely a coincidence that, at this first meeting, Bell had mirrored MT's own preferences, by quoting Abraham Lincoln and by telling her that his favourite poem was Rudyard Kipling's 'If'? These 'coincidences' delighted her. Bell always maintained they were just that. But as the consummate account handler, it's unlikely that Bell would not have arrived well briefed on the preferences of the leaderene – not least by Reece, who already knew them inside out.

It was to MT's credit that she allowed both Bell and Saatchi's to do what they did best. And it was to Saatchi's credit that they created the campaign, which began the undoing of Labour and still stands as the benchmark for political advertising. The famous 'Labour Isn't Working' campaign (later awarded 'Best Poster of the Century' by industry bible *Campaign*) was written by creative Andy Rutherford, who, the story goes, sneaked his work into the art-bag before Bell left for Conservative Central Office to present the ideas. The concept, which was a picture of a long line of people in a dole queue, with the play on words 'Labour Isn't Working', seemed initially destined to fail, given MT's inability to grasp either the humour or the implicit double entendre. 'What's so clever about that?' she demanded sharply of Bell as soon as he laid the work in front of her... In his own words, Bell took a 'pasting'. After the meeting though, she conceded that she thought it was 'wonderful'.

# THE THREE MARKETEERS

But just as they assumed they had the go-ahead, S&S were called back again, this time to explain themselves to Party Chairman Peter Thorneycroft, who questioned the idea of putting their opponents' name in the headline. Bell, whom one colleague has described as an 'Olympic-standard bullshitter', says he 'burbled some reassuring rubbish about it being bang on our dissatisfaction strategy' and got away with it. The poster ran in August 1978 in the remarkably small number of twenty sites across the country. The response was nothing less than a media earthquake and generated millions of pounds' worth of coverage for the modest investment of £50,000. The then Chancellor Denis Healey decried the campaign, accusing Saatchi's of selling politics 'like soap powder' (which wasn't far off because the Saatchis would go on to win the £15 million Procter & Gamble account). He also claimed that the ad was false because the people in the dole queue were Saatchi employees. Actually, writes Bell, they were a bunch of Young Conservatives, gathered together by Michael Portillo, then working with the Conservative Research Department. There's a rumour (though no obvious evidence) that Portillo himself is included in the dole queue.

'All the time, our aim was to make the C2 audience realise they could solve their dissatisfaction by voting for us,' is how Bell succinctly explains the campaign to get Margaret Thatcher elected. Sticking to Reece's original plan, the triumvirate took the fight to the Labour heartlands, which was effectively the popular press (mass-market-circulation tabloids) and TV magazine programming. Between 1978 and 1979 MT appeared on daytime and early-evening TV and radio shows, including *Nationwide*, *Woman's Hour* and Roy Plomley's *Desert Island Discs* on BBC Radio 4, and the *Jimmy Young Show* on Radio 2. She gave a 'cosy' interview to the 'First Lady of Fleet Street', the *Daily Express*'s Jean Rook (upon whom Rita Skeeter, the reporter for the *Daily Prophet* in J.K. Rowling's Harry Potter books, is thought to be partially based).

Perhaps more importantly, she criss-crossed the country endlessly in an energetic 'meet and greet', enabling the public and the press to see her at her most natural; or, as she would term it, 'ordinary'. Local radio phone-ins, factory visits and stump speeches were all faithfully recorded by the red tops. Most important was the support of the *Sun* newspaper (second only in circulation to the *Mirror*), and Bell and Reece massaged their friendship with the editor Larry Lamb (real name Albert – he took 'Larry' after the children's TV show *Larry the Lamb*) and the 'big boss' Rupert Murdoch by setting up meetings with MT. 'We regarded Mrs Thatcher as the Tory most likely to succeed and we were desperate that she should succeed,' Lamb told Bell's biographer, Mark Hollingsworth. A year after MT's success, he would be rewarded with a knighthood.

That, between them, Reece, Millar and Bell created the Margaret Thatcher who has gone down in history as a punchy, clear-minded, polished and at times inspired performer is not in doubt. Without their press strategy and the dial-shifting party political broadcast that they worked on together – the infamous 1979 'Party Before Country' speech – it is doubtful that she could have won over enough of the British public to vote for her. And it was only due to the wiles of Bell that the broadcast did not go out, during one of the greatest downturns in British economic history, with, as MT was insisting, the background filled with elaborate bouquets of spring flowers. It was the sort of potential

# THE THREE MARKETEERS

PR disaster which could have been rivalled only by the likes of British Airways tailfins, Gerald Ratner's 'crap' products and, more latterly, a certain ex-royal's passion for podcasting. Bell circumvented it by agreeing to the bouquets but then telling the camera operator to focus in tightly on MT's face to ensure that the flowers were not visible.

There were times when the triumvirate went too far, flatly turning down a pre-election BBC invitation for Margaret to debate James Callaghan and Liberal Jeremy Thorpe, live, without her knowledge, because they were worried about the optics of avuncular PM 'Uncle Jim' Callaghan being verbally beaten up by, in Reece's words, 'an arrogant bitch'. When she uncovered their deceit, she fired both Reece and Bell on the spot. 'Don't worry,' said a gin-and-tonic-sipping Denis, raising an eyebrow, on their way out. 'She'll be fine in the morning.' She was. By 9am they were back at No. 10 nursing hangovers and appropriately chastened – for the next 24 hours at least.

After the election, as MT left her home victorious, in a blaze of camera flashlights, for her acceptance audience with the Queen, Reece turned to Millar. 'Well, my dear,' he said, 'we seem to have had a minor role in quite an interesting little production. Let's hope it runs. What do you say?'

Over the course of the next eleven years the three marketeers would, to greater or lesser effect, remain involved in the work of 'Making Margaret'. 'We had no hesitation thinking that Margaret was a fabulous woman and leader, the like of which we might never see again. I don't think many others felt quite that way… They felt threatened. And it was easier to hate her than it was to like her,' wrote Bell. Millar was knighted in 1979, shortly after

MT's first victory. His involvement extended beyond her tenure when, in 1991, he was called upon to help with John Major's early speeches. Reece, who had been lured overseas in 1980 for five years by Armand Hammer, returned from the USA to work on both her 1983 and 1987 campaigns (although in 1987 it was from afar since at that point he was working with Bell on Guinness's bid for the Scotch whisky company Distillers). He also became ill in the same year with the throat cancer which would ultimately claim his life in 2001. In 1981, he refused a CBE on the grounds that it offered too little recognition of his services. MT knighted him in 1986.

Of the three, it was Bell who was closest to MT and to whom she would listen most intensely. In 1985 when, as Party Chairman, Norman Tebbit made MT aware of a breaking story uncovered by the *Daily Mirror* of Bell's conviction in 1977 under the Sexual Offences Act for exposing himself whilst masturbating at his bathroom window in Hampstead, she was, as Tebbit recounted, 'shocked', but she remained loyal to Bell and continued, as she wrote in her memoirs, to 'see him socially'. For his part, Bell admitted the conviction but later denied the event ever took place, claiming that his lawyers had advised him to plead guilty to avoid a scandal. MT's friendship with Bell had also not been shaken by his previous and highly apparent cocaine habit, which by 1983, according to his biographer Mark Hollingsworth, had rendered him 'visibly in decline'. Therapy and the re-emergence of his girlfriend Virginia, who had left him and returned to Australia, were factors in his recovery and he would go on to be heavily involved in the resolution of the miners' strike in 1984–5.

Bell was also notoriously the preferred bearer of 'bad news' which, coming from almost anyone else, would send Margaret

Thatcher into a meltdown. When, in 1986, Michael Dobbs, who was working at Central Office, and Saatchi's account director John Sharkey gave a presentation which suggested that the phrase TBW – 'that bloody woman' – was not only being used by her colleagues but also across the country, and presented an indication of her electoral vulnerability, she was incensed. Later she admitted to Bell privately that she was also devastated. 'It might have come better from Tim,' concedes a colleague from that era. 'Because he knew how to present her with bad news and she would take it from him, no matter what it was.' Bell commented: 'It was an extraordinarily insensitive thing to do and showed they understood nothing about Margaret… if you just confronted her and told her that everybody hated her, you couldn't expect her to treat it as if she were being given a bunch of flowers.'

In fact Bell, who had split from Saatchi's, continued not just to 'see' MT, as she admitted, but to advise her privately on her campaign strategy. He needed to keep this quiet because he and Reece were also involved in masterminding the media behind the Guinness bid, which would ultimately fail. His new company, Lowe Howard-Spink & Bell, would controversially (and covertly) create the advertising for the 1987 election, after Thatcher dismissed the Saatchi offering as too negative. It was Bell, too, who could see that MT was in 'ostrich mode' in the run-up to Heseltine's bid for election as PM in the 1990 leadership contest. 'Heseltine's going to fucking well win, Margaret,' he told her, wrongly as it turned out. 'You're exaggerating terribly, Tim. You people just aren't in touch,' she responded defensively.

In the end it was Bell, who outlived both Reece and Millar, who would faithfully visit the woman he loved (whatever love means – to borrow a New Carolean phrase) until the end of her life. It was Bell who would make the media announcement upon her death on 8 April 2013, and Bell who would be amongst those chosen to organise MT's funeral service at St Paul's Cathedral. He was also part of the small, select entourage who attended her cremation at Mortlake Crematorium; after which he said he felt a 'terrible coda – a really awful, black, bleak finality'.

# 6

# Warrior Queen, Gender Blender?

> I can either try as hard as I can to be just like a male Prime Minister, or I can try to be a very different Prime Minister because I'm female, or I can mix the two together.
>
> MT to Tim Bell

'I think Margaret Thatcher was a drag queen,' wrote Ben Walters for the *Huffington Post* in 2013. His point was not that MT was a man in woman's clothing (a cheap shot taken by so many over the years); rather, he was drawing attention to her 'public performance of gender'. By her own admission, MT was at pains to combine male and female attributes, in her style of leadership, her personality and her outward appearance. 'She used her femininity when it suited her,' wrote Tim Bell. 'But then there was the "iron" in her blood, wanting to run the country, get the job done, defeat the enemy.' The latter are clearly not exclusively male qualities; it's just that in leadership positions historically only men had traditionally 'performed' them – with notable exceptions, the most obvious being Boudicca, Joan of Arc, Queen Victoria and Elizabeth I.

Did Margaret Thatcher seek to consciously subvert traditional concepts of gender – both her own and those of the people around her? Certainly, her air of zealotry was a trait that was associated more with men than women. 'I think there was a subconscious element of her being surrounded by men, which created this need to be assertive and confident at all times – rather like a man would have been perceived,' says Ken Clarke. 'She tended to almost position herself *against* other women,' says Norman Tebbit. 'I think she strove to create a strong persona so that people didn't think of her as a woman, they thought of her as a leader.'

What other choice did she have? As the first-ever female PM, there was little doubt that she was going to need to prove herself to both sexes, though clearly on a day-to-day basis it was going to be 'the men' who represented the immediate gender battleground. 'It becomes impossible to separate out "gender" from the cultural intersections in which it is invariably produced and maintained,' wrote Judith Butler in her groundbreaking book, *Gender Trouble: Feminism and the Subversion of Identity* (Routledge 1990). For Butler, gender is 'learned' and 'performative'. Thatcher's persona or performance (if it was that), which developed as she grew in confidence and her leadership grew in longevity, failed to fit any one of the ascribed norms. In this, she created a whole new gender stereotype, beloved of her supporters and despised by political detractors and second- and third-wave feminists alike. She was a big-haired, pearl-toting blonde in a broad-shouldered power suit, wearing fitted skirts, pantyhose and heels, where previously Savile Row pinstripes and John Lobb Oxfords would have been de rigueur. As bossy as she was brave and as seductive as she was strident, she confused, bemused and battered those who still held on to outdated stereotypes of what a woman could and should be. A gift to cartoonists, tabloids and a particular persuasion of Tory (think Alan Clark and his infamously lascivious diaries), she was for some the living embodiment of a whip-cracking dominatrix – the nation's macho mother. For cartoonist Gerald Scarfe, who drew her as everything from a shark to a naked dinosaur 'Torydactyl' with pendulous breasts and pudendum on show, she was 'very, very good material'. In Fluck and Law's *Spitting Image* TV puppet show she was 'guyed' as a pinstripe-suited woman in drag, using a urinal and frothing at the mouth. 'For caricaturists at least, Thatcher was always a good little earner,' Roger Law wrote in *The Guardian* in 2013.

> President Mitterrand says Britain's prime minister 'has eyes like Caligula and the mouth of Marilyn Monroe'. She also has the nerves of a five-star general and, increasingly, the sexual charisma of a woman in her prime. She manipulates her court of bedazzled male advisers with the skill of Elizabeth I.

So proclaimed *Vanity Fair*, the globe's glossiest and most feted celebrity bible in June 1989, dedicating an enormous 21 of its prime shiny pages to an interview with the PM by their ace reporter Gail Sheehy. The interview and subsequent article, for which, thanks to the persuasive powers of Woodrow Wyatt, MT had offered up a few hours, and multifarious 'sources' had opened their Pandora's boxes, established her as one of the world's most enduringly glamorous icons. She was not the cover star though; the blonde *9½ Weeks* actress Kim Basinger scooped that one. Even more telling was the fact that the magazine, owned by Condé Nast, with a readership then of over a million, forwent the traditionally glossy glamorous portrait opener (which would almost certainly have been shot by Annie Leibovitz) for a depiction of MT by illustrator Marie Smith, which seemed to have been informed by both Mitterrand's description and a recent picture of Barbara Bush, America's then First Lady. There was, it seemed, no need for the flourishing eighties drag and queer movement to crown MT as a Queen Bee – *Vanity Fair* had already done it for them.

The paradox at the heart of gay culture's fascination with Margaret Thatcher's gender and persona is and was the notorious Section 28, which prohibited the 'promotion' of homosexuality by local authorities. Incredibly, the legislation was not repealed until 2003 and, whilst no prosecutions under the act were ever made, there is no doubt that the ramifications were far-reaching and stigmatising for an entire generation of queer and non-gender-specific adults. 'I think she would have regarded homosexuality as a private misfortune, not a matter for the police,' says journalist and former MT staffer Matthew Parris,

> but also not a matter for teaching in schools or public declaration or campaigning. I don't believe she ever drove the Section 28 legislation – it was kind of bounced upon government by a private member, but she certainly didn't resist it and her detestation of [GLC leader] Ken Livingstone and his (as we would now say) woke governance was stronger than any opinion she may have had about sexuality.

## WARRIOR QUEEN, GENDER BLENDER?

Parris tells of the moment when he came out to MT: 'She laid a hand upon my arm and said, "Matthew, that must have been very difficult for you to say." I know that she meant it kindly.'

In 2007 Brian Coleman wrote in the *New Statesman*,

> whilst the underlying ethos of Thatcherism (based on individual liberty) might well be pro-gay it was Mrs T's personality which attracted so many homosexual men to the party. In a profession dominated by men with dandruff and hair coming out of their noses or women who appear to have been dragged through a hedge backwards (a la Shirley Williams), the pure elegance, feminine perfection, perfect dress sense and sheer determination to change society drew many gay men to the Iron Lady.

Writer Paul Philip Flynn summed up the 'gay icon' dilemma in *The Guardian*:

> My living, breathing, socialist self can still see the crying eyes of grown men on the street where I lived as an 80s teenager, falling into their withered wives' arms as their jobs fell like skittles under Thatcher's governmental auspices. But my equally sentient gay self cannot help but admire her way with an Aquascutum twinset and the plain fact that her hairspray knew no bounds.

So, was and is Margaret Thatcher really a gay icon? The answer is almost certainly yes (at least for some sectors of the queer population). It was no coincidence that her greatest impersonator, Steve Nallon, is a man, nor is it a surprise that the drag cabaret *Margaret Thatcher, Queen of Soho* (which centres around MT getting lost in

Soho on the eve of the Section 28 debate), written by Jon Brittain and Matt Tedford, has been such a mainstream hit. 'Gay men have always had a penchant for pantomime women – Widow Twankeys and Bette Midlers,' says Matthew Parris. 'She rather fitted the bill, particularly as she aged in power, as almost a caricature of herself.' It wasn't just gay men. One cover of the monthly lesbian magazine *Sappho* posed MT with the Queen. A speech bubble coming from Thatcher read: 'Let's go to the Gates,' referencing a popular lesbian club: the Gateways, on the King's Road, which closed in 1985.

'Femininity is what she wears, masculinity is what she admires,' wrote Beatrix Campbell of MT. This was neither entirely true nor entirely fair. 'Her sex was never irrelevant, certainly not to her. But she was careful about when to deploy it and when she would prefer not to mention it,' says Charles Moore. She certainly had no mentors or role models when it came to being a female leader (although she admired both Golda Meir and Indira Gandhi, another Somerville alumna). In fact, the person she most esteemed was, by her own admission, Churchill, or 'Winston', as she insisted on calling him, as if they were bosom buddies, although they had only met twice and fleetingly.

> Men had a suit they could put on – and I don't just mean that literally. What did women have? Thatcher helped to normalise the idea of what it was to be a woman in power. She offered a visual language – her clothes, her hair, her voice. I think you even saw that in those women who came later in 1997, for example,

says Natasha Walter, speaking of the infamous 'Blair's babes' picture of the new PM surrounded by 96 of his 108 new female

## WARRIOR QUEEN, GENDER BLENDER?

Labour MPs, in their finest, brightest, shoulder-padded plumage. But Walter also ventures that MT's 'normalising' of a woman in power also left future female generations with a problem. 'The question is, can we forge a feminism that doesn't rely on this image of individual empowerment, that can foreground solidarity rather than individualism? Thatcher created a model of female leadership that replicated the hierarchies of patriarchal power structures, and that is a crippling legacy for feminism today.'

Attitudinally, MT's strident approach could hardly be seen as anything other than male; who else at that point could a woman in her position be compared with? In 1979, when she came to power, the Commons had never witnessed a female who spoke with such conviction. And they had certainly never been governed by one. 'Imagine how difficult it was at that point to have had to be so tough,' says Libby Purves, who was herself establishing a career at the BBC at that time.

> It was still very much a man's world. Most women were still saying, 'That's a very good point you are making and I think we should come back to it.' No one (apart from Thatcher) ever said to a man, as Mrs Thatcher would do later (albeit indirectly) to Jacques Delors [then Head of the European Commission, in response to his proposals for European integration]: 'No! No! No!'

('Up Yours Delors' headlined *The Sun* the next day, neatly translating what was perceived to be Thatcher's 1990 anti-EU speech for the nation.)

This shoot-from-the-hip approach was no act. It simply reflected her straight-talking, no-nonsense, self-professed Victorian value system, which she described as 'disciplining yourself to do what is right and important'. She expected her cabinet ministers, colleagues and backbenchers to do the same. 'I don't think it was a matter of sex or gender, rather it was a matter, in her eyes, of morality,' says Norman Tebbit. 'Her religious faith governed her actions.' Factor into this also what I am suggesting was MT's neurodiversity, which famously left her unmoved by, and unresponsive to, the disapproval of others.

> I think by far her greatest virtue, in retrospect, is how little she cared if people liked her. She wanted to win, but did not put much faith in the quick smile. She needed followers, as long as they went in her frequently unpopular directions. This is a political style, an aesthetic even, that has disappeared from view,

wrote Hugo Young, *The Guardian*'s political columnist, in an epitaph to MT which he prepared three days before his own death in 2003. MT's reluctance or inability to show her feelings (and she argued often that she did 'feel', as Jonathan Aitken would confirm, having discovered her weeping at her desk, whilst he was dating Carol) confounded gender stereotypes and manifested as a 'male' strength. Not for Labour politician Denis Healey, though, who described 'her imperiousness, which reminds me very much of Catherine the Great or the Dragon Empress, who presided over the terminal decline of the Manchu Dynasty in China'.

She would have accepted the compliment. Besides, she'd need all of that tough regality in order to prove herself at significant points during her premiership, during which her leadership and more specifically her gender were subject to intense scrutiny and

## WARRIOR QUEEN, GENDER BLENDER?

criticism, particularly in the hot spots of the Falklands War of 1982 and the miners' strike of 1984–5. Her response to the Maze Prison hunger strikers in 1981 had already established a benchmark for what would become her legendary toughness or immovability. Her response to the protest, which demanded the reinstatement of an outdated ruling that 'special category prisoners' (convicted terrorists) be housed separately, with greater privileges than other prisoners (specifically wearing civilian clothing, associating freely with other political prisoners and being exempt from any prison work), is recorded in her autobiography: 'All my instincts were against bending to such pressure.' Despite the global media exposure, she held firm. 'The time has come for President Reagan to use the "special relationship" between the United States and Britain to advise Prime Minister Margaret Thatcher to disengage from Northern Ireland,' urged a piece in the *New York Times*, written by Tim Pat Coogan, the Editor of the *Irish Press*. The Catholic Church, too, weighed into the debate, urging the government to show flexibility. 'I explained the circumstances personally to the Pope on a visit to Rome... He had as little sympathy for the terrorists as I did,' MT writes. When hunger striker and IRA leader Bobby Sands won the seat of Fermanagh and South Tyrone whilst on the strike, she knew that the IRA were, as she puts it, 'advancing'. Sands died on Tuesday 5 May 1981 after 66 days of refusing food. The cause of death in the original pathologist's report was 'self-induced starvation', later amended to 'starvation' after protests from his family. He was 27 years of age. 'From this time forward,' writes Margaret Thatcher, 'I became the IRA's top target for assassination.'

Despite the comparisons, neither Margaret Thatcher nor Elizabeth I actually led their troops into battle. Even if Elizabeth did in fact make her notorious 'weak and feeble woman' speech at Tilbury on 9 August 1588, her 'heart and stomach of a king' (and the rest of her) remained safe behind her own lines, well out of the theatre of war. MT, meanwhile, fought the 74-day Falklands War to recapture the tiny British colony of 1,800 inhabitants in the South Atlantic from Argentinian invaders, in the way of all modern-day British leaders, from behind her desk at No. 10 or at the despatch box in the House of Commons. There were other, biological implications. By now, Margaret Thatcher was 57 years of age. Almost certainly, she would have been menopausal or even post-menopausal, which, with hindsight, might have provided its own set of challenges, alongside running the country and fighting a war. 'Back then, we certainly were not saying things like "I'm menopausal so please make allowances." Can you imagine Margaret Thatcher ever saying, "I can't do PMQs today because I'm having a hot flush?" No, neither can I,' says Gillian Shephard.

Norman Tebbit acknowledges that MT, like everyone else, certainly had her 'off days', which he posits could have been hormone-related. 'Yes, now I think about it, there were definitely times when I thought: this is not a good time of the month to ask her that. Of course, it was not something that was ever openly discussed.' Neil Kinnock, her foil at the despatch box, reflects on what he terms MT's 'erratic' behaviour with a pragmatic shrug: 'Was it her age? Was it some pills she was taking? Was it just her? Whatever it was, towards the end of her time as the PM she would say one thing one minute and contradict herself the next.' But then she was a politician – don't they all do that? I prompt the affable Kinnock. He roars with laughter and sips his cappuccino.

## WARRIOR QUEEN, GENDER BLENDER?

When MP and early hormone replacement therapy campaigner Teresa Gorman, who had long speculated on the source of MT's 'phenomenal energy', plucked up the courage to ask her over tea and biscuits at her home in Eaton Square, soon after her deposition, aged 65, whether or not she took HRT, the response was startling. 'Yes, dear, I have a patch,' MT replied, tapping her bottom as if to indicate the location. And then she confided: 'I've only had it for 18 months. You see, no one told me to come off the pill.' Gorman was astonished. Throughout her premiership it seemed that MT had been administering her own, admittedly rather random, form of HRT, by taking the contraceptive pill into her sixties. 'Denis and I agreed that we could not risk having more children once I became a leader of the party. It was a full-time job. And in those days, I don't think the country was ready for a prime minister on maternity leave,' MT confided. Did doctors really not feel able to tell Margaret Thatcher to stop taking the pill? Or, as a scientist, had she recognised the need to maintain levels of hormones that she would have otherwise lost in her forties and fifties, in order to do her job? Was self-medication the simplest and most private means available to her at that time? There's little doubt that, for most women in their fifties and into their sixties these days, hormone replacement would be considered a viable option, if not a necessity. Particularly if they were running the country. According to Hansard, the first time that the word 'menopause' was used in Parliament was in 1943, in the Lords, in a debate on 'population problems'. It was not mentioned in the Commons until 1964, and it did not clock up its one-hundredth reference until 2017.

With or without the right balance of hormones (and without wishing to use female biology as a means of diminishment

# THE INCIDENTAL FEMINIST

or distraction) it is glaringly obvious that Margaret Thatcher's gender, like that of Elizabeth I before her, presented a fundamental problem to those she was leading, most especially those surrounding her at the top. Despite the insistence of the media, Margaret Thatcher was anything but 'Churchill in Carmen rollers', as one critic dubbed her. Much as she would have liked to believe otherwise, she knew that essentially her sex would count against her during the Falklands War. Although, in a bizarre sense, it also became her superpower.

> Margaret's biggest problem where the Falklands were concerned was that she had never been to war. It turned out, though, that her ignorance was a kind of strength. Anyone who had served would have been far more chary about 'going in' than she was, because they would have understood only too well the potential pitfalls,

says a Whitehall insider who was present throughout the campaign. Another says: 'They were still painting some of the ships on the way down there – we were woefully underequipped and woefully underdefended. We just didn't have the air power. But of course, she would never have understood that. In the end it worked in her favour.'

'When I became Prime Minister I never thought that I would have to order British troops into combat and I do not think I have ever lived so tensely or intensely as during the whole of that time,' Margaret Thatcher later recorded. According to Charles Moore, she later said that, when then Defence Secretary John Nott announced the impending invasion, it was 'the worst... moment of my life'. As a mother, she understood the jeopardy of sending sons into battle (the Queen had announced that Prince Andrew, who was serving with the Royal Navy on HMS *Invincible*, would be aboard). As a politician on the global stage, she recognised the strategic imperative of balancing success with diplomacy; back at home, with her approval ratings plummeting, it appeared that she had little choice. She was also isolated. 'To a large extent she was on her own,' says Robin Butler, her Principal Private Secretary at the time.

> There were a lot of people who were looking for compromise – Francis Pym, the Americans, even Reagan, who was very concerned about US interests in South America. And the French would not give her the protective weapons – the Exocets – she asked for. The armed forces were reported as saying when they were halfway to the Falklands, 'My God, I think she means it.'

Her cabinet, several of whom had seen action during the Second World War, including her deputy William Whitelaw and Foreign Secretary Peter Carington (who would resign the moment the invasion became public) tended towards the 'doveish'. But they were at least military men. Carington's housemaster at Eton had concluded his future was limited: 'For a really stupid boy, there are three possible professions: farming, soldiering and stockbroking.' Yet he had been awarded the MC in the war, likewise Whitelaw. Not so John Nott, the diffident Defence Secretary, who had served in the Gurkhas during the 1950s. It was Nott's 1981 white paper which had recommended cutting back on naval expenditure, the reduction of the surface fleet and the scrapping of the Antarctic patrol ship, HMS *Endurance*. The subsequent Franks Report on the Falklands would suggest that his work 'may have served to cast doubt on British commitment to the islands and their defence'. 'You'll have to take them back,' was MT's response to Nott after he'd broken the news of the invasion on 2 April. 'We can't,' he replied. 'You'll have to,' she retorted.

She resolved to keep Nott in post, in spite of his offer to resign alongside Carington. 'Poor old Notters… was a disaster. He stammered and stuttered and gabbled. He faltered and fluttered and fumbled,' recorded Alan Clark in his diaries (Weidenfeld & Nicolson 2000). She promoted Francis Pym (another MC holder) to be the new Foreign Secretary, in the full knowledge that he was looked upon as her likely successor, but also knowing that his reticent, halting manner and his Tory shire credentials rendered him exactly the sort of 'chap' she did not get along with. 'You hate him. It'll all end in tears,' Carington warned her when she informed him. 'I know,' she said, 'but he's the only one with experience.' She was vulnerable and she knew it. According to Charles Moore, she told Richard Luce (who had resigned alongside Carington and Atkins) years later, 'I felt totally bereft, I felt deserted, very lonely.' The 'imperialists' who were calling for war didn't trust her either, undoubtedly at least in part because of her gender, her class and her relationship with Ronald Reagan. Backbencher Nick Budgen described her at the time as 'at heart… just a vulgar, middle-class Reaganite'.

'I think it was much harder for her than for an ordinary male politician to contemplate some compromise with Argentina, because it would be seen as female weakness that she had not prevailed: she would have lost office,' says Moore.

## WARRIOR QUEEN, GENDER BLENDER?

It was perhaps Denis, who had seen action in the Second World War, who gave her the best advice, which was something along the lines of 'give the orders to the military chiefs and then get out of their way'. It turned out she was good at doing this – probably better than any man.

She had to overcome a credibility gap, and this made her desperately anxious but also much better than she sometimes was at listening. She knew she was ignorant about military affairs (for which she was often laughed at), so she worked incredibly hard to catch up but also showed humility in front of the experts,

says Moore.

Of the armed forces chiefs, her favourite swiftly became Henry Leach, First Sea Lord and Chief of the Naval Staff, who famously appeared in uniform (uninvited) at a crisis meeting in the PM's office, transforming the downbeat mood with an assurance that a task force could be assembled within three days, and the Falklands reached within three weeks. 'Surely you mean three days?' asked the PM. 'No,' said the First Sea Lord firmly, 'I don't.' Leach told friends that during the crisis his phone would occasionally ring at 2 or 3am and he would know exactly who was on the other end. '"Henry, I just need to know one thing." "Yes, PM." "Can we win?" "Yes, PM." "Ah," she would say. "Goodnight then."'

Alan West (Admiral/Lord West of Spithead, or 'Westie' to his friends) describes himself as 'a unit commander and very low down the pecking order during the Falklands'. 'I do know,' he says, 'that she gave a promise to the Chief of Defence Staff and the First Sea Lord that she would see the war through, and she was as good as her word. More than that, she was robust.' West, who would ultimately go on to head up the Royal Navy, came to know Margaret Thatcher well. 'She was very good to brief. She would look straight at you and ask direct questions. You had to be spot on with your responses. You knew if you'd got it wrong she'd lose all faith with you.' West briefed Thatcher on US airstrikes against Libya in 1986. 'She asked me: "Do you think this is the right thing?" I said, "I'm just here to provide a briefing, it's not my job to have an opinion." Her response, which was exactly as it had been to the First Sea Lord during the Falklands, was: "I absolutely want to hear what you have to say."'

In 1989 she told Brian Walden: 'The best compliment they can give a woman is that she thinks like a man. I say, she does not, she thinks like a woman.' MT might well have been referring to her leadership during the Falklands campaign. 'She definitely sought confidence in her decision-making. On the question of whether we should seek to retake the Falklands, she went around the table to ensure she had the unanimous backing of her cabinet,' says Norman Tebbit. There was a great deal at stake. In 1979, MT had resisted negotiations suggested by the Foreign Office, who were proposing a 'leaseback' of the islands to Argentina, similar to that of Hong Kong. According to Jonathan Aitken, 'The stubbornness of her attitude and her inexperience in foreign affairs killed off all opportunities for the conflict to be avoided.'

That was certainly one way of looking at it. But as far as MT was concerned, the Falkland Islanders' desire to 'remain British', and the fact that 'British sovereignty has strong legal foundations', as she put it, was what counted. Or at least that was the way she spun it.

## WARRIOR QUEEN, GENDER BLENDER?

> I think she really felt it would be such a humiliation for Britain if we lost, and she felt she simply couldn't accept that the Argentinians could simply take the Falklands. It would also of course have been a political disaster, but it was never my impression that that was what she was most worried about,

says Robin Butler.

'We must recover the Falkland Islands for Britain and for the people who live there who are of British stock,' she told ITN, before exhorting, 'Do you remember what Queen Victoria once said? "Failure – the possibilities do not exist." That is the way we must look at it.' But not everyone did, least of all one of MT's favourite bêtes noires: the BBC, which she claimed was not 'on our side'. In her book *Pinkoes and Traitors* (Profile 2015), Jean Seaton details the biggest controversy, which was how the BBC spoke about British troops. When reporter Brian Hanrahan described 'our forces' as he reported from the task force, the editor of Radio News, Larry Hodgson, put up a memo on newsroom noticeboards. 'Please do not say "our forces",' it read, 'when you mean "British Forces". It is contrary to BBC style.' A subsequent memo headlined 'NOT OUR TROOPS' went out, stating: 'We should try to avoid using "our" when we mean British. We are not Britain, we are the BBC.'

Seaton also details another, more light-hearted incident that nonetheless serves to underline the BBC's relationship with MT, which, in those days at least, was laced with sexism.

> In September, after the end of the war, Mrs Thatcher came to have dinner with the BBC Board of Management… she harangued… the BBC chiefs (all men) about the ways in which

they had failed the nation. In a brief respite, while people left the table for the lavatory, one BBC executive whispered to another, 'Thank God the Director General has gone to get the SAS – they're the only people who will get us out of this.'

On 5 April 1982, under MT's command, the British government sent a naval task force 8,000 miles into the South Atlantic to take on the Argentine forces in advance of an amphibious assault on the islands. The British fleet ultimately included some 38 warships, 77 auxiliary vessels and 11,000 soldiers, sailors and marines. Paraphrasing one commentator: it was a long way to go for a couple of thousand people and an awful lot of sheep.

The conflict, which lasted 74 days and ended with the Argentine surrender on 14 June 1982, would test Margaret Thatcher's 'mettle', as Enoch Powell so famously put it. But it would also test her emotional reserves. Could a woman – and one with no experience of war – stand up to what was in effect a rogue junta with (what seems in hindsight) a perfectly reasonable claim to a bunch of Argentinian-owned islands, which had been invaded and colonised by the British in 1833; an American President whose administration had more than a weather eye on keeping South America 'onside'; an insecure Europe (with the exception of a surprisingly supportive Mitterrand); a 'wobbly' Security Council and sniping from the Labour sidelines?

There was speculation from all sides that she couldn't handle the pressure. She must have known that, as for the US administration with Vietnam, there was a likelihood that the popular consensus of the British people would change once the so-called 'body bag' effect hit. In other words, once young servicemen began to die (though most would have no graves and no repatriation), the effects of a war so far away it could hardly be conceived of would become all too real. Her response was to double down. To become even more resolute, to underscore, or 'big up' in modern-day parlance, her reputation as an *Iron Lady*, in terms both of negotiations and her role as quasi-commander of the armed forces (technically that role was Queen Elizabeth II's). 'Get me a drink,' Al Haig, President Reagan's Secretary of State, is said to have commanded an aide as he walked into his Claridge's suite after Falklands negotiation talks with MT; 'that's a hell of a tough lady.' In her memoirs, MT wrote: 'We now had to stand firm against the pressure for making unacceptable compromises while avoiding the appearance of intransigence.'

That Margaret Thatcher was playing against female type cannot have escaped anyone. That she led from the front and won (if there are ever truly any victors in war) certainly destroyed any number of traditional female stereotypes in perpetuity. 'Margaret Thatcher's authoritarian leadership style directly contradicted the idea that women are by nature more consensual, more pragmatic,' wrote Helen Wilkinson.

> It was therefore oddly dissonant with one of the central planks of feminist advocacy in the eighties and nineties, namely the idea that if women were to come to power, their values (feminine values) would civilise society and politics: competition would be replaced by co-operation, strutting egos with sweet reason, as men too would gradually discover their inner feminine selves. Instead, Thatcher showed the world that women had an equal right to be hard, tough and even nasty.

# THE INCIDENTAL FEMINIST

In short Margaret Thatcher was a 'badass'. To prove it, in 2019, BuzzFeed News published a picture column entitled 'Margaret Thatcher's 19 Most Badass Moments' – amongst them, the infamous 'ride in the tank' at Hamburg, near the East German border, in 1986, the 'iron lady' speech of 1976 and her defence of the decriminalisation of homosexuality in 1966.

She might have talked and played tough, but the Falklands War exacted an emotional cost. Perhaps it's a crass and sexist suggestion to make (mea culpa) but it appears, at least from the comparative evidence available, that it took a greater mental toll on her than it would have on a man in her position. And it was the losses, not the stressful diplomacy, or the pressure of keeping up with the armed forces strategies, or the need to keep Parliament, the British people and world opinion onside, that cut deep. 'When blood was shed, some of her critics were fiercer against her because of the image of a woman causing death being unnatural,' says Moore. 'It was during the Falklands that she showed her enormous distress. She was in a terrible state, overwrought and anxious – highly emotional over the loss of lives,' says Robin Butler. Speechwriter Ronnie Millar tells of the moment MT received the news of the sinking of HMS *Sheffield*, hit amidships by an Exocet missile, with, at that point, twenty men lost. 'I was with her in the study,' writes Millar. 'She made no sound, just stood with her body half turned away, fists clenched, struggling for control. Then, almost but not quite silently, she was weeping.' Gillian Shephard recalls: 'I think she felt very alone. She was very isolated. She expected support from Reagan which was not forthcoming – he sat on the fence. I think she was very surprised by Mitterrand, who was the one who really stuck with her.'

# WARRIOR QUEEN, GENDER BLENDER?

Says Jonathan Aitken: 'I don't think she slept at all during the Falklands campaign really. She was always hanging around the radio, listening for any news at all. Interestingly, I also think this is the time that she felt closest to her children and they to her.'

Her nervousness and exhaustion found its way into the public sphere after John Nott's announcement to the cameras outside No. 10 on 25 April 1982 (notably, an opportunity she could have taken for herself but resisted) that the island of South Georgia had been retaken: 'Be pleased to inform Her Majesty that the White Ensign flies alongside the Union Jack in South Georgia. God save the Queen.' At the news that 'so far no British casualties have been reported', a brief smile of relief had flitted across Margaret Thatcher's tense, pale face. As she and Nott turned to go back inside, a reporter asked: 'What's next, Mr Nott?' At which Thatcher's exhaustion and frustration at the rapacious media and the events of the past few weeks boiled over. 'Just rejoice at that news and congratulate our forces and the Marines. Goodnight, gentlemen. Rejoice.' The wording was unfortunate and her political opponents made much of it, with Denis Healey later accusing her of 'glorying in slaughter'.

'Her nervousness led to that statement and "rejoice" was taken in absolutely the wrong way. I think she was just so thankful that there had been no loss of life,' says Butler. Later, MT had her own say on the incident: 'I meant that they should rejoice in the bloodless recapture of South Georgia, not in the war itself. To me, war is not a matter for rejoicing. But some pretended otherwise.'

At its end, 649 Argentine military personnel, 255 British troops and three Falkland Islanders were killed in the conflict that returned the islands to British control. Is it too much to suggest that it was the victory in the Falklands which won MT the 1983 general election? Her ratings, which at the beginning of 1982 had been the lowest of any Prime Minister in the history of polling, jumped from 41 per cent in April to a resilient 59 per cent after the conflict, according to a report by data researchers Ipsos using data from their Public Affairs Archive. But the report also states that MT's ratings and the Tory poll share had begun to climb in advance of the invasion, thanks to perceived improvement in the economy. 'History ought perhaps to recall the Labour Party's 1983 manifesto ("the longest suicide note in history") as being more decisive in shaping 1980s British politics,' the report suggests, before conceding that, even so, 'images of the British–Argentine war will linger longer in our collective memory.'

At approximately 10.15pm on 14 June 1982, Margaret Thatcher rose to tell the House that 'they are reported to be flying white flags over Port Stanley'. ITN's *News at 10* triumphantly broke the story live on air. The BBC's flagship *Nine O'Clock News* programme failed to get the scoop. They'd been prevented from doing so by an MT-imposed press blackout, which had been in operation since the news had begun filtering in during the early afternoon. 'When I went to sleep very late that night, I realized how great the burden was which had been lifted from my shoulders,' MT recorded in her memoirs.

That Margaret Thatcher could extend her supposed 'female pragmatism' to the point of ruthlessness was never in doubt. Her so-called Victorian morality aside, had she invaded the Falklands because she had seen that every other option left her vulnerable to the point that she would readily be deposed? 'I think the Falklands victory saved her prime ministership very definitely,' concludes Simon Jenkins, who later became editor of *The Times*. 'When I subsequently interviewed Ted Heath and James Callaghan, they both confided that they wished that they had had a "Falklands". The war transformed Margaret Thatcher's reputation both in the UK and internationally.'

If the Falklands had taken her unawares, Margaret Thatcher's clash with the National Union of Mineworkers in 1984–5, which would become emblematic of her battle with all heavily unionised activity, was over a decade in the making. It would again underscore her gender, in sharp contrast to that of those she was confronting (miners' wives notwithstanding). In truth, 1970s Britain had been a mess – literally and metaphorically, economically, politically and socially – with everyone from refuse collectors to train drivers, postmen, health workers and miners on strike. Resilient unions, backed by seemingly unbreakable trade union legislation, had held successive governments hostage. Between October 1978 and March 1979 ten million working days were lost to industrial action. By 1980 British trade unions had 12.2 million members – a little over a fifth of the total British population.

'Heath had failed to thwart the unions in '74, Callaghan in '78,' says Michael Heseltine, 'so in '79, when she came in, there was a government which already knew what was necessary. Against the unions, as with so many other issues, she used her gut as much as she used strategy. She had very strong views and a determination based on her convictions.' Nonetheless, in 1981, when the miners came out on strike again, MT's pragmatism kicked in. 'We were already trying to build up coal stocks by then and it cost us a great deal of money,' says David Howell, then Energy Secretary,

> but Scargill saw what we were doing and he got the lads to strike immediately. At which point, Mrs Thatcher told me personally, 'We are not ready. Give them what they want.' In my inexperience, I closed the whole thing down very quickly and it reflected very badly on me.

Howell admits that, at times of crisis, MT routinely briefed against her ministers, including him.

> She could be extremely undermining. Whilst she'd told the press that the '81 miner's agreement was a skilful retreat, she told everyone around the cabinet table that I'd been too weak. I saw her brief against a lot of people during my career including Peter Carington at the Foreign Office. This was the way she ruled. It made a lot of people very unhappy.

Unhappy or not (and Howell's claim was repeated or underscored by many who had worked with MT), he points out that it is a gross overstatement to say that Margaret Thatcher was single-handedly responsible for bringing down the mining industry in Britain and closing all of the mines. 'This was a movement which actually began in the late 1960s when coal was going out of fashion; much of it was borne by the outrage of miners that imports of coal were growing and yet mines were being closed.' In fact, the closure of mines, which was part of the west's deindustrialisation programme, had begun in 1947 as

## WARRIOR QUEEN, GENDER BLENDER?

the USA and then Europe began the painful process of slowing production and making workers redundant. Between 1947 and 1994, some 950 mines were closed by UK governments. Clement Attlee's Labour government closed 101 pits between 1947 and 1951; Macmillan (Conservative) closed 246 pits between 1957 and 1963; Wilson (Labour) closed 253 in his two terms in office between 1964 and 1976; Heath (Conservative) closed 26 between 1970 and 1974; and Thatcher (Conservative) closed 115 between 1979 and 1990.

Did the fact that Margaret Thatcher was, and still is, vilified for mine closures and the destruction of mining communities across the north of England have anything to do with the fact that she was a woman? Almost certainly, if you take the data as evidence. Was she guilty as charged? Yes and no. That mining was a patriarchal industry, which would inevitably bridle at being effectively 'governed' by a female, was not in doubt; rather the question was, who out of the two outsized personalities of MT and Arthur Scargill, the leader of the Yorkshire miners and president of the National Union of Mineworkers, would triumph? And it was very definitely personal.

> I had never had any doubt about the true aim of the hard Left: they were revolutionaries who sought to impose a Marxist system on Britain whatever the means and whatever the cost... The hard Left's power was entrenched in three institutions: the Labour Party, local government and the trade unions,

she writes in her autobiography. 'Predictably, it was the National Union of Mineworkers, led by its Marxist president, Arthur

Scargill, who were destined to provide the shock troops for the Left's attack.'

Union militancy had brought down Ted Heath's Conservative government in 1974. Margaret Thatcher could never forgive the unions for this. What's more, she saw the miners as militancy manifest. 'She was determined not to go the way of Ted Heath. She was ready for them,' says Robin Butler. And so, a union of 170,000 men effectively took on one woman (and the National Coal Board (NCB)).

MT and Arthur Scargill almost certainly never met, but Scargill's short-sighted, wilful resistance to yielding, negotiating or agreeing to allow a strike ballot (which would have weakened the government's position markedly) undoubtedly triggered her more ruthless, obstinate tendencies. 'For her, he was a kind of pantomime villain,' says Neil Kinnock. 'She genuinely thought he was a menace to the British Constitution.' Kinnock, who also famously despised Scargill, is not backwards in coming forwards on MT either. 'I could not stand the woman. Politically or personally. Her whole existence was a pretence,' he says. She in turn seemed to delight in her ability to trounce him at the despatch box. 'His Commons performances were marred by verbosity, a failure to master facts and technical arguments and, above all, a lack of intellectual clarity,' she writes. It probably didn't help that Scargill and Kinnock bore a vague resemblance to one another. Plus, they were both possessed of the ability to continue to pontificate and argue when everyone else had succumbed to ennui. MT viewed Scargill's behaviour as undemocratic (it was). His behaviour also engaged her tactical, practical brain and her clear rationale that 'right' should always prevail. 'The miners' strike was the perfect example of her ability to not rush into decisions,' says Stephen Sherbourne. 'She thought everything through. She was incredibly tactical. She was happy to pull off the road for a bit and wait until it was the right time to get going again.'

Working with the Scottish-born 'take-no-prisoners' chairman of the coal board (1983–6), metallurgist and industrialist, Ian MacGregor, a former chairman of British Steel, and Energy Secretary Peter Walker, MT had plotted to build up enough coal and coke to keep the country (and the steelworks) running in anticipation of another strike. In December 1983, MacGregor announced that he aimed to cut the workforce by 44,000. As a result, he extended the existing redundancy scheme in January 1984, which paid out £1,000 for each year of service. 'A man who had been in the pits all his working life would get over £30,000,' Margaret Thatcher wrote in her autobiography: roughly £120K in today's money. Another strike was called after the NCB announced the closure of Cortonwood colliery in Yorkshire on Thursday, 1 March 1984, prompting a mass walkout.

> Coal stocks were about 35 to 40 per cent higher than ever in history by the end of February of 1984. What the government didn't count on was the madness of Scargill or the fact that the miners would for the first time in the history of a national strike do so without a ballot,

says Howell.

Scargill's undemocratic approach divided the workforce, but it didn't stop him from calling an all-out strike on 12 March 1984. It would take a year for the strike to end, during which time it was not only Scargill's reputation which would be tarnished. In what has become known as 'the Battle of Orgreave' on 18 June, when the police took on the mass of picketers bussed in to prevent coke – the high-carbon fuel derived from coal – being moved from the British Steel coking works in Orgreave, South Yorkshire, shocking levels of police violence towards the miners were captured on camera. The bloody conflict implied government approval, if not clear consent, for the use of physical oppression and attack by riot and mounted police against the mineworkers who had initially protested peacefully.

The confrontation involved thousands of police armed with riot shields and batons (and organised charges of mounted police into the fleeing strikers); 28 officers and approximately 100 miners were injured, while 95 miners were arrested and 55 charged with riot, which at the time carried a life sentence. 'We had already given them [the police] the equipment and the training they would need, learning the lessons of the 1981 inner-city riots,' writes MT in a retrospective quasi-admission of responsibility.

But there was violence on the other side too, in the form of intimidation in mining villages, not only of miners – so-called 'scabs' – who had continued working, but also of their wives and children. Shop owners in the coalfields were warned not to supply working miners with food, and their children were threatened in school by the offspring of striking miners. The brutal and bloody beatings by the police divided the public. On the one hand the police response appeared heavily out of proportion; on the other the miners, who were, as Neil Kinnock puts it, 'easily led', were striking undemocratically and ultimately seen to be taking on 'their own'. The strike turned deadly in 1984, when miners

David Jones and Joe Green were both killed whilst picketing, in Nottinghamshire and Yorkshire respectively.

In November 1984, a Welsh taxi driver, David Wilkie, was killed when two miners pushed a concrete block from a footbridge onto a taxi in which he was driving a non-striking miner to work. The miners, who were initially convicted of murder, had their charges reduced to manslaughter.

On top of the violence the government had a burgeoning PR problem. Everyone, including MT, could see that MacGregor's skills increasingly did not run to public relations – internal or external. Peter Walker was said to despise him; in return MacGregor described meetings with him as 'unpleasant'. Scargill nicknamed him the 'Yankee Steel Butcher', in part because he was irascible and unmoveable but also because he'd spent a long time living in the capital of capitalism: the USA. Tim Bell, who was brought in by MT to beef up the optics, said MacGregor 'was incapable of showing sympathy. The press was full of stories about miners' families starving and going to the soup-kitchens. MacGregor would act as if it wasn't any concern of his.'

Bell worked with the incorrigible, Claridge's-based old Etonian David Hart, scion of the Ansbacher merchant bank, who amongst other things set up military-style protection for non-striking miners threatened by NUM gangs and helped fund the breakaway Union of Democratic Mineworkers. Hart, whom Bell states played 'an inestimable part in our successes', was exactly the kind of male MT was drawn to – a dangerous, soldierly cove with a heavy 'tache and a curiously unstoppable flow of funds, despite being a former bankrupt. Hart would travel to the coalfields in his chauffeur-driven Mercedes and take snuff with the miners (many of whom were addicted to the stuff, using it as a substitute for cigarette-smoking, which was banned below ground), convincing them he was 'one of them', but all the while sending reports from the trenches to both MT and *The Times*.

For all of his bluster, Hart really was effective. It was he who arranged for Scargill to be presented with a court order on the floor of the Labour Party Conference after he persuaded his good friends, billionaire John Paul Getty Jr and the industrialist Hector Laing, to donate money to the fund for the working miners' attempt to sue the NUM. When a High Court judge ruled the strike was illegal without a ballot, Hart collected the server of the legal process in a chartered helicopter (his favourite mode of travel) and delivered him to Blackpool, just in time to serve the writ to Scargill in full view of the TV cameras on 1 October 1984.

Next up was the Conservative Party Conference. 'As usual, by the end of the week of our 1984 Party Conference in Brighton I was becoming frantic about my speech,' writes Margaret Thatcher. Much of her brain power that week had been applied to the fact that the National Association of Colliery Overmen, Deputies and Shotfirers (NACODS) were threatening to strike. As the official safety union, without them no pit could legally continue to function and the strikers would stand a real chance of defeating the government. It was a clever move and the possibility of it going ahead flummoxed MT.

Perhaps it was this added distraction which meant that she was still putting the finishing touches to her speech at approximately 2.54am on 12 October, assisted by her Principal Private Secretary, Robin Butler, when a bomb, which had been placed

## WARRIOR QUEEN, GENDER BLENDER?

one floor above the PM's room three weeks beforehand by IRA member Patrick Magee, exploded. 'Those who had sought to kill me had placed the bomb in the wrong place,' states MT with her customary blunt directness, devoid of any emotion, in her autobiography. Others were not so fortunate. Five were killed: Deputy Chief Whip Sir Anthony Berry, Eric Taylor, Roberta Wakeham, Lady Jeanne Shattock and, a month later from her injuries, Muriel Maclean. Norman Tebbit and his wife Margaret were badly injured. Margaret was paralysed from the waist down and would never walk again.

'[MT] was supremely calm,' says Butler, who began to take charge of the official papers moments after the bomb exploded and witnessed her immediately moving to the bedroom to check on Denis's welfare. He briefed her a few hours later. 'I told her, this looks pretty bad and you can't possibly continue with the conference. People have died.' She took no notice. She slept for perhaps one hour in her clothes at the Police College in Lewes. She changed into her conference suit (which had been gathered from her suite the night before by the faithful Crawfie), brushed her hair, made herself up, and at precisely 9.30 that morning, one day before her fifty-ninth birthday, she walked steadily onto the conference platform. 'Her response right from the start was: "Right, they've tried to kill us and we must show them that they haven't,"' says Butler. 'If she was fearful, she did not betray it.' She delivered her hastily rewritten post-lunch speech perfectly, for which she received a standing ovation. 'Not particularly good,' recorded Douglas Hurd in his diary, in what can only be described as a fit of churlish chauvinism, 'but she had had no sleep and is tearfully applauded for what she is.'

What she was, was the seemingly fearless female leader of a nation which had grown used to attacks on native soil. But perhaps not one this close. British public opinion, which had been wavering over MT's perceived treatment of the miners, immediately swung in behind her. But in this rare case, appearances, where MT was concerned, were deceptive. After the IRA released their chilling acknowledgement of responsibility – 'Today we were unlucky, but remember we have only to be lucky once. You will have to be lucky always' – she took to carrying a torch in her handbag everywhere she went, fearful of being trapped in another bombing and being unable to find her way out. At Chequers that weekend, after the Sunday service, TV cameras caught her tearfully dabbing at her eyes as she left the church. The events of 48 hours before had finally caught up with her. 'This was a day I was not meant to see,' she told her daughter Carol.

On 28 October 1984, *Times* journalist Jon Swain revealed that Arthur Scargill and Roger Windsor, the NUM's chief executive, had been holding secret talks with the Libyan government to solicit funds. (Documents released 23 years later revealed that Scargill had also been in talks with top officials at the Kremlin.) Scargill's credibility, which was by then in question, bottomed out. By the end of the year 70,000 striking miners had returned to work. On 3 March 1985, a delegate conference voted for an orderly return. There was no agreement over pay, pit closures or overtime. There was also no amnesty for convicted pickets.

By 1994, when the coal industry was privatised, just 7,000 miners remained in their jobs in an industry which in 1984 had employed 187,000 miners. The repercussions across the north of England, Scotland and Wales were dire, as communities were hollowed out, devoid of jobs, hope and meaning. 'Look, it wasn't how I would have done it. The aftermath needed to be dealt with,' says Gillian Shephard. It was remarkable how little attention was paid by society in general, and politicians in particular, to the mining locales, once the pits were closed. For Helena Kennedy, broadcaster, barrister and Labour member of the House of Lords, the answer was clear. She told me:

> Companies should have been given real incentives to open businesses providing new employment in those areas. Money should have been poured into those communities for retraining as ambulance drivers, as paramedics, as sports instructors, as healthcare workers. School support teams could have been created where men could provide support for boys with problems. These men needed to be told they had value and respect. Money could have been found but these were not Mrs T's voters. Communities became shells. No wonder young men in these communities turned to drink and drugs – the sense of hopelessness was passed down to further generations.

Was Margaret Thatcher to blame? Should the fact that she was a woman have made a difference? Not if gender parity was the benchmark. But there's an argument to be made that it wasn't. A male making the decisions MT made would have been regarded as a 'tough decision-maker'. As a female making the same decisions, the dice were loaded against her. 'The old working class were shrinking – old industries crumbling. The closure of mining had started under the previous Labour administration, though it was all blamed on her,' says Edwina Currie.

But that is not the popular or prevailing narrative. 'When it came to the conditions of ordinary working-class people, Thatcher represented a break from patrician one-nation conservatism. Frankly, she was more vicious,' says Frances O'Grady. 'In my view, Thatcher didn't break class ceilings; rather, she tried to break working-class spirit.' Is that true? 'Margaret Thatcher badly needs some political revisionism. Yes, she could be cruel, but she was not uncompassionate,' says Jonathan Aitken. 'No one ever looks at what she actually did for the workforce and for people who actively wanted to work. Everyone focuses on the miners – and she did a lot for those miners who were threatened and wished to stay in work.'

Helen Wilkinson's work for the think tank Demos (*No Turning Back: Generations and the Genderquake*, 1994) revealed that in fact during the 1980s some of the greatest shifts in attitude and aspiration where work was concerned had occurred amongst younger women in the socio-economic groups C1 and C2. In the book *On the Move: Feminism for a New Generation* she wrote: 'Confident young working-class women joined the trade union movement in the 1980s, and have the confidence to make their voices heard. Their confidence has undoubtedly been partly inspired by Margaret Thatcher's example.' Wilkinson points to MT's industrial and economic policies, her demolition of union power, her deregulation of the labour market and her willingness to embrace the increasingly flexible and increasingly globalised economy, which she says 'accelerated the shift in power from men to women, from masculine into feminine values in a way that would have been hard to imagine Old Labour's policies having done'.

## WARRIOR QUEEN, GENDER BLENDER?

When the Institute for Fiscal Studies published their paper on women's employment in the UK in 2018, the authors Barra Roantree and Kartik Vira illustrated that the past 40 years had seen an almost continuous rise in the proportion of prime working-age women (25–54) in employment – up from 57 per cent in 1975 to a record high of 78 per cent in 2017.

Whilst she might have halted the cycle of industrial decline and encouraged more women into the workplace, MT's victory over the miners proved pyrrhic. It was a lose–lose. The general public felt uncomfortable from the start with the concept of female political might, putting the man on the street – or rather, down the mines – out of work. As John Campbell points out:

> Despite Scargill's tactics there was real sympathy for the miners and particularly for their wives, seen as long-suffering heroines of their communities' doomed struggle. Collections for the miners' families raised at least £5 million… conscience money, in large part, contributed by those in work to allay a sense of guilt about those who were losing their livelihood through no fault of their own. There was still a romance about redundant miners.

Little, if any, media coverage was devoted to the miners' redundancy packages.

At the end of 1984 BBC Radio 4's *Today* programme ran a poll in which listeners voted Thatcher and Scargill respectively their Woman and Man of the Year.

# 7

# Onward Christian/Scientist

People turn round to me and say, look, you're the first woman Prime Minister at No. 10. I turn round and say I'm the first science Prime Minister at No. 10. That doesn't half shake them.

MT, July 1984, reception at No. 10 launching a campaign to encourage more girls to take up science

To understand Margaret Thatcher – to really understand her – you have to comprehend three things: firstly, to put it plainly, that she was the daughter of a lower-class England shopkeeper; secondly, that she was a devout Nonconformist Christian; and thirdly, that she was a scientist. Furthermore, she'd been a working scientist before she became a politician and a Christian before she became anything else,

says Norman Tebbit. Tebbit's succinct analysis offers the most clarity in the shortest number of words of any Margaret Thatcher interview I conducted. 'Margaret,' he says, 'weighed all of her decisions and tested all of her proposals against the standards of Christianity. And then she analysed them as a scientist would.'

Many would argue that to be a 'believer' and a scientist were two conflicting notions. But it's easy to forget that MT's time in office would be the last of any British PM to fully engage with, and be informed by, religious beliefs. It was certainly the last to assume that, in Britain, 'religion' meant Christianity.

> Back in the 1980s Britain was still assumed to be a Christian country. These were the days when the religious correspondent of the *Times* was in fact the Church of England correspondent; when the General Synod proceedings were reported verbatim in the newspapers, and when charities were fronted by churchmen, not celebrities,

said Dr Eliza Filby in an interview with the think tank Theos about her book *God and Mrs Thatcher: The Battle for Britain's Soul* (Biteback 2015). 'We don't do God,' the bullish Alastair Campbell famously told an American journalist who was interviewing Tony Blair in 2003, thereby confirming that whilst Anglican Tony Blair (who would convert to Catholicism soon after leaving office) definitely *did* do Religion with a capital R, he and the Labour Party would not be allowing the hand of God a say in policy-making. At least not publicly.

MT had no such qualms. In fact, she positioned her entire political ethos as the struggle between good and evil, describing her beliefs as 'the most marvellous evangelical faith'. Her religious strictures, at least in the early days, were flexible; some might even describe them as 'wet'. She voted liberally on abortion under controlled conditions in 1966 and for the decriminalisation of homosexuality in 1967, but later in her career she failed to take up either cause positively.

She was always, as her detractors are swift to point out, in favour of the death penalty. In 1969 she voted to restore capital punishment and spoke out in support of it again in 1979 and 1983. This fact notwithstanding, 'she seemed to confuse her semi-libertarian form of individualism with Christianity,' wrote David Mills in the American religious journal *First Things* in 2013. 'Economics are the method; the object is to change the heart and soul,' MT told the *Sunday Times* in 1981, representing a steelier, more salient resolve. She even eyed the welfare state with a Methodist's rationale, in part blaming what Keith Joseph called 'the Father Christmas state' for eroding an individual's desire to work. As historian Florence Sutcliffe-Braithwaite explained on the website History & Policy (April 2013): 'Thatcher wanted to re-establish an economic and legal framework and a cultural ethos which rewarded what she saw as the "Victorian" or "bourgeois" values of thrift, self-reliance and charity among all classes.'

Eliza Filby traces the crystallisation of Margaret Thatcher's religious and political views to her 1968 Conservative Party Conference speech when she uttered one of her most memorable lines: 'The point is that even the Good Samaritan had to have the money to help, otherwise he too would have had to pass on the other side.' In the writing of the speech, she'd drawn on the works of philosophers Popper and Hayek, amongst others, but for Filby 'it was to her Bible she looked... for legitimacy and as a way of popularising these ideas'. MT was clear about her religious motivation: 'I believe in what are often referred to as "Judaeo-Christian" values: indeed, my whole political philosophy is based on them,' she writes in her autobiography. For a woman of such a strong, self-proclaimed faith it was ironic that the Church very often positioned itself directly against her. In turn, she was extremely reluctant — and as a lay preacher's daughter some might say scared — to take on the Church directly. When a government report proposed deregulating Sundays, so that stores could open, sporting events be run and licensing laws overthrown, she wrote in the margins of one memo on the subject: 'I should leave this topic alone for the time being.' In another, relating to a private member's bill on the same issue, she describes it as 'the last thing we need at present'.

'Perhaps some policy mistakes could have been avoided if the bishops were prepared to engage with Thatcherism instead of winning cheap applause by misrepresenting it,' wrote one commentator in the *Telegraph* in 2015.

In the wilful distortion of Thatcher's views, the Church was not alone. In perhaps the most stunning misrepresentation of the words of a twentieth-century leader, a quote from a seemingly innocuous interview with the journalist Douglas Keay, of the then bestselling magazine *Woman's Own*, in 1987, which reflected the combination of MT's religious and political beliefs, has been routinely decontextualised and weaponised ever since.

Keays' question, paraphrased for reasons of copyright, was as follows:

> When I first interviewed you six or seven years ago you used almost the same words. Government statistics show the divorce rate under 35 is nearly 50 per cent, abortions have nearly doubled. We seem to have more violence, we have the yuppies of

the City, sort of violent with money. We have competition and free enterprise and it seems somehow to go together with greed.

MT's response came in two parts, partly because, halfway through, Keay interjected with a comment which, according to the archive, seems to have been mistranscribed. Here's the second, salient part of her response, subsequently edited for publication by Keay:

> I think we have gone through a period when too many children and people have been given to understand 'I have a problem, it is the government's job to cope with it!' or 'I have a problem, I will go and get a grant to cope with it!' 'I am homeless, the government must house me!' and so they are casting their problems on society and who is society? There is no such thing. There are individual men and women and there are families and no government can do anything except through people and people look to themselves first. It is our duty to look after ourselves and then also to help look after our neighbour and life is a reciprocal business and people have got the entitlements too much in mind without the obligations, because there is no such thing as an entitlement unless someone has first met an obligation and it is, I think, one of the tragedies in which many of the benefits we give, which were meant to reassure people that if they were sick or ill there was a safety net and there was help, that many of the benefits which were meant to help people who were unfortunate – 'It is all right. We joined together and we have these insurance schemes to look after it.' That was the objective, but somehow there are some people who have been manipulating the system and so some of those help and benefits

that were meant to say to people: 'All right, if you cannot get a job, you shall have a basic standard of living!' but when people come and say: 'But what is the point of working? I can get as much on the dole,' you say: 'Look. It is not from the dole. It is your neighbour who is supplying it and if you can earn your own living then really you have a duty to do it and you will feel very much better!'

How different Margaret Thatcher's legacy might have been, if the media takeaway from this interview had been 'Margaret Thatcher says "Help thyself and then thy neighbour"' or 'There's too much entitlement and not enough obligation'. And not the half-quoted, oft-quoted, daft-quoted 'there is no such thing as society'.

MT was also no proselytiser. 'She never rammed her faith down your throat, nor was she the type to drop God into every conversation or policy,' says Caroline Slocock.

> She was an ideological politician but with a very strong sense of personal duty, which may have derived from her religious upbringing. When she said 'we' I suspect she wasn't using it in the royal sense as people thought, rather I think she was trying to project a higher cause bigger than just herself.

Which explains a great deal but fails to account for MT's infamous quote at the birth of her son Mark's first child: 'We have become a grandmother.' (A quote which allegedly set alarm bells ringing at the Palace.)

Perhaps, in part, MT's inconsistency could be put down to the fact that her Christianity was what the *Church Times* called

## ONWARD CHRISTIAN/SCIENTIST

'selective but genuine'. By the time she became leader of the Tory Party she had already switched, with encouragement from Denis, from Wesleyan Methodism to what some might term the more intellectual and socially ambitious Anglicanism. Any faith would be hard-pressed to argue with what MT stated was one of the great principles of Judaeo-Christian inheritance: tolerance. In a speech to the General Assembly of the Church of Scotland in May 1988, she said:

> People with other faiths and cultures have always been welcomed in our land, assured of equality under the law, of proper respect and of open friendship. There's absolutely nothing incompatible between this and our desire to maintain the essence of our own identity. There is no place for racial or religious intolerance in our creed.

But her judgements patently did not always reflect her Christian beliefs, no matter how one interprets them. One devastating example is illustrated in the 2024 inquiry into the infected blood scandal. Almost 3,000 people died and 30,000 Britons were infected with HIV and hepatitis C (accompanied by other attendant health problems and the associated stigma) after being given contaminated blood products in the 1970s and 1980s. The inquiry, led by Sir Brian Langstaff, pointed the finger directly at Margaret Thatcher's Conservative government, and, by implication, at the PM herself. 'Margaret Thatcher, as well as subsequent governments and health secretaries, continually said infections were "inadvertent" and patients were given "the best treatment available on the then current medical advice",' Sky News reported. The inquiry had concluded that this was not true and that the factual basis for the claim was unclear. 'The line, which was wrong from the very outset, then became entrenched for around 20 years: a dogma became a mantra. It was enshrined. It was never questioned,' said Langstaff. (For more on the infected blood scandal, see Chapter 8.) It is hard to imagine how a woman who prided herself on being the first scientist to become PM, over and above being the first female, could really have been ignorant of such matters.

Is it a coincidence that both Angela Merkel (Chancellor of Germany 2005–21) and Margaret Thatcher trained as scientists, or that both of their fathers were in some sort of religious ministry (Merkel's father was a Lutheran pastor and theologian)? Probably not. Both claimed to have been heavily influenced by their fathers, and both were possessed of a scientific and religious rigour and steeliness, without which it is likely that neither would have succeeded. Merkel obtained a doctorate in quantum chemistry and worked as a research scientist until 1990. Thatcher was also a research chemist, first at British Xylonite (BX) Plastics in 1947 and then in 1950 at J. Lyons and Co., where, contrary to popular myth, there appears to be no evidence that she ever worked on the process of making soft scoop ice-cream.

A career in science was swiftly thrown over, however, and in 1951, having married Denis, she resigned from Lyons and began to study law. She was called to the Bar in February 1954, and on 8 October 1959 she was elected MP for Finchley. Wrote Hugo Young:

> These two jobs, lasting barely three years in all, constitute the totality of Margaret Thatcher's first-hand contact with the world of commerce and industry... In any case, Prime Minister

## ONWARD CHRISTIAN/SCIENTIST

Thatcher never tried to make political capital out of these fugitive involvements. They were incidental to her political ambition and she has never pretended otherwise. They made her a living whilst she devoted most of her psychic energy to the greater and more glamorous task.

For a woman who spent so little time as a scientist (and had confided to a friend as early as her university days that she 'should have studied law') Margaret Thatcher set a great deal of store by her qualification and often drew upon her experience in the field when making decisions.

'In my experience she saw the world as a scientist would all of the time,' says Margaret King.

> Her thoughts were rational and always with a scientific slant. Once she used an ornamental prism which had been given to her as a gift and was standing on a coffee table at No. 10 as a means of explaining her views of the public and the press to me. 'Now, Margaret, you see the sun coming through that prism? What colour is the ray coming through to you?' I replied: 'Orangey yellow.' Then she says, 'So I'm standing here and Mr B [her advisor] is standing next to you. I'm seeing green. Mr B is seeing cerise. That is how people see newspapers. Everyone has a different vision.'

Jon Agar, Professor of Science and Technology Studies at UCL, argues that MT's first career as a chemist sometimes influenced her third as a politician (*Science Policy under Thatcher*, UCL Press 2019). When she was Education Secretary in 1971, she agreed to a proposal tabled by Lord Rothschild that government funding of science should be treated more as a business case, having initially been resistant. Agar had earlier posited, in a 2011 paper for the Royal Society's *Notes and Records*, that this decision clearly defined MT's hard-line policies:

> It was precisely because Thatcher knew what scientific research was like that made her impervious to claims that science was a special case, with special features and incapable of being understood by outsiders, and therefore that science policy should be left in the hands of scientists. Such a strategy of persuasion and protection might have considerable purchase on a science minister with no direct experience of the working life of a scientist, but not Thatcher.

The ramifications of MT's decision would haunt her whilst Prime Minister. In January 1986, a half-page advertisement ran in *The Times* announcing the creation of a new organisation: 'Save British Science'. The ad, which had over 1,500 signatories, decried the lack of funding, the brain drain and low morale within the British science community, laying the blame directly at the door of the Thatcher government. In a 2013 *Nature* journal article entitled 'We are still saving British science from Margaret Thatcher', eminent physiologist and biologist Denis Noble details how the 1986 group, who travelled to London for a press conference, were knocked off the front page by Michael Heseltine, who resigned the same day over the Westland crisis. However, the campaigning group still exists and is now called Campaign for Science and Engineering (CaSE). 'Did we make mistakes?' writes Noble, answering his own question: 'Perhaps the most serious was to accept (as did later governments as well) too much of the Thatcher government's agenda: to make science justify itself by its economic impact.'

A great deal of MT's lifelong passion for science and scientific rigour stemmed from her respect for her former tutor at Somerville, chemist Dorothy Hodgkin, whom she revered almost above anyone, other than 'Winston'. Under Hodgkin, only the third female to ever take a Chemistry first at Oxford, and ultimately the first to ever take paid maternity leave, MT wrote her fourth-year dissertation on X-ray crystallography of the antibiotic cocktail gramicidin. In 1964, Hodgkin would win the Nobel Prize in Chemistry for her crystallographic analysis of the structure of molecules, leading to penicillin development. At the time of writing, she remains the only British woman to win a Nobel Prize in science.

In 1948, MT came down from Oxford having been awarded what Charles Moore describes as a 'respectable second-class degree'. During her time at No. 10, a black-and-white portrait of Hodgkin hung on the wall of MT's study and the two continued their relationship, corresponding frequently via letters. 'Lady T was terrified of one person and one person only and that person was a woman: Dorothy Hodgkin,' says Charles Powell. 'When she would visit No. 10 Margaret would ask me to be in the meeting with her and she would quite literally sit on the edge of her chair, saying nothing, whilst Dorothy laid into her.' Hodgkin's left-wing political views made her a natural Thatcher adversary and she would, over the years, in correspondence and in person have absolutely no compunction about taking on the PM. Whilst writing Hodgkin's biography, author

# THE INCIDENTAL FEMINIST

Georgina Ferry found a tattered piece of paper in Hodgkin's archive, held at the Bodleian Library in Oxford, headed 'Notes for Margaret', which read: 'Object: to rethink relations with the Soviet Union on the basis that friendship is possible and would be to everyone's advantage – trade – science – art – the lot.' At one Downing Street reception, MT was observed sitting next to Hodgkin, who suffered from acute rheumatoid arthritis and used a wheelchair, solicitously cutting up her food for her. 'We just took a different view,' MT later wrote sanguinely of their conversations and friendship. 'She couldn't dissuade me, and I couldn't dissuade her.'

'Mrs Thatcher would occasionally hark back to science, despite the fact that she had worked as a chemist so briefly,' says a former advisor, 'and it would throw a spanner into briefings. You'd be painstakingly explaining something to her as swiftly as you could and she'd say words to the effect of "Hurry up for goodness' sake – of course I understand – I am, after all, a scientist."' She was reportedly sceptical of President Reagan's plans for SDI (the Strategic Defence Initiative, or 'Star Wars' as it became known) because, with her 'science hat' on, she doubted its effectiveness in ending the Cold War, and also Reagan's claim that it would effectively bring an end to global nuclear deterrents. In December 1984, according to Hugo Young, she spoke for 90 minutes (although records suggest it was actually more like 45) at a Camp David meeting 'with a directness which no other leader, it was said from the Reagan side, would have been permitted'. She told Reagan and his attendant aides and ministers that it was a mistake to continue, saying that the Star Wars defence was unattainable: '"as a chemist" she said she knew it wouldn't work,' writes Young, who quotes one of the Americans present saying: 'It was a great Thatcher performance.'

On a lighter note, as a scientist MT would probably have been delighted that the credit for the ongoing 4 May theme or meme of 'May the Fourth be With You' belonged to the Conservative Party. The organisation took out a half-page newspaper advert in the London *Evening News* after MT won the 1979 general election on that date, which stated: 'May the Fourth Be with You, Maggie. Congratulations!'

'She certainly possessed a scientist's perspective. I don't know of any other leader who spoke up so early about the climate crisis. I think she was the first,' says Caroline Slocock. John Gummer recalled:

> Science proved to her that climate change was happening so she stood up against everybody else and said, 'This is what's happening and we've got to do something about it.' She also persuaded the President of the United States [then George H.W. Bush] to attend the first global climate summit in Rio in 1992 which she had called for whilst still in office.

She was in fact the first global leader to countenance the veracity of the climate change theory after hearing about it at the inaugural UN environment conference in Stockholm and then by having it explained in greater detail by diplomat Sir Crispin Tickell, who had studied the subject at Harvard. 'She very much felt herself to be a scientist among non-scientists, and of course she certainly felt that as a woman in a man-made world, she had to make her point,' he later told *The Ecologist* magazine of her 8 November

1989 speech to the UN General Assembly, when she proved herself prophetic on the matter. 'The problem of global climate change is one that affects us all and action will only be effective if it is taken at the international level,' she told the assembly. 'It's no good squabbling over who is responsible or who should pay. Whole areas of our planet could be subject to drought and starvation if the pattern of monsoons and rains were to change as a result of the destruction of forests and the accumulation of greenhouse gases.' Invoking Charles Darwin, she also told the General Assembly that the UK would take responsibility for a new centre for the prediction of climate change. The Hadley Centre for Climate Research and Prediction (the Met Office Hadley Centre for Climate Science and Services as it is now known) was set up in 1990 under the auspices of MT. It has been at the forefront of climate research ever since.

When in 1985 Oxford University denied Margaret Thatcher an honorary degree under the spurious guise of protesting against government cuts in education, it was the seat of learning which appeared closed-minded, not the Prime Minister. This rendered her the only post-war PM to have been denied an honorary degree (though later Tony Blair too would be denied, also in protest). There was a suspicion, however, that underlying the protest was intellectual snobbery and resistance to change, rather than a relentless march towards educational excellence. Put simply, the intellectual establishment did not like Margaret Thatcher and she, in return, did not think much of them either.

During her time in government the balance of power between the educational system – i.e. those doing the teaching – and the government undoubtedly shifted. Ultimately, the way MT saw it, parents should be allowed a say in terms of where and how their children were schooled. The 1979 Education Act enabled local authorities to maintain grammar schools (although in fact the number of comprehensive schools almost tripled under the Conservatives); the 1980 Education Act gave parents greater powers – both on governing bodies and the right to choose a school for their children; and the 1988 Education Reform Act phased in the National Curriculum with three core subjects (maths, English and science), six foundation subjects (history, geography, technology, music, art and physical education) and a modern foreign language at key stages 1 to 4 (ages five to sixteen). In 1986 GCSEs replaced O levels. From 1984 to 1987, the government battled with teaching unions (and was mostly victorious). In 1987 the Teachers' Pay and Conditions Act imposed a new salary system and conditions of employment.

'You don't stop someone becoming a fellow of an academic body because you dislike them,' stated the principal of Somerville, Daphne Park, disagreeing with the dons' protest over the honorary degree. MT, for all of her misgivings about intellectuals, was said to be privately deeply hurt. Downing Street issued a statement: 'If they do not wish to confer the honour, she is the last person to wish to receive it.' 'It was probably the thing that bothered her most,' says Charles Powell.

Contrary to the view of most intellectuals and academics, both academia and science made modernising strides under MT. During her tenure, student loans were introduced, extending the opportunity for more students from a greater variety of backgrounds to attend university. The introduction of the RAE (Research Assessment Exercise) in 1986, to which the dons were so opposed, created greater accountability for public funding. 'Before Mrs Thatcher, universities were very similar to public utilities – run for the benefit of staff with government money,' said Professor Terence Kealey, former advisor to MT and vice-chancellor of the University of Buckingham. 'She was determined to introduce a much higher level of accountability.' David Willetts, Universities and Science Minister at the time of MT's death, said: 'As a scientist she understood the value of research... that is why, as prime minister, she overruled official scepticism and made Britain a full contributor to the Large Hadron Collider.'

MT exacted her own quiet but weighty revenge. In 1999 she was made a Companion of the Elite Guard of Cambridge Benefactors in acknowledgement of her fundraising efforts for the university, to which the Thatcher Foundation endowed a £2 million chair in 'enterprise studies'. Margaret Thatcher's extensive collection of her personal and political papers was donated to the Archives Centre at Churchill College, Cambridge, in 1997. The centre was purpose-built to house the papers of her hero: Winston Churchill.

In 1988, MT gave vent to her resentments over Oxford's rejection three years previously by taking a swipe at intellectuals in a TV interview she granted her 'friend', gamekeeper turned poacher Brian Walden. Walden, once an MP and sometime contributor to MT's speeches, flattered himself that he knew the PM better than any other journalist. 'Of course, she reflected, revolutionary doctrines, like communism, usually came from intellectuals and academics,' he wrote in the *Sunday Times* of 8 May 1988, about their interview. She said:

## ONWARD CHRISTIAN/SCIENTIST

They think they have a talent and ability that none of the rest of the human race has. That is the ultimate snobbery, the worst form of snobbery there is. Only put them in charge and the poor will have everything. So the poor put them in power and discover the rulers have everything and the poor have nothing.

# 8

# Madness, Madonna and MT

## *Pop, Profanity and Power under Thatcher*

Yes, it is nice they know your name, isn't it?
MT, *Smash Hits* interview, March 1987

Was Margaret Thatcher the grit in the creative oyster that was 1980s Britain? Is creativity within popular culture really an act of rebellion? MT's relationship with culture and the arts was never easy. She began her time in office with a 4.8 per cent cut to Arts Council grants and ended it with one of 2.9 per cent, with the Arts Council becoming a government body. She wanted museums, arguably one of the most defining manifestations of a flourishing nation, to stand on their own two feet, and encouraged sponsorship. Dame Elizabeth Esteve-Coll – the first female director of a national art collection, who took over the V&A from Sir Roy Strong in 1988 – was pilloried by the so-called intelligentsia for her Thatcherite approach. (For which read: they didn't like it when a female was swiftly able to achieve what no man had been able to since the museum's inception.) Under Esteve-Coll's auspices visitor numbers at the V&A rose from 900,000 to 1.35 million. Critics carped about commercialism – the V&A advertising campaign 'An ace caff with quite a nice museum attached' – created by who other than Saatchi & Saatchi – came in for particular criticism. Ultimately though, for all of their grumbling, the heads of every other museum would swiftly follow suit.

In 1981, MT cut university spending by 8.5 per cent, thereby cementing her reputation as the enemy of the Literary Left, by whom, she had rightly presupposed, she was regarded as nothing short of an anti-intellectual at best and a philistine at worst. Not everyone agreed. Philip Larkin told his friend Kingsley Amis that watching MT debating at one of her infamous 'arts gatherings' in 1982, of which there were quite a few over the years, 'was like watching a top-class tennis-player… just bang, back over the net'. Amis had previously written to Larkin after meeting MT in 1977, saying: 'I thought her nice and bright but by God she doesn't half hate lefties.' The artist duo Gilbert and George both 'came out' as Thatcherites, to furious criticism from colleagues. 'In the art world, us saying we were Thatcherites was the worst thing you could say. Like saying you were a Nazi paedophile or something. They still don't forgive us for that,' George told Michael Prodger in *The Critic* in 2019.

Right-wing writers like Anthony Powell were rather more reductive in their praise: 'I find Mrs Thatcher very attractive,' wrote Powell, who questioned other guests at the same dinner. 'Physically desirable was the universal answer… including Vidia [the novelist

## MADNESS, MADONNA AND MT

V.S. Naipaul].' Female writers, by contrast, were almost universally unkind (though Iris Murdoch was notably a fan). Fiction writer Angela Carter wrote, in what seemed like a dismissal of her entire sex, that Thatcher 'coos like a dove, hisses like a serpent, bays like a hound'. The apotheosis of intellectual anti-Thatcher snobbery was perhaps reached in 1986, when historian Lady Antonia Fraser and her husband, Harold Pinter, held a meeting at their home in lofty Campden Hill Square, for what was effectively the anti-Thatcherite literati. Attendees included Ian McEwan, David Hare, Margaret Drabble, Angela Carter and Salman Rushdie. They called themselves 'the June 20 Group', which led some to draw parallels with the similarly named 20 July Group which had plotted to assassinate Hitler on that date in 1944. According to Fraser, though, it was simply a nod to the birthdays of McEwan and Rushdie, which fell on either side of that date.

Other than inflaming the press, the group had no effect whatsoever. In any case, the creative industries in 1980s Britain, particularly the 'populist' ones (of the type that those in the June 20 Group would most disdain), were flourishing. Whether this was because of, or in spite of, MT is moot. But on both sides of the Atlantic there was an explosion of creativity (often taking the form of social and political protest). To name names on the American side (just a few): Keith Haring, Jean-Michel Basquiat, Jeff Koons, Prince, Madonna, Michael Jackson. In the UK, artists like Tracey Emin, Damien Hirst, Rachel Whiteread and Jenny Saville and musicians including George Michael, Queen, U2, the Human League, Sade, the Police, Elvis Costello, the Style Council and Madness all reflected the mood – a mixture of gloss and gloom. Movies, too, mirrored the zeitgeist. Indeed, the man responsible for perhaps the most poignant of characterisations of the class-, sexual- and social-conflict-ridden Britain of the 1980s, *My Beautiful Laundrette* – Hanif Kureishi – famously claimed that MT had 'no understanding of what a central place the arts have in British life, or how good Britain is at producing books, films, theatre and music.' As critic John Harris of *The Guardian* pointed out: 'The paradox, then, was delicious, because Thatcher, her ideas, and their impact on society all served to create a cultural earthquake.'

Iain R. Webb, Professor of Fashion and Design at Kingston School of Art, began his career at the pop culture and style magazine *Blitz* in the 1980s and then went on to work at *Harpers & Queen* and was the first and only (male) fashion editor of *The Times*.

> I was the gay son of a milkman – who'd have thought I'd make it in Thatcher's Britain? There were lots of people like me who felt like outcasts within society either because of sexuality, race or class, but there was also an outpouring of creativity at this time – maybe because we all felt we had nothing to lose. And, of course, ironically, we did have the Thatcher work ethic and drive, which the middle and upper classes did not have. It sort of gave us an advantage over 'them'.

There was, then, a creative urgency about the eighties, which few other recent decades have possessed. Julie Burchill arrived in London in the mid eighties.

> It was the most wonderful time to be young and in the media/arts – very much like the sixties, I imagine. I wrote that 'we were all Thatcher and [Malcolm] McLaren's children' and there

was something so honest about 1980s capitalism, as opposed to the mealy-mouthed habit of modern corporations showing off their sensitivities,

she says, admitting that she breathed the rarefied air of a small group of 'Soho pleasure seekers' (for which see the infamous Groucho Club founded in 1985: only literary types allowed – strictly no advertising people). Nonetheless,

There was a get-up-and-go feeling in the country as a whole. I'll never forget going home to Bristol in 1986 to find my father – an avowed communist – showing off about having bought shares in the newly privatised British Gas, especially in the light of that awful 'Tell Sid' ad campaign.

The spectre of AIDS loomed increasingly large. 'Yes, the threat of AIDS was hanging over the entire gay community,' says Webb, 'and remember in the early eighties no one knew what it was or how to treat it. People began dying. I think that kind of terror bonded everyone in the creative industries together in a way. We were united by two common enemies – Thatcher and AIDS.' The threat of the disease – initially misnamed GRID (Gay-Related Immune Deficiency) and often called a 'gay cancer' – which would come to be known as AIDS (Acquired Immune Deficiency Syndrome) was tangible and would affect an entire generation – LGBTQ and straight. By the end of 1984, Britain had recorded 148 cases of AIDS and 46 deaths – amongst the first was a young man called Terrence Higgins, who died in 1982, and it is from the trust named after him that this data was drawn.

It took the government until 1985 to issue any form of health advice to the medical profession. MT's response to AIDS was both conflicted and inadequate, although, for a woman who pursued the unforgiveable Section 28, any personal prejudices against those homosexuals close to her appeared to be non-existent. One of her closest allies, Ronald Millar, was flamboyantly homosexual, and a member of her cabinet, Nicholas Eden (son of Anthony), the 2nd Earl of Avon, former aide-de-camp to Queen Elizabeth II, Undersecretary of State for Energy 1983–4 and for the Environment 1984–5, died of AIDS-related causes, shortly after resigning because of 'ill health' in 1985.

As a scientist, MT very quickly understood the risk of AIDS; as a practising Christian she was concerned about endorsing any form of 'risky' sexual behaviour, particularly amongst the young. She vetoed a ministerial broadcast on the threat of AIDS to the nation but in 1987 sanctioned a national leafleting programme and a TV advertising campaign, nicknamed 'Monolith', replete with sounds of thunder and lighting, images of an exploding volcano, the chiselling of a gravestone and acres of pouring lava (presumably extraordinarily oblique references to sex). Some 23 million homes received leaflets bearing the heading 'AIDS: Don't Die of Ignorance'. Few of us who were young at the time can forget the advertising campaign, which closed with the black tombstone, with the word AIDS chiselled onto it, crashing to the ground and actor John Hurt intoning: 'If you ignore AIDS it could be the death of you.'

Equally as damning as MT's response to the HIV virus that caused AIDS was the fact that the government was slow to offer any form of AIDS testing programme (when the US and many

European countries had already done so). Britain also continued importing infected blood products, particularly Factor VIII, which was used as a blood-clotting agent for haemophiliacs. In 2021 Norman Fowler, who was Social Services Secretary (with responsibility for health) from 1981 to 1987, told the Infected Blood Inquiry that he believed that neither MT nor the Treasury were prepared to offer compensation to people who contracted AIDS from infected bloods because 'then the floodgates would have been opened'. According to the Haemophilia Society, in the 1970s and 1980s about 6,000 people with haemophilia and other bleeding disorders were treated with contaminated clotting factors containing HIV and hepatitis viruses. Some of those infected their partners, often because they were unaware of their own infection. Since then more than 3,000 people have died. Around 1,250 people were infected with HIV, including 380 children. Fewer than 250 are still alive.

The gay community was already under attack from the general public, which laid the blame for AIDS firmly at its door. By the time Section 28 arrived in 1988, it was possessed of a kind of siege mentality. 'I think we knew Section 28 was coming,' acknowledges Webb, who remembers being at Bang nightclub (the biggest gay club in Europe at the time) in 1979 on the evening that MT was elected PM.

> The police raided the club. They came through from one end to the other. They had no powers to do anything, they just wanted to show us a police presence. The message was, 'There's plenty more of this coming down the track.' It was chilling, but later

Section 28 would serve as a kind of catalyst for us all to be even louder and prouder.

Two groups of lesbian activists took matters very publicly into their own hands. In February 1988, after the House of Lords had voted in favour of the bill, which, to reiterate, actually made it illegal for schools and local authorities to teach 'the acceptability of homosexuality as a pretended family relationship', two activists abseiled into the chamber on washing lines bought from Clapham Market. In another headline-generating protest, on 23 May 1988, the night before Section 28 came into force, a small number of women invaded the BBC studio where presenter Sue Lawley was broadcasting the *Six O'Clock News* live, wearing T-shirts that read 'Stop the Clause'. One handcuffed herself to a camera, another to the news desk. The Editor of News at the time, Tony Hall, described the protest as 'intolerable'.

Webb's most searing memory of that time is that, whilst attending one of the Section 28 demonstrations in London, he spied a drag queen, who had climbed up a lamp post along the march route, immaculately attired as Margaret Thatcher in Tory-blue suit and pussy bow, complete with lipstick and big hair, urging the marchers on with her large, black, gold-clasped handbag. 'That summed it all up for me, perfectly.'

The more it seemed that the exploration of one's sexuality was being threatened, the more the blending of gender was explored by the pop culture of the eighties. The New Romantics were a musical movement with make-up and brittle, big-haired femininity underscored by a glossy, broad-shouldered brightness, which included groups like Culture Club, Adam and the Ants, Duran Duran and Spandau Ballet. One of the first openly gay bands, Frankie Goes to Hollywood, came to be seen as pop representations of the Thatcher success story. In reality, this wasn't always the case. As DJ Stuart Maconie told American National Public Radio (NPR), Gary Kemp, Spandau's guitarist who had written 'Gold', later became a member of Red Wedge, the left-wing musicians' organisation created to help Labour get re-elected. 'I know that it angers Gary Kemp to this day... that he's seen – because of the way that music sounds, because it sounds so kind of well-upholstered and shiny-suited – that he's seen as being an arch-Thatcherite when in fact he was a Labour supporter.' It can't have helped the atmosphere on the tour bus that Spandau's lead singer, Tony Hadley, was a self-professed Conservative Party supporter and an ardent admirer of MT.

To say that women in popular culture were overlooked during the Thatcher eighties is an obvious understatement. 'Though AIDS was new and scary, we all knew we were on the same side: against ignorance,' says Julie Burchill. 'Women could see gay men as oppressed and sexually censured just like they were.' A few American women began to inhabit roles that made some inroads into the stereotypes: Linda Hamilton in *The Terminator*, Sigourney Weaver in *Alien* and Melanie Griffith in *Working Girl*. And then along came Julia Roberts in the blockbusting *Pretty Woman* of 1990, undoing all of their good work with her role as the pretty prostitute who gets her guy and gives up her day (and night) job. In Britain, only Julie Walters, starring in *Educating Rita* in 1983, struck out for female independence via education. Meanwhile, playwrights took on MT with gusto, with Caryl

Churchill's *Top Girls* (1982) and *Serious Money* (1987), David Hare and Howard Brenton's *Pravda* (1985), Jim Cartwright's *Road* (1986) and Alan Ayckbourn's *A Small Family Business* (1987). Not for nothing did the Brazilian concept of the Theatre of the Oppressed become popular in 1980s Britain.

Plenty of eighties creatives were lyrically adept at skewering their so-called villain, and, as John Harris has pointed out, perhaps no one did it better than the Jam, whose vocalist, the sharp-suited mod Paul Weller, wrote a peerless take-down of the early Thatcher years, which had been mired by urban riots from Bristol to Toxteth, striking miners and unemployment, in the 1982 hit 'A Town Called Malice'. The Jam were of course not alone: UB40 (named for the Unemployment Benefit Attendance Card) sang about being a 'One in Ten' (out of work), while the Specials' 'Ghost Town' was about the evisceration of towns across the English Midlands as manufacturing in Britain continued its inevitable shrinkage. And who could forget George Michael and Andrew Ridgeley's 'Wham Rap' chant of 'DHSS, DHSS' (which for the young amongst us stands for Department of Health and Social Security)?

Although much noise is still being made about the decline of the manufacturing industry under MT, the shrinkage actually occurred relatively slowly whilst the Tories were in power. In 1970 manufacturing was 20.57 per cent of GDP, by 1979 it was 17.62 per cent and when MT left office it was 15.8 per cent. But that didn't help those who were out of work in the early 1980s, when unemployment exceeded three million. And then there was the gender pay gap, which stood at around 66 per cent until 1987, although the next five years saw the most significant improvement in women's relative pay (up to 70 per cent by 1992). 'When Am I Going to Make A Living?' Sade sang in 1984. In what could have been a call and response from across the Atlantic, in 1985 Madonna replied with a hit ironically endorsing the predominant eighties value of 'cold hard cash' in 'Material Girl'. By 1987, eighties excess would breed the unforgettable celluloid greedmonger, the unscrupulous Gordon Gekko from Oliver Stone's *Wall Street*.

Musicals were more MT's thing than Madonna and she rightly regarded Andrew Lloyd Webber as one of the great British success stories of her era. Lloyd Webber 'owned' the West End with his musicals, which dominated the theatre world during the 1980s. In celebrated theatre critic Michael Billington's book *State of the Nation*, he writes that the musical represented 'Thatcherism in action': what it celebrated was the triumph of individualism and profitability. Where British theatre in previous decades had been famed for its writers, actors and directors, he commented in *The Guardian* in 2013, 'in the 1980s it became identified with its musicals – *Cats*, *Starlight Express*, *Les Miserables*, *The Phantom of the Opera*, *Miss Saigon*'.

Was the criticism of Lloyd Webber and his success (of which there was much) simply another form of elitist snobbery? After all, as MT might have said, there was nothing wrong with a musical. There was an element of both justification and irony to all of this carping from the 'lofty lefties'. In fact, the success of some of their number was undoubtedly down to the Thatcher government's Enterprise Allowance Scheme, which paid £40 per week for up to twelve months to any and every small-scale, working-age entrepreneur who could provide a business plan and a self-funded £1,000 in savings or loans. At its peak 100,000 young people were enrolled in the scheme, which would employ over 325,000 people in total. A study at the time from the World Bank found that for every 100 people taking part, 64 jobs were created. According to a report from the Royal Society of Arts, the EAS created 325,000 jobs at a cost to the Treasury in today's money of £4,200 each. Eighteen months after signing up, 65 per cent of recipients were still running the business they had started, and a fifth of them had started employing someone who was not part of it. A quarter of them were under 25. Beneficiaries of the EAS included Tracey Emin, *Viz* magazine, Alan McGee's Creation Records, Julian Dunkerton of Superdry, Turner Prize winners Jeremy Deller and Rachel Whiteread, sculptor Edmund de Waal and singer Jarvis Cocker.

Much as they might have distrusted her, the younger literary set were publishing works which, whilst critical of the government, also managed to achieve a glossy edge. Amongst them were Martin Amis's *Money: A Suicide Note* ('*Money* seethes with Swiftian disgust at the corrupting effect of filthy lucre and the private hell of lonely gratification,' said the *New York Times*), Alan Hollinghurst's *The Swimming-Pool Library*, Julian Barnes' *Metroland*, Ian McEwan's *The Child in Time* and, from across the Atlantic, the biggest of them all, responding to the 'excesses' of the Reagan/Thatcher year: Tom Wolfe's *The Bonfire of the Vanities*. Notably, the most lauded novelists of MT's time in office were almost all men, although Anita Brookner won the Booker Prize for *Hotel du Lac* in 1984, and Sue Townsend had phenomenal success with the quasi-infantile *Secret Diary of Adrian Mole, Aged 13¾*, which tells you something about the paucity of successful women writers during this literary decade. Perhaps more prophetically, from across the Atlantic came Margaret Atwood's *The Handmaid's Tale*.

If any author could be seen to span the Thatcher decade, it was Salman Rushdie, who began the 1980s with his celebrated Booker Prize winner *Midnight's Children* (1981) and ended it in hiding with round-the-clock police protection, sanctioned by MT, after a fatwa was issued in response to his 1988 novel *The Satanic Verses*. Rushdie, whose politics in no way aligned with MT's ('Nanny-Britain, strait-laced Victoria-reborn Britain... thin-lipped, jingoist Britain, is in charge,' he wrote in a 1983 essay in the *New Statesman*), may later have regretted naming one of his characters in *The Satanic Verses* 'Mrs Torture'. Later, he recalled MT's solicitousness on the two occasions they met whilst he was in hiding as 'touchy-feely... auntie-like... and quite disarming'. (Rushdie later credited MT for his decision not to name his attacker in his memoir *Knife*, which charted his experience of being stabbed on 12 August 2022, before he was about to give a lecture at Chautauqua Institute in New York State, likening it to MT's reluctance to give IRA terrorists the 'oxygen of publicity' during her time in office.)

Four TV shows in Britain perhaps defined the eighties: Alan Bleasdale's *Boys from the Blackstuff*, a 1982 drama set in Liverpool and described aptly by Apple TV as 'profoundly moving human dramas [which] follow in turn the attempts of five working-class heroes to survive', especially memorable for the character Yosser Hughes, whose catchphrase 'Gizza job' underscored both the prevailing plea of the 1980s and what the British Film Institute described as 'a lament to the end of a male, working-class British culture'. The 1981 Granada TV adaptation of Evelyn Waugh's *Brideshead Revisited*, which exploited middle-class Britain's continued reverence for and fascination with the aristocracy (it was also spectacularly good television), was in stark but successful contrast to *Only Fools and Horses*, written by John Sullivan, which tracked the fortunes of two South London 'chancers' and their comically hopeless attempts to fulfil their dreams and become millionaires during the Thatcher 'have it all' eighties. Not forgetting MT's own particular favourite: *Yes Minister* and then *Yes, Prime Minister*, a wry, tongue-in-cheek look at the way Westminster and the country was – and still is – run: by civil servants.

Whilst these television dramas were male-biased and featured male heroes or anti-heroes, they also reflected the gradual erosion of the post-war male stereotype and traditional male power, which was perhaps inevitable (and for many of us entirely welcome) in a country where a female was finally calling the shots. *Blackstuff* charts the decline of a whole male-dominated way of life, whilst *Only Fools and Horses* showcased male vulnerability, albeit cloaked in side-splitting comedy. The antithesis to the show's characters of Del Boy and Rodney Trotter was Harry Enfield's 'Loadsamoney' – a satire on the get-rich-quick world of aspiring working-class Thatcherites. Meanwhile in *Brideshead* (voted tenth in the list of 100 greatest ever television programmes by the BFI and one of *Time* magazine's greatest TV shows of all time; *Blackstuff* and *Yes Minister* also made the BFI top ten) the only real winner is Julia Flyte, who gets the vast family estate rather than her brother but tragically, thanks to the rigours of Catholic guilt, does not get her man. In *Yes Minister* no man wins (and there were very few female characters) but the bureaucratic machine triumphs. Experimental comedies like *The Young Ones*, *The Comic Strip Presents* and *Blackadder* also began to explore 'man as fool'. Perennially victorious and universally feared in the second series of the historical comedy *Blackadder* was Richard Curtis's version of Queen Elizabeth I, 'Queenie', played by Miranda Richardson with more than a knowing wink towards an irascible, domineering female with a fawning court of male suitors, all of whom feared for their heads.

It is perhaps not a coincidence, though, that arguably the best TV show of the post-Thatcher 1990s starred a woman – Helen Mirren as Detective Chief Inspector Jane Tennison. In Lynda La Plante's *Prime Suspect*, Mirren plays a hard-bitten workaholic with a taste for drink, whose wry sense of humour, biting satire and 'boss girl' demeanour leaves no one in doubt as to who is in charge. She doesn't actually say 'Why do I have to do everything myself?' as MT allegedly once did, but the implication is hard-wired into all seven series, for which Mirren won three BAFTAs and two Emmys. Could Tennison, whose frustration over the barriers of her sex and class are all too apparent, have been written without Britain previously experiencing an entire decade with a female in charge? Highly unlikely.

If Morrissey of the Smiths was to be believed, everyone in the 1980s was 'miserable now'. Except that they really weren't. Two major popular media events dominated the decade – the marriage of Prince Charles and the then Lady Diana Spencer in 1981, and Live Aid in 1985. Both unleashed a remarkable amount of unbridled joy into the atmosphere of a country either in the grips of a right-wing regime or enjoying a kind of renaissance, depending upon both your politics and your economic situation. Live Aid, which followed on from the original Band Aid, was put together by the lead singer of the Boomtown Rats, the scruffy ball of intellectual energy and four-letter words that was (and is) Bob Geldof. It's hard to divine whether Britain's unbridled enthusiasm for Live Aid came from the music itself or the fact that we as a country could still pull off a stunt of showmanship so ridiculously ambitious, with stages in London and Philadelphia (and Phil Collins, thanks to Concorde, appearing on both), as to be virtually impossible. If you're a boomer or Gen Xer you'll probably remember where you were on that hot afternoon in July 1985, either in the stadium or joining the estimated 1.5 billion globally who watched the TV coverage as Bowie, Queen, Elton John, George Michael, Alison Moyet, Sade, Dire Straits et al. took to the stage. Geldof's original response to the BBC's report on the famine in Ethiopia, from their foreign correspondent Michael Buerk, was the Band Aid single, 'Do They Know It's Christmas?' Geldof and co-writer/producer Midge Ure's urgency impressed MT, because their ethos chimed directly with her own. 'What fascinated me was this,' she told *Smash Hits* in a 1987 interview: '[It was] not only "Why doesn't Government give more?" but "What can I do as a person?" That was his [Bob Geldof's] approach.' '"Do They Know It's Christmas?" crushed all argument; it gave miners' benefit records like the Council Collective's "Soul Deep" an air of axe-grinding and pettiness. People striking to save their jobs couldn't compete with the media-swallowing story of Band Aid, and the images of starving children,' wrote music historian and musician Bob Stanley from the band Saint Etienne.

If Band Aid and Live Aid irrevocably changed celebrity charitable giving forever, the introduction of a young, beautiful, blue-blooded British ingénue into the staid, moulding environs of Britain's Teutonically derived royal family radically altered the image of Britain – at least to the outside world. Suddenly, Britain was glamorous! With its female PM and now its captivating princess, who obligingly popped out the heir and the spare within a few short years of getting hitched, Britain was the place to be (or at least the place for the paparazzi to be). Peter York and Ann Barr satiated the outpouring of interest in 'Di's tribe' with their bestselling *Official Sloane Ranger Handbook*, detailing what they wore – navy blue, Barbours and pearls, pie-crust collars, striped shirts (for both sexes) and Hunter wellies – how they spoke – 'wa wa' – where they lived – Kensington and Chelsea – and where they drank – the White Horse, Parsons Green, aka 'the Sloaney Pony'. The greatest irony of the Sloane Ranger, as Peter York wrote in *The Oldie* magazine in 2022, was that

> Sloanes were widely confused with aristocrats, whereas they were really a sub-set of the upper middles. They seemed then to be an important, settled layer – arguably the marzipan one – in our national cake, with the monarchy at the top and the toffs providing the icing. If the Sloanes became suddenly, unwittingly, fashionable in the early 1980s, by the end of the decade – after the Big Bang (1986) – they couldn't have been more out, more wrong. The go-for-it, free-market era did more to

undermine Sloane culture than all the various post-war Labour governments, high taxation and the three-day week.

Ever since the 1980s it has been routine, if not de rigueur, for those with intellectual pretensions to dismiss Margaret Thatcher as a woman devoid of a cultural hinterland. This point of view is as much (again) based upon classism, intellectual snobbery and political leanings as it is on supposition. Yes, MT liked musicals and yes, she also read Dick Francis, but wouldn't you, following an afternoon in the Commons or a meeting with Deng Xiaoping? Here was a woman who had sung in the Bach Choir at Oxford, proclaimed her favourite composer was Béla Bartók, and had consumed volume upon volume of political theory and philosophy including Hayek, Popper and Friedman. She also loved poetry, including that of T.S. Eliot, Larkin, Kipling, Whitman and Longfellow, some of which she could quote at length. She was famously passionate about opera (hardly a pedestrian pastime). The only holidays she would religiously pencil into her diary were those to visit friends in Salzburg whilst the opera season was in full swing. 'This was one of the few times we could be reasonably sure she would not return early, as she was wont to do,' says Charles Powell. 'She really did love her opera and not much got in the way of it.' She loved the paintings of Constable and Turner, but was notoriously distrustful of the contemporary 'School of London', describing Francis Bacon as 'the man who paints those awful pictures'. Her choices for her 1978 *Desert Island Discs* with the programme's creator Roy Plomley included Beethoven, Dvořák, Verdi, Mendelssohn, Mascagni – and 'Smoke Gets in Your Eyes' by Irene Dunne. Music, she told Plomley, is 'what I go to when

I want to take refuge... from a very logical life I've lived and I've always been trained to live'.

In 2016, Miriam Gross wrote a piece in *The Oldie* entitled 'Mrs Thatcher, Culture Vulture'. In it she referred to an investigation into MT's intellectual prowess, published in the *Telegraph* on 10 January 1988. The author of the original piece (entitled 'Why Britain's Eggheads Look Down on Mrs Thatcher'), Graham Turner, had talked to, amongst others, Anthony Burgess, who by then lived in Monaco and 'went so far as to claim that "she is never to be seen at concerts, plays or operas".' 'There is no doubt,' Turner writes, 'that Mrs Thatcher provokes feelings of almost pathological malevolence among the intelligentsia.' The author Robert McCrum, notes Gross, 'writing in *The Guardian* the day after she died, judged that "Margaret Thatcher was the most Philistine PM in decades".' Just two examples of the narrative bandwagon onto which most 'Thatcher haters' from the arts and popular culture would fling themselves, with little or no journalistic due diligence – as if being what they regarded as 'culturally backwards' (which in any case she most definitely was not) made you a lesser person and somehow unfit to lead. 'Government spending [on the arts] in total actually went up, not down, during her time in office. But some in the arts world did better than others,' writes Gross.

And yet the trope that MT ruined the arts in Britain prevails, with those who consider themselves artistically superior often making statements of unqualified, blinding stupidity. Gross notes that Peter Hall, director of the National Theatre under MT, records in his memoirs that: 'I saw the Thatcher government dismantle the performing arts, spoil our education system and partially destroy our great tradition of public service broadcasting.' Gross concludes, as those who had done any level of research into the progression of the arts during the Thatcher years might: 'What?? Mrs Thatcher's bourgeois gentility seems to have driven Left-leaning arts people completely over the top. But, for all their contempt, there is more than enough evidence to show that she was certainly no philistine.'

And yet, the pressure of conforming to the view that one cannot be an artist or creative of any kind and be seen to be sympathetic to or appreciative of MT – either as a PM or an individual – continues. Take the examples of Geri Halliwell and Madonna. In April 2013, just after the death of MT was announced, Halliwell, a member of the Spice Girls – the group who had declared MT to be 'the first Spice Girl, the pioneer of our ideology' – posted on Twitter (now X): 'Thinking of our 1st Lady of girl power, Margaret Thatcher, a greengrocer's daughter who taught me anything is possible… x.' Hours later, responding to the immediate and vituperative backlash, Halliwell deleted the tweet, apologising for any offence she had caused. 'I was weak under fire,' she later said. 'She (MT) had the courage to stand by her convictions. Not like me.'

In 2015, Madonna suffered a similar fate when she tweeted a picture of MT followed by one of her quotes: 'If you just set out to be liked, you will be prepared to compromise on anything at any time and would achieve nothing.' She added: 'Thank you Margaret Thatcher! #unapologetic #rebelheart'. Less than 24 hours later, this particular 'unapologetic rebel heart' had presumably responded to criticism from her fans and deleted her tweet.

And still it goes on. In 2023, Turner Prize winner Jesse Darling used his acceptance speech to complain about Margaret Thatcher, who, he claimed, had 'removed art from schools on the grounds that it was not "economically viable"'. Setting aside for a moment that fact that Darling had presumably not left junior school when MT was deposed, his erroneous claim underscores the problem with the 'nasty Mrs Thatcher' trope, which these days, via social media, spreads amongst the (presumably uninformed) with pandemic ease. The *Observer* critic Rachel Cooke was moved to report on Darling's speech: 'Such talk, received so rapturously (and so unquestionably) by the art world, seems very odd to me. There are plenty of people, elected and non-elected, who are far more deserving of our ire when it comes to the arts right now.' Acknowledging that Darling's pronouncement was inaccurate (in the 1980s art and design were compulsory for children up to fourteen) she reminds us that in the run-up to the imposition of the National Curriculum in 1988, MT's Education Secretary, Kenneth Baker, had argued for the subject to be studied up to the age of sixteen. 'Try to imagine anyone, whether Labour or Tory, so much as suggesting such a thing now.' At the time of writing, art and design is only compulsory for Key Stages 1 and 2 in the National Curriculum: that's those who are five to eleven years of age.

# 9
# Knights, Rotters, Bounders and Cads

On the shoulder of every Prime Minister sits a Brutus.

MT to Margaret King, 28 November 1990

'All of Margaret Thatcher's favourite men and those she promoted, sometimes way beyond their abilities, looked as though they'd walked out of a 1950s B-movie,' says Neil Kinnock. 'Put it this way, if Ronald Reagan had looked like Marlon Brando she would not have had much time for him.' Whilst Kinnock's reductionist explanation does neither him nor the former PM any favours (and he acknowledges this with a smile), it's easy to see where he is coming from. Margaret Thatcher liked good-looking men. But she also liked men who flattered, and those with brains, tenacity and, to put it bluntly, balls. Sometimes, all of the aforementioned qualities ended up in one package, but more often they did not. She was also a fan of men in uniform, men with military bearing or pasts (Fergus Greer, the photographer whose picture of her graces the front of this book, says he wore his regimental tie for the shoot and she commented on it immediately) and also men with titles. 'She was a great appreciator of the aristocracy – men with inherited titles fascinated her and the bigger, the better,' says a friend. 'She really thought these people were a link to Britain's historic past. I suppose she was right in a way.'

Contrary to popular theory, MT was not shoring up vestiges of her own past (i.e. a father figure) when she struck up alliances, political, strategic and otherwise, with powerful, useful or entertaining men. She was seeking advancement, and often not on her own behalf but on the part of the entity to which she was indentured: Great Britain. This is not to suggest that male politicians do not do exactly the same thing in forming power partnerships (see Blair and Brown, Starmer and Rayner). But the men who performed a substantive role in MT's life whilst she was in power – those who were in her thrall and others she gathered around her metaphoric and sometimes literal coffin-shaped cabinet table – had many things in common, the most significant of which was that they fervently believed in the new type of conservatism that 'the boss' stood for. Certainly, there were plenty who took risks and behaved offensively in other areas of their lives, mostly concerning women, money and power. (What else was there?) But almost all, including the statesmen amongst them, at one point or another summoned deep reserves of what could pass for old-fashioned gallantry and fealty, to keep her in post. Naturally, she took full advantage of the tendencies of this particular type of male to defend the female in their midst. And, when the luminosity of their star dimmed, as it almost inevitably did (with the exception of the statesmen), they, the party, the press, and more often than not the electorate, knew exactly what to expect.

## THE STATESMEN

'She was sexy – speaking woman to woman,' says Margaret King, 'and close up she really was very attractive – gorgeous skin and eyes.' Plenty will attest to MT's appeal. 'She had good breasts – I'll give her that,' says one politician and detractor. 'Nice legs and ankles,' says Aitken. But perhaps no one would or could have appreciated MT on the global stage more than Ronald Reagan, fortieth President of the United States, 1981–9. 'She adored him,' says Charles Powell. 'They agreed on pretty much everything. She hugely admired his communication skills and he in turn admired her decision-making and her ability to think through issues.' The two first bonded when Reagan, then governor of California, was passing through London on a brief tour of Europe to underline his knowledge of foreign affairs for his presidential bid. She was Leader of the Opposition. 'I liked her immediately. She was warm, feminine, gracious and intelligent and it was evident from our first words that we were soulmates when it came to reducing government and expanding economic freedom,' he said. 'I look forward to renewing our friendship when we meet in Washington next month,' she wrote effusively in her letter of congratulations on his landslide victory of 4 November 1980. When he granted her the highly contested and distinguished honour of being the first western leader to visit him on home soil, on 25 February 1981, he knew exactly what he was signing up for. At the end of their state dinner, held with great pomp in the White House, MT ended her speech invoking her all-time hero. 'You spoke of Winston Churchill,' she said, resplendent in high-necked black taffeta, pearls and white evening gloves as she turned to Reagan. 'We all do. Nearly fifty years ago, Winston told our two countries that together there is no problem we cannot solve. We are together tonight. Together let us prove him right.'

'She had a sort of, it sounds a bit explicit to say, a sexual attraction to Ronald Reagan,' said Charles Moore, in conversation with Peter Robinson on the Hoover Institution's current-affairs programme *Uncommon Knowledge* in 2021.

> I don't mean it was in any sort of naughty way. But she liked this tall, impressive-looking actor. She liked his charm and she thought he was the sort of classic American, and he liked what he saw as a classic English lady in Margaret Thatcher. And there was definitely a sort of elegant flirtation there and a sort of almost private communication which was beyond officialdom. I think that was important.

There's little doubt that the romantic, old-fashioned star power of the handsome, elegant ex-movie actor reminded MT of her happiest childhood days when, during her visits to the cinema, 'I roamed to the most fabulous realms of the imagination.'

'I sometimes thought I was directing *Gone with the Wind*,' reflected Bernard Ingham drily in his book *Kill the Messenger* (HarperCollins 1991). It helped that the two were always seated next to each other at international summits. 'The fact that the United Kingdom and the United States were seated side by side

## KNIGHTS, ROTTERS, BOUNDERS AND CADS

because of the alphabetical protocol for participating nations cannot be underestimated,' says Charles Powell. But the happy couple did not always see eye to eye – not over the Falklands, for which Reagan sat on the fence until the last moment (trying to keep President Galtieri onside as a buffer against Cuban and Russian intervention), nor on, amongst other things, the US invasion of Grenada, on 25 October 1983, which Reagan green-lit at 2am from the Eisenhower Cabin, Augusta National Golf Course, Georgia, wearing his pyjamas and slippers. In a frantic transatlantic phone call, an incandescent MT later reminded 'Ron' that Grenada remained a member of the British Commonwealth, with Queen Elizabeth as its titular monarch. 'She's upset,' wrote the President in his diary, 'and doesn't think we should do it. I couldn't tell her it had started.' Nicholas Wapshott (*Ronald Reagan and Margaret Thatcher: A Political Marriage*, Sentinel 2007) relates what happened next, after MT called the President in his study, quoting Robert McFarlane, national security advisor. Once she found out that the invasion had already gone ahead, 'it was not a happy conversation'. The conversation, which was all one way (hers), gained notoriety when an account leaked of the President covering the mouthpiece with MT's barking still audible: 'Isn't she marvellous?' he said, smiling, to members of his national security team.

Perhaps the couple's greatest achievement was their joint role in the collapse of the Soviet Union. Neither could have achieved it without the other, and it was Gorbachev's fascination with MT that facilitated his relationship with Reagan. The two first met, according to Jonathan Aitken, at the funeral of Yuri Andropov, who had succeeded Leonid Brezhnev as General Secretary. The young member of the Politburo, noticing that the PM was freezing after standing for over an hour in the VIP enclosure in Red Square, approached her and escorted her to a warm room. On their next meeting, she would recall Gorbachev's gallantry: 'I remember how you took care of me. It was frosty and I was wearing thin stockings and a light suit.' She realised after some research that he was earmarked as a potential future leader of the Soviet Union. She invited him to Britain – to Chequers no less, much to the alarm and bemusement of her Foreign Office advisors, who had little idea at that time who he was. As Aitken points out, the visit owed much to MT's intuition, as did her opening salvo over pre-luncheon drinks, when, as he recalled in his book, *Margaret Thatcher: Power and Personality* (Bloomsbury 2013), MT did not hold back:

> I want there to be no misunderstanding between us. So I must tell you that I hate Communism. I hate it because it brings neither freedom, nor justice, nor prosperity to the people. But if you Russians must have it, then you are entitled to it – secure within your own borders.

Gorbachev spoke to Aitken for the book and recalled how over lunch the argument between them became very hostile: 'She was accusing the Soviet Union of all sorts of unfair things… she became so heated that at one moment she turned away from me. So I turned away from her, too. We were almost back to back.' He confessed to Aitken that when he caught his wife Raisa's eye and she mouthed 'it's over', he considered leaving. But he told himself that, since they were guests, the conversation should continue.

# KNIGHTS, ROTTERS, BOUNDERS AND CADS

I said quite firmly to the Prime Minister: 'Mrs Thatcher, I know you are a person with an acute mind and high personal principles. Please bear in mind that I am the same kind of person.' She reacted with just a nod, so then I said, 'Let me assure you that I have not come here with instructions from the Politburo to persuade you to become a member of the Communist Party.'

With that, MT burst into laughter and the entire table followed suit. Tensions arose again over what MT described as 'your trade unions helping our miners with money' and later Gorbachev's suggestions for mutual nuclear disarmament. 'Do not waste my time,' warned MT, 'on trying to persuade me to say to Ron Reagan: "Do not go ahead with SDI." That will get nowhere.' (In fact it would be Ronald Reagan who would later come dangerously close to a deal with Gorbachev over nuclear disarmament at their second Reykjavik summit on 11–12 October 1986 – much to the horror of MT, who was not consulted and believed fervently in the notion of nuclear deterrents to maintain global stability.)

It was Bernard Ingham who fed MT the line 'a man we can do business with'. She uttered it the next day in a post-Chequers BBC interview: 'I like Mr Gorbachev. We can do business together.' And so they would. 'It was an appreciative relationship,' says Powell, 'and long after they both left office Mr Gorbachev would visit her every time he came to London. He was very kind to her, kinder than most other leaders after she stepped down.' As General Secretary of the Communist Party from March 1985 to August 1991, Gorbachev would be the only person ever to hold the additional title of President of the Soviet Union (1990–1).

# THE INCIDENTAL FEMINIST

If Ronnie and Margaret were flirtatiously close, there was also a frisson of sexual energy between MT and Gorby. 'Thatcher had a definite womanish feeling towards Gorbachev,' recalled Ambassador Leonid Zamyatin diplomatically. Her triumphant visit to Moscow for talks with Gorbachev (coupled with plenty of historic photo opportunities and a TV debate in which she calmly pasted three Moscow journalists), with more than 100 million viewing her visit on state TV, probably quickened Reagan's pulse, too. She was embraced by the Russian people as a modern-day Catherine the Great. By the time he arrived in Berlin in 1987 to utter his 'Mr Gorbachev, tear down this wall' speech – the same city where, in 1963, his predecessor, President John F. Kennedy, had historically proclaimed '*Ich bin ein Berliner*' – the drawing back of Churchill's 'iron curtain' was already in play. As Wapshott points out, Hungary's boundaries with Austria were no longer being enforced and Eastern European citizens were already crossing the Austrian border illegally into the west. In 1990 Reagan paid a post-presidential visit to Russia to see for himself the results of 'glasnost' ('opening'), the accolades for which belonged to Gorbachev, but bathed both himself and MT in its reflected glory. 'Seventy-seven per cent of Russians say they want to live in a free and democratic country,' Gorbachev told *Time* magazine. 'That is the legacy of perestroika [the restructuring of Russia's political and economic system].'

'I don't think Margaret Thatcher can ever have been more surprised than in 1982 when the first leader to call, endorse and support her actions in the Falklands was François Mitterrand,' says Gillian Shephard. 'We never really like to admit it, but Mrs Thatcher was very influenced by the French and French ideas.' The notoriously 'Latin' relationship which existed between France's first socialist President of the Fifth Republic and MT (yes, it seems he really did say she had the mouth of Marilyn Monroe but the eyes of Caligula) tends to cloud our comprehension of the power of their partnership, which achieved much, as Mitterrand's biographer Denis MacShane reminds us. It included the building of the Channel Tunnel, the passing of the Single European Act and the enlargement of the European Community to take in the then poorer nations of Spain, Portugal and Greece. Working with Helmut Kohl, whom MT never really warmed to – 'too pudgy and… well, German', says a source – the three (together with perhaps MT's most despised combatant, Jacques 'No, No, No!' Delors) created the Europe which remains – notably, without the UK – to this day. 'He likes women, you know,' MT is said to have commented to her then Cabinet Secretary, Robert Armstrong, after her first meeting at Chequers with Mitterrand in May 1981. 'There was always a little bit of a flush to her cheek and a sense of heightened emotion after a Mitterrand visit,' remembers Charles Powell.

## THE STRATEGISTS

'Margaret particularly liked clever strategists,' says Norman Tebbit,

> and she used them to their best advantage. Take Airey Neave – he was exactly the kind of man she liked – military, brave, clever and revered – he'd escaped from Colditz, been awarded the

Military Cross. He saw the potential in her that not many, including she herself perhaps, saw. Airey saw that she could become leader.

Indeed, without the influential, risk-taking Neave (Eton and Merton, Oxford), MC, DSO and holder of the Croix de Guerre (who escaped Colditz, wearing a fake uniform and sporting the fabled 'arse creeper', a cigar case containing maps and money stowed inside his, ahem, rectum), who had already served in Ted Heath's government and was MT's Shadow Secretary of State for Northern Ireland, as her campaign manager, it was unlikely that she would have had the proverbial cat in Hades' chance of becoming PM.

For all of his military bravado, Neave was not a typical MT 'man'. 'He was a curious fellow,' says Jonathan Aitken. 'There was something almost crablike about him: he did not walk, he scuttled – one never felt one could pin him down. His secretive dealings were conducted in the smoking rooms and the dark corridors of Westminster.' When Neave died on 30 March 1979 after a bomb, placed by the Irish National Liberation Army (INLA) under his car, exploded on the ramp of the House of Commons car park, MT was bereft. She and Neave were more than political partners, they were friends who had known each other since MT began her pupillage in Fred Lawton's Chambers in 1953, where Neave was already practising. She swiftly cancelled her plans for a party political broadcast that evening and grieved in solitude. A month later, she would fulfil Neave's wish and plan to become PM. 'I don't think she was ever able to replace Airey,' says Tebbit, 'but throughout her career she would form liaisons or partnerships with the sort of men, whom, like Airey, she could lean on or who could help her in some way – Ian Gow was another.'

It was the assassinations of Neave and Gow, who both died tragically in car bombings at the hands of Irish republican paramilitaries, which effectively bookended MT's prime ministership. In Gow, the perennially witty, nattily attired, Winchester-educated son of a Harley Street doctor, who served in the 15th/19th Hussars, MT had found another clever, charming man she could lean on, and who would become part of the PM's trusted inner circle. From 1979 to 1983 he was her PPS. 'He served her not just with loyalty but with love... Gow fought the prime minister's corner with the fervour of a romantic crusader,' read his *Guardian* obituary. 'The Platonic ideal of a PPS,' said the *Telegraph*. When he resigned from his post as Minister of State for the Treasury, in protest over the Anglo-Irish Agreement of 1985 (in which the Republic of Ireland was given a consultative role in Northern Ireland for the first time), Gow, MP for Eastbourne, recognised that as an outspoken critic of the IRA he was a marked man. His continued refusal to yield to the strictures of security reflected his desire to not be cowed by terrorists: he maintained his listing in the telephone directory, published his address in *Who's Who*, would not countenance the idea of a bodyguard, ignored the standard protocol of checking under his car for explosive devices before setting off and often left the keys in his car overnight. He died on the morning of 30 July 1990 outside his home in East Sussex, when 2kg of Semtex placed by the IRA under the driver's seat of his Austin Montego detonated. His wife Jane Gow (now Dame Jane Whiteley) witnessed the aftermath. On 1 August 1990, the IRA released a statement claiming that Gow had been targeted both for his unionist views and because he was a 'close confidant' of MT. 'You will never win,' said his widow in a statement read out by a police officer. 'We have lost the dearest person in the world, but it will not diminish our resolve to be as strong as he was in fighting this terrible wickedness.' Gow was the last MP to be murdered until the death of Jo Cox in 2016.

## THE KNIGHT OF THE SHIRES

Bluff and avuncular, the Rt Hon. the Viscount Whitelaw KT CH MC (Winchester and Trinity, Cambridge), known as Willie Whitelaw, deputy party leader and effectively MT's deputy PM, was, in the words of one fellow Tory, 'properly posh'. A man who grew up in a grand home, Monklands, in Nairn, Scotland, a Cambridge golfing blue who described himself as a 'farmer', Whitelaw is often rightly credited as the man who held the Tories together under MT's divisive rule. Known in the 'Dear Bill' letters in *Private Eye* as 'old oyster eyes' or 'Lord Lake District', his hale and hearty, tweedy appearance, coupled with his marbled vowel sounds, family connections and military service (he commanded Churchill tanks in Normandy), qualified him perfectly to be the unofficial 'deputy PM' as well as the Home Secretary from 1979 to 1983. When MT decided that his time in cabinet was up, she made Whitelaw a viscount to maintain his allegiance, and ruthlessly 'kicked him upstairs', as Charles Moore puts it, into the House of Lords. She couldn't bring herself to tell him about his demotion so she asked the then Chief Whip, Michael Jopling, to break the news. She had good reason to keep him onside: he was able to smooth the waters between the 'Old School' Tories of the shires – particularly those dissenters with titles and a tendency to complain about MT, loudly and in public – and the 'new' Tories favoured by MT, like Norman Tebbit, Cecil Parkinson and David Young. 'Willie occupied a unique role,' says David Howell. 'He was the bridge between the sneering aristos and those who were sneering about the aristos. He was the pacifier of the zealots and the confronter of the super-Conservatives.' When Whitelaw stood down for medical reasons in 1988, MT threw him a drinks party and uttered the much-repeated phrase 'every Prime Minister needs a Willie'. Sceptics suggested that this throwaway quote was the perfect example of the PM's inability to comprehend a joke, while others who were present suggest that she knew exactly what she was saying. Either way, she was proved correct. Once she lost the services of Whitelaw, the peacemaker, her power base began to crumble.

## THE PRODIGAL SON (NOT MARK)

Charles Powell was perhaps her ideal man. 'He was the son she always wished she had,' says one politician, pointedly referring to the fact that her own son Mark's questionable endeavours had caused the PM endless anxiety. Not so the Oxford-educated Powell, who was at her side (and some said in her ear) almost daily for seven years. The patrician son of an air vice-marshal, and a descendant, so it is alleged, of Sir Hugh de Morville, one of the assassins of Thomas Becket, Powell forms one of half of the political Powell power duo. His brother Jonathan, previously Tony

Blair's Chief of Staff from 1997 to 2007, is at the time of writing Sir Keir Starmer's UK National Security Adviser. 'Charles and Jonathan are rather similar,' their mother Ysolda told the *Telegraph* in 2001. 'They all [sic] have the same push to get to the top, they all want to be the boss. I don't know why. We didn't say, go out and rule.'

For some, Powell was the meddling bureaucrat who went native. The civil servant who, in accordance with normal diplomatic strictures, should have moved to another post after a few years, but at MT's insistence, and his own desire, stayed put. Her refusal to countenance the loss of Powell was regarded by many as one of the early signals that she was losing touch with her power base and the outside world. 'He interfered in almost every aspect of policy-making (domestic as well as foreign),' wrote Richard Vinen in *The Literary Review*, reflecting on Powell's leading role in the third volume of Charles Moore's biography of MT, *Herself Alone*. As Vinen points out, Powell once suggested 'breezily... that the prime minister might care to sack both her foreign and home secretaries'. 'It was sometimes difficult to establish where Mrs Thatcher ended and Charles Powell began,' wrote Sir Percy Cradock (*In Pursuit of British Interests: Reflections on Foreign Policy under Margaret Thatcher and John Major*, John Murray 1997). Powell's role in the 1985 Al-Yamamah arms-for-oil trade deal with Saudi Arabia (one of the biggest arms contracts ever landed by the UK) for BAE Systems was also the focus of an investigation conducted by the *Guardian* newspaper. He later became a paid advisor to BAE Systems.

Powell was one of the very few men (perhaps the only other was her press secretary Bernard Ingham) in whom MT placed absolute trust. He described working for her as turbulent, and described her as a 'radical'. But when it came to taking his advice about her own position, she ignored him completely. 'After the 1987 election I did write to her, saying that that experience had been so rough on her and her health that she should not stand again,' says Powell. And MT's response? He laughs. 'She said, "Thank you for your note." It was never mentioned again.'

'Ultimately I think that both Powell and Ingham were part of the problem,' says Stephen Sherbourne. 'As excellent as they both were, they were also shielding her from what was really going on. They forgot she couldn't walk on water and allowed her to lose touch with her backbenchers and with the country as a whole. Everything was filtered through them.'

'I remember as a junior diplomat going through a big demonstration in a motorcade with Mrs Thatcher,' Charles's younger brother Jonathan told the *Telegraph*. 'As she got out of her Rolls-Royce I heard her say, "Wasn't it nice to see all those people waving at us?" I suddenly realised how cut off you can get in politics.'

It was Charles Powell who once stated that MT did not have a happy day once she left office: 'There was a distinct touch of *Sunset Boulevard* to her later years.' Whether this was true or not, Powell's loyalty was absolute. He visited her regularly at the Ritz, timing his visits for 'teatime'. 'We used to argue over who had eaten more chocolate biscuits,' he said. She appointed him Knight Commander of the Order of St Michael and St George (KCMG) in her retirement honours list of December 1990.

# THE INCIDENTAL FEMINIST

## CRIMINALS, FAWNERS AND FORNICATORS

For a woman who regarded the majority of men with a jaded, wary eye, MT was surprisingly vulnerable to male sycophancy – even if the sycophants were simpering and spineless. The relationships were of necessity (on her part at least) mutually beneficial – that said, there was a certain commonality: 'They were either good-looking, erudite, wealthy, titled or charming – it always worked best if they possessed a combination of some or all of the aforementioned. Oh yes and tall; they had to be tall,' says a former advisor. Of these men there was seemingly no shortage and, despite their (frequently) appalling behaviour (which ran the gamut from indiscretion to desertion and criminal behaviour), MT was remarkably willing to entertain them. That she was lonely, there was little doubt. By their own admission, away from the rigours of politics, she and Denis pursued different social lives. When his services as PM's husband were not required, he went out for dinner and drinks, either with work associates or golfing and rugby chums, whilst MT worked long into the night alone in her office. At this point, she would welcome courtiers, often with a large glass of whisky. And the courtiers were always of the opposite sex. 'She liked men, and she preferred our company to that of women, but there's little doubt that she thought us the weaker sex,' says Matthew Parris.

Prime examples of an MT 'weaker sex type' included Cecil Parkinson, Alan Clark, Jeffrey Archer, Woodrow Wyatt and advisor Tim Bell. There is no point in pretending that Thatcher was not acutely aware of the shortcomings of all of these men, and they stand as glaring examples of her inability to resist the fawning flattery of ambitious and sometimes immoral individuals, who preyed on her narcissistic need for approval. That MT pursued friendships or associations with wholly unsuitable men is not in doubt. That she failed to see through their smokescreens of venal charm is mystifying.

Tim Bell merits another mention (although he has been previously discussed) because several interviewees were clear that he and MT had a fairly unusual extracurricular 'friendship', which involved Bell placing his hand on her knee under dinner tables across the capital and more. My Journalism 101 interrogative of 'How do you know this?' was always met with the same response: 'Because he told me.' Bell adored MT and made no bones about it, once telling Denis: 'I love her.' Part of the adoration was, by his own admission, the thrill of proximity to power, which accompanied their friendship. His association with and work for MT also made him very rich. In addition, she had the distinction of standing ready to overlook his shortcomings, when many others did not. These involved variously, but not exclusively, his criminal conviction for exposure, his behaviour with women, his abuse of drink and recreational drugs, and his creativity (by his own admission) with the truth. But a lover to MT? He was unlikely to have got to what the Americans delicately term 'third base' (or even first or second). And that's presupposing that he didn't make the whole thing up. 'It would have been just like him to do that,' says a former close colleague from the advertising world. 'He was good at "big fish" stories.'

It is easy to see why Cecil Parkinson (or 'Smarmy C' as he was known in *Private Eye*) was one of her favourites. The son of a railway worker, educated at Lancaster Royal Grammar School, and then Emmanuel College, Cambridge, he was an athlete during his university days, awarded a blue for athletics (220 and 440 yards). With the permanent appearance of a man who had just left the gym, his glowing cheeks, slicked-back hair, strong jaw and Savile Row suits assured him of female attention. But it was also his abilities and confidence which endeared him to MT. A self-made man without any of the hard edges of a Norman Tebbit or the insecurities of a Jeffrey Archer, he was an efficient, effective and intelligent politician. Above all, he was loyal. She included him in her Falklands War cabinet, not because he had any experience of war (he didn't) but because she knew she could count on his backing. 'There were moments,' reports Hugo Young of that time, 'when Parkinson, seeing the fraughtness in her face, felt that what he really ought to do was put a manly arm around her.' As a slick party PR operator, Parkinson proved his worth and, as Party Chairman, was given much of the credit for masterminding MT's 1983 election victory. It was rumoured that as a result she intended to reward him by making him Foreign Secretary, thereby anointing him as her distant successor.

But Parkinson's weakness (and she should have known – perhaps upon reflection she would allow that she did) was women. During the party conference in October 1983, his long-term mistress and one-time parliamentary secretary, Sara Keays, went public with their twelve-year affair, giving an interview to *The Times* claiming that Parkinson had promised to leave his wife for her and then reneged on the deal. When, according to Charles Moore, Parkinson told MT of his 'very big personal problem', she was bemused. 'What's that got to do with anything?' she asked. 'They tell me Anthony Eden leapt into bed with any good-looking woman. You can sort this out.' So much for female solidarity.

Colonel Hastings Keays, Sara's father, put paid to Parkinson's career by sending MT a letter, revealing that his daughter was pregnant with Parkinson's child. As a result, Parkinson was 'de-shuffled' and given the lesser department of Trade and Industry. Within months he would resign. Sara Keays' fight for maintenance for their daughter Flora, who had both mental and physical challenges, was protracted and painful, with a judge finally awarding her £20,000 per annum in 1993. At that point, Keays also agreed to Parkinson's stipulation, backed by an injunction, that no further information about Flora or her schooling could be published until she turned eighteen. She initially approved of this in her desire to protect Flora, but soon came to see that it in fact protected the wily Parkinson.

When Parkinson died in 2013, Flora's support payments ceased and Keays was forced back into the courtroom. Her own political ambitions had also been thwarted by Parkinson and the party; it was later revealed that he had also intervened to have her name removed from a shortlist of parliamentary candidates in Bermondsey. 'The events of 1983 ended my career,' she told Beatrix Campbell. 'The party refused to have anything to do with me and never gave me any reason for taking me off the candidates list.' Whilst Parkinson's career never entirely recovered, he was embraced back into the fold of Tory politics and ennobled in 1992 as Baron Parkinson of Carnforth. In 1997 he was made Conservative Party Chairman once again by William Hague.

Jeffrey Archer and Alan Clark were, in a way, two sides of the same coin (though it's doubtful either would have appreciated being written about in the same sentence).

More than any others, these two stand as glaring examples of MT's serial inability to resist the fawning flattery of ambitious and sometimes immoral men. Whether their access to her resulted in anything measurable politically is questionable, although as Deputy Chairman of the party in 1985–6 Archer at least proved an effective fundraiser. As for Clark… well, there's no telling quite why MT favoured Clark other than his aristocratic background (he was the son of Lord Kenneth Clark, the art historian made famous by his *Civilisation* TV series), his quick wit and his savage charm. He *was* fiercely loyal – the quality which counted most to MT – 'a gallant friend' is how she referred to him at one point in her diaries. She rewarded that loyalty with a junior cabinet post, making him Minister of State for Trade. In return he flattered her relentlessly, publicly admitting that he found her 'attractive' but that he didn't want to 'jump on her'. She never thought him to be a particularly effective politician and was studiously deaf to his impassioned pleas that she make him Foreign Secretary. Is it possible that she was unaware of Clark's position as a Nazi sympathiser? Unlikely. In which case, it renders their 'friendship' even more confounding.

In 1996, the publication of the Scott Report revealed that, whilst in post under Thatcher, Clark had permitted the export of machine tools manufactured by a British company, Matrix Churchill, to the pariah state of Iraq, which, writes Ken Clarke in his memoirs, 'were fairly obviously for the manufacture of weaponry'. At the 1992 trial, the government's defence collapsed when

Clark admitted to having been 'economical with the actualité' in response to parliamentary questions about the export licences to Iraq.

Clark's astronomical self-importance and his vicious snobbery shine through in his notoriously indiscreet diaries, in which he reveals himself to be not only a serial adulterer (once having sex with the wife of a judge, socialite Valerie Harkess, and her two daughters, in what was later known as the Harkess Affair after the *Sun* newspaper claimed that the three women attempted to blackmail Clark) but also a depraved man with a predilection for extremely young women. 'Girls have to be succulent – and that means under 25,' he writes. He was 65 when the diaries were first published in 1993. Clark's biographer Ion Trewin includes a diary entry written about his wife-to be, Jane Beuttler, then aged fourteen, in 1956 (Clark was 28). 'This is very exciting. She [Jane] is a perfect victim, but whether or not it will be possible to succeed I can't tell at present.' Clark married Jane in 1960 when she was just sixteen years of age and he just less than twice her age. It's hard to imagine that after their marriage Jane had anything approaching a happy life, but she appeared to have made peace with her lot. When Valerie Harkess sold her story and called Clark 'a pathetic, lecherous, dirty old man', Jane responded: 'Quite frankly, if you bed people that I call "below-stairs class", they go to the papers, don't they?' Perhaps then, the Clarks deserved each other?

Was it the wit that made Alan Clark's *Diaries* a bestseller? 'Had Alan Clark not been a bounder, his diaries would not have been the great entertainments they are,' wrote Andrew Marr in all of his white male resplendence in *The Guardian* in 1999. Back then, most men and presumably a significant number of women would have found them amusing. Today, they read as an indictment of the times and the confessions of a rightly condemned man.

Whilst plenty have testified (some on the witness stand) to Jeffrey Archer's legendary economy with the truth, he was (and at the time of writing remains) another gold-standard MT charmer. A successful, self-made man more than once over, he penned his first novel, *Not a Penny More, Not a Penny Less*, to ward off the bankruptcy which forced him to resign from Parliament in 1974. He returned to politics in 1985, when MT, who valued his energy and commitment, made him Deputy Chairman of the Conservative Party. He resigned his position in 1986 when the *News of the World* published a front-page story about an Archer intermediary handing an envelope of cash to a prostitute on Victoria Station in order that she leave the country. They had the pictures and the tapes to prove it: 'Tory Boss Archer Pays Off Vice Girl' was the headline.

When the *Daily Star* went further, and directly accused him of paying for sex with the 'vice girl', whose name was Monica Coghlan, Archer sued. He won the 1987 court case, positioning himself as a philanthropist who wanted to 'help', rather than a client of Coghlan's. In his summing-up the judge, Mr Justice Caulfield, clearly smitten with Archer's 'fragrant' wife Mary, who had given evidence, asked the jury to consider whether, in view of Mary's attributes, Archer seemed to be the type of man 'in need of cold, unloving, rubber-insulated sex in a seedy hotel round about quarter to one on a Tuesday morning after an evening at the Caprice?' The jury were perhaps the only group of people in Britain who failed to reach the correct conclusion.

## KNIGHTS, ROTTERS, BOUNDERS AND CADS

Archer won damages of £500,000. His further trial in 2001, initiated by the fact that two defence witnesses changed their statements and admitted to lying on his behalf, found him guilty of perjury and perverting the course of justice, for which he served two years of a four-year sentence. Far worse than that, he was suspended from the Marylebone Cricket Club for seven years. He retained his title: Baron Archer of Weston-Super-Mare (John Major had ennobled him in 1992) and his membership of the House of Lords. Later the journalist Greg Lowe described the experience of interviewing him thus: 'He disarmed me with the skill of a fast-talking dodgy geezer who talks you out of your hard-earned cash, whilst trying to fondle your wife.' Monica Coghlan, the prostitute who worked the streets by her own account to raise her son, did not live to experience her exoneration. She was killed in a car accident weeks before the 2001 trial began.

'I was in love with her, yes, but I suppose in the best platonic manner because – well, she was a marvellous girl… her skin was glowing and she had very fine legs,' Woodrow Wyatt said of his relationship with Margaret Thatcher in 1996. A former socialist, who never actually joined the Conservative Party but became one of MT's closest confidants, Wyatt was a scurrilous gossip, with a fascination for women, champagne and cigars, and friends in (very) high places. Despite his pretensions – of which it seems there were many – he was, like almost all of MT's courtiers, far from aristocratic. Named after the American President Woodrow Wilson, and the son of a prep-school headmaster, Wyatt was a self-confessed snob, defending his stance to *Independent* newspaper journalist Geraldine Bedell: 'Being a snob is about liking the best.' Unlike MT's other courtiers he was, to borrow the phrase that she once used about Denis, 'not a very attractive creature'. The perennially bow-tie-sporting Wyatt often sent her notes for her speeches and the two were said to have spoken at least twice a week for the entirety of her time in No. 10.

Other than flattery, there is no obvious reason for her to have taken him into her confidence, although he certainly mingled with the so-called top drawer and, as a newspaper columnist, he wielded power. A favourite of the Queen Mother and a sometime 'fixer' for Rupert Murdoch ('Rupert rang… He asked me whether I thought Arnold would get his way about the Plessey bid [an electronics company manufacturing computer systems, amongst other things])… [and] whether he should go and see or tell Mrs T about it'), Wyatt used his position as chairman of the Horserace Totalisator Board (aka the Tote) as an entrée into the society to which he aspired to be accepted. 'Kingsley Amis to lunch. Arrives on the dot. Refuses champagne unless it is old,' he writes on Thursday, 18 September 1986. On Thursday, 18 June 1987, he writes of Princess Diana: 'I'm not surprised that Prince Charles is bored with this backward girl who couldn't even pass any O levels… Queen Elizabeth [the Queen Mother] spoke mostly to me. I told her about the Archbishop of Canterbury coming to the Jockey Club… she didn't really like the idea.' In April 1990: 'Spoke to Margaret at about half past eight in the morning and asked her how the meeting with Bush had gone. She said it had gone very well and they are beginning to realize we are their staunchest ally.'

Wyatt once said of MT, 'Margaret is what Napoleon said about Josephine. She is all woman.' According to his daughter Petronella, writing in the *Evening Standard* on the death of MT in 2013, her mother was less keen. Having once suspected MT and her husband of having an affair, Verushka Wyatt had the temerity to voice an opinion at her own dinner table, with Thatcher present, only to receive the following forceful riposte from the PM: 'Be quiet, dear. Your turn will come.' In 1987 MT ennobled Wyatt as Baron Wyatt of Weeford.

## THE TRAITOR?

If it was the resignations over the matter of Europe by both her Chancellor Nigel Lawson in October 1989 (which weakened her) and her Deputy PM Geoffrey Howe in November 1990 (which undid her), they were not the first snipers to inflict damage. That particular distinction belonged to another would-be assassin, who first winged her in 1986 and then returned a few years later to finish the job. The press had already nicknamed Michael Heseltine 'Tarzan', not so much because of his good looks, flowing blond hair, piercing blue eyes and loping, snake-hipped stride but because, during a parliamentary debate in 1976, when the opposition were on the losing side of the vote, he had seized the ceremonial mace and shaken it menacingly at the government Chief Whip. 'Heseltine made himself look like a fanatic from *The Planet of the Apes*,' writes Jonathan Aitken of that moment. 'Among MPs there were more frowns than laughs… Tarzan's excesses seemed a contempt of the House, because the mace is the symbol of the Crown in Parliament.'

Michael Ray Dibdin Heseltine, the son of a factory owner and Territorial Army colonel, and whose great-grandfather worked his way up from a clerk to become a manager at Tetley's and on to owning a grocery chain, was and remains a very successful businessman. But his status as a rising star and an emerging captain of industry failed to impress many Tory Knights of the Shires, who regarded him as 'nouveau'. Alan Clark memorably described him as 'an arriviste, certainly, who can't shoot straight and in Jopling's damning phrase "bought all his own furniture"'. In the face of such significant handicaps, Heseltine muddled through, managing to serve successfully as MP for the safe Tory seat of Henley for nearly 30 years (1974–2001), until he retired from the Commons.

Despite this impressive record, it was his controversial resignation from his cabinet post as Secretary of State for Defence in MT's second cabinet in January 1986 which made him a household name. The fate of the failing Westland Helicopters (worth a paltry £30 million or so) was, for want of a better metaphor, a strange hill upon which Heseltine would choose to die. As head of Defence, he firmly believed that Britain's only helicopter manufacturer should be sold to a European conglomerate and he duly put together a deal between British Aerospace and GEC. This was in the full knowledge that MT favoured a merger with the American-owned Sikorsky, whilst, outwardly at least, she insisted that the decision should be Westland's. When she refused to allow Heseltine to put his case for Westland to the Cabinet, he resigned in what can only be described as a fit of pique. The subsequent inquiry into the strategic leaking of related documents on both sides became known as the Westland Affair and implicated the two of them. Heseltine says he did not intend to resign over Westland.

# KNIGHTS, ROTTERS, BOUNDERS AND CADS

It just mushroomed. Resigning certainly wasn't what I planned, but I did think I should be able to put my case for Westland to the cabinet, which Margaret refused to allow me to do. I remember thinking to myself, 'If you think this matters you can't allow yourself to be humiliated in this way.' It was a matter of honour. And so I left.

As he strode up Downing Street, scattering journalists and cameras in his wake, MT must have experienced conflicting emotions. Although she claims in her memoirs that she expected Heseltine's resignation, she also confesses that she had thought him too big a beast to sack herself: 'Michael was at that time a popular and powerful figure in the party.' As the public fallout from his 22-minute resignation speech outside the Ministry of Defence continued (and Trade and Industry secretary Leon Brittan's head rolled) she must have known that she was dealing with her own version of the Terminator. And that, just like Arnie, Heseltine would be back. From then on, she would constantly be looking over her shoulder.

Ironically, there was much more that united Heseltine and Thatcher than divided them. Both were effective politicians, unwavering in their views. Both had the capacity to inspire loyalty and admiration in their colleagues. They were, much as he would have hated to admit it, from similar backgrounds (although the Heseltine family's social and economic advancement had begun two generations earlier than MT's). Both would go on to make a great deal of money – he from his businesses and she from her post-PM books and lecture tours. Publicly, each condemned the other. 'Michael's sense of priorities was gravely distorted by his personal ambitions and political obsessions,' MT writes in her autobiography. He, meanwhile is blatant. 'I never liked her,' he says, 'but then you don't need to like the person you are in politics with. You are colleagues, not friends.'

And yet, did they protest too much? There was something all too strident and palpable about their bristling public disregard for each other. Indeed, some conjecture that there was actually a sexual chemistry between them, which they strove to conceal with a mutual disdain. It makes sense. Today, 'Hezza', as the press came to know him, is by turns both negative and positive about her. 'I think my relationship with her was extremely good,' he says of their early days in government together, 'she told the Chief Whip I was her natural successor'. But later, he says the relationship soured. 'She wasn't what she seemed and her decisions and views were much more complicated than people thought. The poll tax, which was an absolute disaster, is the perfect case in point. Her style was lecturing and hectoring. Mine was not.' On paper, he was perhaps her ideal man. 'They certainly put on a good act when they were together – they seemed to like each other – they were coquettish even,' says Margaret King. 'That chemistry was real,' says another observer. Heseltine denies this: 'There was never any element of her feminine wiles with me,' he says flatly.

Theirs was a tempestuous relationship right from the get-go, when, much to her chagrin in 1979, he bluntly refused her offer of a cabinet post as Secretary of State for Energy, arguing that he wanted to remain as head of the department he had shadowed: the Environment. She capitulated – a rarity – telling her Private Secretary: 'I don't like one-to-one confrontations with Michael.' Heseltine went on to play key roles in the government's Right to Buy scheme, the regeneration of Liverpool in the early 1980s and the government's battle against the Campaign for Nuclear Disarmament (CND). 'I think I was the most interventionist minister the country ever had – and this was all with Margaret's approval.'

He was never destined for the top job, though. And perhaps, even after Westland four years earlier, he knew this. 'I thought it was Shakespeare who said, "He who wields the knife will never wear the crown," but apparently it was me… heh, heh, heh.' He is laughing his pantomime-baddie laugh, but somehow it doesn't seem that convincing. 'Absolutely, I would very much like to have been Prime Minister,' he says, unable to keep the regret from his voice. He probably should have been. His bid for the leadership was thwarted though, when, having won enough votes in the first round of the contest on Tuesday, 20 November 1990, to force MT's resignation two days later, he lost out in the second round to John Major, who became PM on Wednesday 28th. Was Heseltine's failure to win over the party due to his actions over Westland in 1986 or his direct challenge to MT in 1990? Probably a combination of both. 'I divided the party,' he admits ruefully. 'I could not unite it. John Major had a lot of friends – he was the insider and I was the outsider.'

But perhaps he was always destined, like MT, to be outside the fold. It was what made them both, in their own ways, revolutionaries. But it was also, as it turned out, their fatal flaw.

# 10

# All the Prime Minister's Men

We would have what I would describe as a modest amount of amorosity, for lack of a better word.

Tony Bray, one of MT's early Oxford boyfriends, describing their physical relationship

Let's give it a go. That's the girl.

Denis Thatcher to himself on deciding to propose to MT

Was Margaret Thatcher a virgin when she married? Does it matter? Yes and no. And not necessarily in that order. Up until the publication of the first volume of MT's authorised biography in 2013, it had been assumed that Denis Thatcher was her first and only real love. This is because the story of MT's love life was in her gift to tell. And for as long as she was alive, she remained famously tight-lipped about her romantic past. In her autobiography she skims over the personal side of her time at Oxford and by page 48 of the hardback she has met Denis: 'It was clear to me at once that Denis was an exceptional man,' she writes firmly, as if that is the end of the discussion. Perhaps it should be; but the real story of MT's early dating history reveals a great deal about the ambitions, pragmatism and unusual thought process (some might say emotional detachment) of Britain's future first female PM. More importantly, it sheds light on the foundations of her overall attitude to men. For, whilst she surrounded herself with them, relied upon them and was famously both flirtatious and combative with them, Margaret Thatcher never entirely trusted any member of the male sex, with the sole exception (perhaps) of her husband.

The 'there was only ever Denis' narrative served MT extremely well and she was at pains to perpetuate it. The couple had even tried to keep their engagement a secret during Margaret's bid for a Dartford seat in the 1951 general election, but local agent Beryl Cook leaked the news just before election day, thinking it would give MT a boost. Unsurprisingly, it did not do the trick. During her eleven-year search for a seat, MT would continually be dogged by questions about her suitability for office as a woman, so it's not really surprising that she wanted to draw a veil over her private life. The last thing she needed was any damaging speculation. This was, after all, the 1950s, when a woman getting married was tantamount to her putting on an apron and becoming a baby-making machine. It was exactly the kind of thing that Tory grandees and MT's detractors could and would use against her during her early political years, as proof of her unsuitability to be an MP, let alone hold the highest office in the land.

In 1985, whilst she was in office, questions about MT's early love life surfaced in a book called *Five at 10*, by Diana Farr (André

Deutsch), which discussed the relationships of five No. 10 spouses. They were swiftly quashed and later denied altogether. The one man who clearly was the love of her life, Dr Robert Henderson, the superintendent of Dartford Southern Hospital, was quoted in the book. 'Margaret and I were very close,' he told the author. He later revised his story when approached by the *Daily Express*, telling them: 'We were never romantically involved.' Whatever his reasons (and we might guess that *someone* had had a word with him), Henderson was simply not telling the truth.

Charles Moore sniffed this out and more besides when, during the writing of *Not for Turning*, Volume 1 of his biography of her, he was granted access to a stash of letters written between MT and her sister Muriel during the years 1944–8, which shone an entirely new light on 'the virgin Tory candidate' and the resolute emphasis on her innocence, during her Oxford years and beyond. Looking at those same letters today it becomes patently obvious that MT fell deeply in love once, if not twice, before meeting Denis. What is less clear is whether she was actually in love with Denis when they married, or whether, with her typically pragmatic or neurodivergent attitude, she simply judged him to be her best bet. Much of this uncertainty is down to the fact that the letters between the sisters have a large gap in their continuum, which, given the frequency of their previous correspondence, points to a number having been removed – perhaps to preserve MT's modesty – before they were made available.

Her hunch (if that was what it was) that Denis would serve her well turned out to be possibly the best decision she ever made. Without exception, everyone interviewed for this book was united in the singular belief that without the love, support and (to put it brutally) money of Denis Thatcher, MT could never have become Prime Minister. 'I think she wanted to marry an older, socially grander man and she admired certain qualities – upright, good bearing, someone who had had a good war. She knew Denis could stand on his own two feet – he had the money and she wanted a secure base for her life,' says Moore.

That is not to say, though, that the young MT did not harbour doubts about the divorcee, ten years older than her, when they met at a dinner in Dartford thrown in March 1949 in her honour by a director of Denis's family paint company, Atlas Preservatives, where Denis was MD. Denis was also present at the dinner and she writes to Muriel about 'a Major Thatcher, who has a flat in London (age about 36, plenty of money)'. After dinner, Denis took her to catch her train. 'He drove me back to town at about midnight,' she writes.

> As one would expect, he is a perfect gentleman. Not a very attractive creature – very reserved but quite nice. He's not very fond of meeting 'people' – he says he doesn't get on with them awfully well. We arrived back at Liverpool Street at about 1am and packed me into the milk train, which left at 3.40. Altogether, it was quite a thrilling evening.

For his part Denis, too, had paid attention, later saying his first impression of Margaret was 'a nice-looking young woman, a bit overweight'.

It was Charles Moore who outed Tony Bray as MT's first love, having followed the trail of letters between the sisters to Tony himself. Moore tracked him down to a small red-brick house on an estate in Sussex, which appeared on camera alongside Bray and Moore in BBC2's documentary *Young Margaret, Love Life and Letters* in 2013.

Bray, by now a cheery, sensitive, retired stockbroker who sheds a tear over Margaret whilst reminiscing, was a student at Brasenose College, Oxford, when he met a young MT at an Oxford University Conservative Association meeting. He was studying a six-month 'general sciences' course, which combined military training and science lectures. Moore describes him as from a 'solidly bourgeois background... short and not particularly good-looking', whilst Bray described Margaret as 'very thoughtful and a very good conversationalist'. He told Moore that he felt she had a 'degree of loneliness' and he admired her 'elegant, dark hair' (as it was at the time). She was, he said, 'a plump, attractive girl in a well-built way'. From her style of kissing, he deduced that he was her first relationship. Later he said that they had enjoyed a 'modest amount of amorosity'. Whatever Bray meant by this, as a gentleman, he did not divulge. And whether she experimented sexually with him or not (and it was likely, given her naivety and her religiosity, that she did not do *that* – or anything close), it remains quite possible that, by the time she married, Margaret Thatcher was not a virgin.

What Tony very definitely *did* do for Margaret, possibly for the first time in her life, was show her how to have fun. As such, she was smitten. 'We had a marvellous time,' she writes to Muriel, brimming with excitement over the Randolph Ball in Oxford. 'Tony hired a car and we drove out to Abingdon.' Entering the Crown and Thistle pub she claims, with her characteristic, straightforward reportage, that 'everyone looked up and stared'.

As she describes her appearance – in a borrowed royal-blue velvet cloak and her hair with 'the front part piled up on top' – it is unclear whether the attendant company stared because they were in awe of, or appalled by, her outfit. Either way, Margaret was discovering that it felt good to be noticed. She continued to see Tony, mentioning him frequently in her letters to Muriel. They even broke new ground by staying for a weekend with her parents, which Bray remembered as 'all right'. But for Margaret, this kind of gesture was immensely significant, and it is likely that she thought it indicated his long-term intentions.

After he left for Bovington Camp in April, she and Tony continued to write, but the correspondence tailed off once Tony was posted to Germany for a commission in the Royal Inniskilling Dragoon Guards. When he failed to respond to Margaret's barrage of letters, she exhibited every sign of a shaken young lovelorn by writing to Tony's mother, desperate to find out whether something terrible had happened to him. In fact, Tony told Charles Moore, he had decided to let the relationship 'fizzle out'. He was concerned he said, that a life with Margaret would not be 'fun'. He got that right. Margaret, who undoubtedly felt spurned, spent her final two years at Oxford and beyond, as Moore points out, fundamentally alone, and there's little doubt that her first experience of love left her shaken and more than a little cynical.

In 1948, Bray would write to her again in Colchester, where she was working in her first job at BX Plastics, leaving her feeling vindicated. 'The letter was very weird and sentimental,' she writes to Muriel, but that didn't stop her from meeting up with him again. Was it curiosity, lingering love, or simply that she felt like being taken out for a night on the town? Probably a mixture of all three, and it involved a level of deception with her parents. On 5 September 1948 she wrote guiltily to Muriel to clarify: 'In point of fact, I was not meeting "a crowd of old college cronies" in London yesterday, but Tony. He had written to say if I was ever in London to let him know – so I thought we might have the evening out yesterday.' After taking tea together at Fullers in Regent Street, Tony took her to see the musical *Carissima* and then on to dinner at Kettner's: 'quite a fashionable West End restaurant… I really enjoyed the evening very much – though I wouldn't dream of re-striking up the association with Tony.'

She wasn't being entirely truthful and continued to see him. 'I saw Tony twice during the weekend I was in Oxford,' she writes in a letter to Muriel dated 18 December 1948. 'I did theatre and dinner with him on Saturday evening… and went out to tea on Sunday.' (A paragraph in this letter has been tantalisingly redacted on behalf of the family on 'medical grounds', leaving us to speculate what could have been wrong with MT at that point, particularly as she'd clearly spent a lot of time with Tony.)

She was looking around, too. She'd been caught out once by Tony and she wasn't going to let it happen again. She was prone to crushes – she'd developed one at Oxford on a young Worcester College man called Neil Findlay, which had taken the best part of an academic year to dissipate; this time it was David Papillon of Lexden Manor, from a prominent Colchester family and active in the Young Conservatives. (Moore notes in his biography that, unbeknown to MT, Papillon was homosexual: 'Throughout her life she remained innocent about such things.') 'There was a whole host of Christmas cards awaiting me… including one from David Papillon!! In his own handwriting too. I sure was surprised but I calmed me down [*sic*] by assuming that he sent them to all persons active in the Conservative cause,' she writes to Muriel. And there is one more salvo from Tony: 'I had a valentine from Tony!' she tells her, in February 1949. After that, the trail goes cold. Bray told Moore he had begun to see another woman, taking her skiing even whilst he was still seeing Margaret. In June 1950 he got engaged, to Valerie, the woman who would spend the rest of her life with him. 'It's no good thinking over the chances you missed,' MT told Charles Moore firmly when he tried to pursue the topic of Bray for her biography.

If Margaret was unable to completely gloss over her relationship with Tony Bray, she would find it easier to control the narrative about her second boyfriend, Scottish farmer Willie Cullen. This is because when Margaret decided, after a short time dating him, that he did not fit the bill, she offloaded him onto her sister in a jaw-dropping series of moves so calculated that it puts Jane Austen's Mrs Bennet to shame. The 'Scotch farmer', as she initially described him to Muriel, met Margaret at a Conservative group party and from then on pursued her with an intensity that she seemed to find both uncomfortable and delicious, first turning up unannounced at her office at BX Plastics in Colchester and then phoning to press her for dinner. She describes their meeting to Muriel on 23 January 1949: 'I expected to be bored to tears but in fact he was really rather sweet, with quite a sense of humour.' Cullen laid out his prospects on their first date, rather like a reverse dowry.

> His farm is worth £25,000, he has 3,000 £1 shares of ICI… a thousand of something else, five hundred of this <u>and</u> that and so on and so forth… And being a Scotman [sic] he left a ninepenny

tip for the waiter. I could have fallen through the floor. That's how people with money keep it! He's had a new Rover on order for three years.

Cars were important to MT and she noted carefully in her letters what each of her beaus drove, as though the car embodied the man (in Denis's case in particular, it would). Her Scottish farmer was insistent too, in a way she hadn't experienced before: 'he drove me home in his present rather old car – and got quite ardent on the way… He speaks with a frightfully Scotch accent. I'm afraid he's going to be an awful nuisance,' she writes hopefully.

On 13 March 1949 she writes to Muriel that she is continuing to date William Cullen, but with an ulterior motive:

> Went to the flicks yesterday evening with my farmer friend and got him all primed up to meet you sometime. I showed him the snapshot of you and I together – and he said he could scarcely tell the difference so I should think we could easily substitute me for you. When can you come down for a weekend?

And then, on the 17th of the same month, she meets Denis for the first time at the aforementioned constituents' dinner, but continues to send out encouraging signals to Willie – or William as she often refers to him – accompanying him to the local Caledonian Ball in place of his regular date: his sister: 'I think I set some tongues wagging.' He showers her with gifts. This she likes: 'a pair of nylons… he never takes me out without producing a box of chocolates with some sweets!' The distraction is welcome as she is working hard. 'Politics do take up a tremendous lot of time and I am only too glad to have a little relaxation arranged for me without my having to do anything about it.' On the matter of sweets, Cullen's judgement was sound. Confectionery – perhaps a hangover from the post-war years of rationing – was always the way to MT's heart. ('She absolutely loved chocolates. It was one of the only battles she didn't win,' says a former assistant.) On 6 April 1949 she writes to Muriel triumphantly: 'Bill has announced that he wants to meet you. I shall be in my old tweed suit and blue coat. I expect you'll have your highwayman coat on but don't come too exotic underneath.' They are headed to meet Bill's mother for the first time. She adds excitedly that he had bought her 'a lovely bottle of French perfume… it's one of the frightfully expensive ones – called Crêpe de Chine.' A couple of letters later she sounds resolved on her decision about Bill, if a little patronising:

> I shan't marry Bill… I am not in love with him and a marriage between us would falter after 2 or 3 months. We have completely different outlooks, and quite different sorts of friends. While I get on all right with his, he would feel out of water with mine.

We don't know how Muriel initially felt about the suggestion that she take on MT's cast-off or indeed how the meeting between her and Willie went, because the letters are only one-way (Muriel surely has either kept or destroyed her own), and the next few letters seem to be missing. By the time we catch up with Margaret again, she is very definitely still dating William. They have an outing to Flatford Mill, 'one of the beauty spots of Essex that Constable was always painting', and he has been 'marvellous' whilst she was unwell, 'coming over every other day with butter, eggs and grapes etc'. It seems to be getting more serious as they make up a foursome with Willie's sister May and her fiancé. And then, in mid May 1949, events take a different turn. Margaret writes to Muriel that she and William have lunched together in full view of the farming fraternity and 'all heads were turned towards us'; but then she introduces someone new into the mix. She says she has met the 'medical superintendent of the Southern Hospital… He's a most unusual chap and, like a number of his profession, still a bachelor. He's over 40 so he'd do quite nicely for you… He said I was to 'phone whenever I felt fed up with politics but of course I shan't,' she writes, before adding: 'William says he hasn't heard from you. Do write to him as quickly as possible… I told him that I went up to the Southern Hospital with a doctor who impressed me very much – and he wrote back and said, was I giving him a hint to get out!' Meanwhile, Denis is also beginning to appear on the scene as a contender:

> Tonight I am going out to dinner and theatre with Denis Thatcher. It will be my first non-political night out for ages. He has just returned from a trip in West Africa. I am going to the Paint Federation Ball at the Grosvenor at the end of November with him.

We cannot know what next transpires, because again, more letters between the sisters are either missing or have been intentionally removed from the file. Nonetheless, the transfer of William's affections from one sister to the other is almost complete, when we next find Margaret writing to Muriel in January 1950:

Dear Muriel, I have written to William in the vein I told you. He wrote a letter to me – much warmer in tone than his others… We are meeting in London on Saturday afternoon to talk over the various aspects of 'we three' and it will then be broken off between he and I, for good and all.

She seems to be attempting to allay Muriel's fears: saying she thought it would be better if she saw Willie in person as 'it would be easier, for when we meet again in a different relationship… if we parted in the flesh – not by letter – as friends. Hope you approve.' As if to reinforce that she has now entirely moved on she introduces Robert into the conversation: 'In the evening I met Robert on the Dartford Station… He spent his Christmas with an enormously wealthy family who have five daughters of marriageable age, one of which is a doctor. The prospects don't look very hopeful, do they?'

By February 1950 matters are settled. 'Dear Muriel, I saw your engagement in the *Telegraph* this morning,' she writes on 14 February 1950 on her personal general election letterhead, which sports a headshot of her in the left-hand corner. She has recently moved jobs from BX Plastics in Colchester to J. Lyons and Co. at Hammersmith, enabling her to be nearer to the Dartford constituency where she is standing as the Tory candidate. And she has also taken a temporary sublet on a flat in London. By now, she is seriously dating Robert Henderson, who, as Charles Moore points out, at 47 was just over twice her age. A talented surgeon, Henderson had developed the 'iron lung', the go-to treatment for polio victims in the 1940s and 1950s, and took over as medical superintendent of Southern Hospital in Dartford in 1940. Moore describes Henderson as a 'thin, drily amusing man [who] loved roses and country life, a good party and especially a good Bloody Mary. Physically, he resembled Denis Thatcher, although he was shorter and considered to be better looking.'

Margaret is falling in love and is elated. She writes to Muriel of their outings: 'By the way, after Polling Day Robert and I are dining and dancing at the Berkeley. He gave me a choice of three; the Savoy, the Bagatelle or the Berkeley… My new white frock is simply lovely and I have every intention of wearing it on that night.' She draws a shaky illustration of the frock, both back and front, to display its allure to Muriel. And then the 'loved-up' couple go away for a night: 'I am going down to Eastbourne for the weekend. Robert is coming to join me on the Sunday, staying overnight and he will drive me back on the Monday. Needless to say, I'm looking forward to it tremendously.' (What are the chances of it having been a chaste night away? I'd say, by the excitable tone of her letter: zero.) In another letter, she strikes a note of caution: 'I go out with him most weekends and one night during the week. But whether it will even come to anything I very much doubt for he thinks the difference between our ages very great.' She has reservations, too, about his resistance to introducing her to his friends (which, as every woman knows, is the kiss of death). She introduces him to Muriel and Willie, indicating her own levels of seriousness about the relationship. In an undated 1950s letter she tells Muriel: 'It was awfully nice to see you both on Sunday night. I wanted Robert to meet Will and it was an ideal opportunity. I gather they got on like a house on fire.'

But then… 'Robert is not at all well. In fact, he's going into hospital on June 12th to be operated on,' she writes on Wednesday

31 May 1950. From her description, the condition sounds like cancer: 'They are removing part of the tummy and duodenum.' After the operation, Robert leaves for Aberdeen to convalesce. Whilst he is away, she dines with Denis. 'We drove down to the Mitre Inn at Hampton Court,' she reveals.

Is she hedging her bets and 'running' two men at the same time? Almost certainly. And why not? For Margaret, this would not have seemed like a calculated move; rather, with her exceptionally rational mindset, it would have appeared to be entirely the sensible thing to do. She seemed to have no intent of playing one off against the other, and it's clear that she was in love with Robert but also curious about the potential lifestyle that Denis had to offer. Charles Moore points out that there's no evidence that Robert and Margaret ever physically consummated their relationship. But equally, there's no evidence that they did not. Indeed, Margaret's later response to Robert's behaviour seems to suggest that this was, for her, an exceptionally meaningful relationship. The kind of relationship which involves the losing of one's virginity. We cannot know for sure, because the pertinent letters from the sisters at around this time are noticeably also missing from the file. And in any case it is not likely that MT, with her resistance to the discussion of all matters sexual, would have committed something like this to paper, even to her sister.

What the letters do reveal is that, after a couple of trips back to Dartford that autumn (when Margaret visited him from London – which raises the question of where she stayed), Robert fades away, literally and metaphorically. It seems she waves him off to Madeira in February 1951, where he is travelling as the ship's doctor. 'He was looking very much in need of a rest,' she writes, to Muriel.

The following week she writes again with news of another date with Denis: 'I went to Twickenham with Denis Thatcher and a couple of his friends to see England v. Scotland. I am not thrilled at watching either rugger or soccer, but I was pleased to go this time never having been to an international before.' By now, she has taken a more permanent mews flat: 101 St George's Square Mews, Victoria SW1, which she seems to spend weeks scrubbing: 'it has been empty for 3 months and is absolutely filthy.' Nonetheless, it is shipshape by the time Denis visits her there for a drink, before accompanying her to dinner and then to the Festival of Britain. She's patently still holding a candle for Robert, though, and she tells Muriel (in a letter undated, but likely from May) excitedly: 'Tonight Robert is coming up and we are going out for dinner. Last time he came I created a slap-up dinner, four courses, just to show him! But I can't rise to that every time.'

And then, just as swiftly as the relationship between Robert Henderson and Margaret Thatcher began, it vanishes. He is never mentioned again, except by one other person: Margaret's father. So, what happened? The clues are in the letter which Alf Roberts writes to Muriel, dated 25 September 1951. 'Next, which will be more surprising, Margaret and Dennis [sic] Thatcher are becoming engaged... and likely to be married first week in December.' He tells Muriel that he had 'heard from Margaret that he had asked her to marry him and that she was considering it but wanted to see me first'. Given the closeness of the sisters, the unwavering regularity of Margaret's letters to Muriel and their confessional nature, it is not possible that Muriel was unaware of the breakdown of the relationship between Margaret and Robert.

Nonetheless, the pertinent letters detailing the breakdown are missing too. Alf Roberts goes on: 'The Robert business upset Margaret very much, but that will pass.' We can read between the lines here and say almost unequivocally that Robert must have called a halt to the relationship, causing MT grave distress. On the rebound (although she did think it through) she decided to marry Denis, who later admitted to Charles Moore that 'she didn't leap at it'. As Moore also points out, all of MT's previous mentions of Denis in her letters to Muriel were 'either neutral or mildly unflattering'. 'I can't say I really ever enjoy going out for the evening with him. He has not got a very prepossessing personality.'

It is likely, then, that MT rationally calculated that Denis was a good bet – as indeed he turned out to be. 'We had a lot in common,' she later said. 'He was on the financial side, I was interested in economics. He was in the paint and chemicals business, I was a chemist.' These are hardly the words of a smitten lover. But then, Robert's rejection of MT seems to have tempered her enthusiastic approach towards the opposite sex, and for all of her flirtatious coquettishness, about which many have spoken and many more written, with the exception of Denis (though he occasionally gave her pause for thought) Margaret Thatcher never entirely trusted a man again. When Charles Moore approached her directly about her relationship with Robert, MT would not be drawn.

> I was prompting her, because at this point she couldn't always remember things that clearly, but when I said his name, she told me immediately that he was much older than her. But when I suggested that perhaps she and Robert might have got

married – or that at least they had both thought as much at one point, she said, 'I wouldn't disagree with that.'

Major Denis Thatcher (retd), MBE (military), son of Tom, a New Zealand weedkiller manufacturer, and Lilian, daughter of a South London horse dealer, had also had his heart broken by the time he met Margaret Roberts in 1949. The cause was not the Second World War, for which Denis was mentioned twice in despatches, but a woman, 'a stunning girl in a blue silk dress', also called Margaret, to whom Denis had been married for six years, throughout the war. 'It was one of those wartime marriages,' she later said, 'which never really got off the ground.' After they divorced in 1948, the first Mrs Margaret Thatcher would marry again almost immediately. This time, she married a baronet, Sir Howard Whitby Hickman, with whom she had, much to Denis's distress when he found out, been having an affair. 'The breakdown of his marriage shattered him totally and he seemed rudderless,' a former school friend reflected.

That Denis was divorced would also have given the young MT pause for thought, particularly where her father and her constituents were concerned. But Alf Roberts was surprisingly and uncharacteristically accepting of Denis's past. 'Dennis [sic] has had an unfortunate experience,' he writes to Muriel. 'He was married during the war, but after only about five weekends' leave spent with his wife she left him… I told Margaret she could disregard this as he was in no way at fault and actually he is an exceedingly nice fellow also of course very comfortably off.' Until she was elected Tory leader, few constituents would ever discover the truth. The couple had a pact (perhaps unspoken) never to mention it. The story was broken in 1979. 'I even learned from the pages of a tabloid newspaper the astonishing news that my father had been married and divorced a few years before he met my mother,' writes Carol. 'Don't mention it to your father,' MT warned Carol. 'He won't talk about it. It's a wartime thing.' As Moore points out, MT was never entirely comfortable with being the 'second' Mrs Thatcher.

Both MT and Denis, then, came to their marriage with reservations and resolution. 'Let's give it a go' is how Denis later described his decision to propose. 'Denis was an absolutely wonderful partner but he was also a very selfish man,' says a friend.

> Their relationship was very traditional – you could call it patriarchal. The woman who was running the country really also was cooking the bacon and eggs for him every morning before she began the work of government. He never considered that this was in any way wrong. In fact, he expected food on the table, that the children be seen and not heard and that he be allowed to live his own life – playing golf, refereeing rugby matches and prolifically sinking G&Ts after the sun went down (and later in life well before).

Denis also had a 'wobble', as MT might have put it, in 1964 when he had what is now generally acknowledged to be a nervous breakdown. 'I think by that point Denis had been working very hard, he had yet to find his way entirely as a political spouse and he was also under a great deal of pressure,' says Moore. The pressure came from the fact that he was providing for his mother, whom he adored, his sister and his aunt – all of whom had shares in his company, Atlas. 'None of them had any real money other than that which they could draw out of the company... it seemed to me that the whole depended on the life of one man,' he told Moore. The doctor prescribed complete rest and, shortly afterwards, Denis left for South Africa – 'God's own country' – by boat. He did not return for two months. Moore says that Denis always denied that his crisis had to do with MT's career, and a friend suggests that it was the couple's marriage, rather than the politics, which proved the proverbial straw (although presumably the two were almost indivisible?). 'I think he needed to get away and think about whether, given all of the stressors, it would and could work out.' Was anyone else involved? The friend looks away. 'We can't know for sure, of course, but if I had to guess... I'd say possibly... probably – in Africa.'

If MT was alarmed, she did not show it, at least not in public, where her new role as an MP engulfed her. Moore says that she was reticent to discuss this period of her marriage, allowing only that she was 'very glad to have come through it... I think it's reasonable to suppose that when Denis left she did not know whether he would return to her,' he says.

That the relationship largely worked there was absolutely no doubt. The Thatchers had, almost without exception, one of the most successful marital and thus working relationships of any political first couple. MT seemed to relish her role as doting wife almost as much as she adored her job as Britain's first female PM. 'DT', as she always called him, was her second priority after her work – but he was a close second. He never minded, in any case. It was part of the deal.

> Her very first instinct after the bomb went off was to go straight into the bedroom to check to see whether or not Denis was OK. It was a terribly risky thing to do – there was broken glass everywhere and falling masonry. We didn't know if another bomb was going to follow – but her first and only thought really was for him,

says Robin Butler, her Principal Private Secretary at the time, of the seconds following the 1984 Brighton bombing. 'I think her response pretty much summed up their relationship.'

Not that Denis didn't often give her pause for concern. Many found his straight-talking approach hard to fathom; others found him perpetually amusing. 'Avoid telling them [the press] to "sod off". It makes them cross,' was the advice he gave to Cherie Blair and Cate Haste for their book (*The Goldfish Bowl: Married to the Prime Minister 1955–1997*, Chatto & Windus 2004). He then went on to describe what he termed 'an unfortunate incident' at a rugby dinner in South Africa in 1979, when he declared that the British Lions should be able to play in South Africa despite the ongoing sanctions: 'If those chaps who are playing the other game [i.e. Association football, or soccer] can go to Russia, as sure as hell we can go to South Africa.' His remarks caused a mini-tempest in the press back home in Britain, but, to his relief, 'the wife' kept schtum. 'Front page of the *Daily Telegraph* – she didn't say a word,' he said admiringly.

There's little doubt that Denis was fundamental to his wife's success. 'Denis was widely acknowledged as the only person who could really tell her what he thought and she would be guaranteed to listen,' says Stephen Sherbourne.

Often during speechwriting bouts at say one in the morning, when we'd all be desperate for bed and she would want to continue, despite our heavily dropped hints of yawning, stretching and closing notebooks, Denis would come in. 'Bed,' he'd say firmly. 'This is just a speech, it's not the Ten Commandments.' She would obediently follow, to our great relief.

He could also calm her and get her to see reason. 'Not a vote in the box!' he would advise if ever she was agonising over a decision that he could see would not move the electorate. When she became too heated, he was there too. Tim Bell writes of a moment at Chequers when, after he had requested an extra 'million or so' for a communications budget, MT lost her temper and began shouting. 'She was getting herself into quite a state. I think that this was the occasion when Denis leant across to her, put his hand on her knee and said, "Steady, Pet – friends."'

As a consort he was textbook. Rather like the late Duke of Edinburgh, following along a few paces behind, occasionally exasperated by the ridiculousness of proceedings, not to mention the turgidity, he was forgiven the odd explosive outburst, explicitly un-PC comment and general irascibility of approach. 'I don't know what reception I'm at but, for God's sake, give me a gin and tonic,' he once said. His humorous, no-nonsense likeability earned him independent fame as one half of the fictional 'Dear Bill' column, penned for *Private Eye* magazine by Richard Ingrams and John Wells. His fictional other half was generally taken to be his great friend and golfing partner, journalist and *Telegraph* editor, Bill Deedes. 'Dear Bill,' reads one 'letter' from 10 Downing Street, dated 7 October 1983,

> Did you ever read about the man who was buried in a coffin for six months with only a tube connecting him to the outside world for some damn fool scientific experiment in France or somewhere? Well, after my five-continents-in-four-days tour with Margaret I know exactly what he felt like when they brought him up.

The letters were so successful that they were published in book form. They also spawned a stage play, *Anyone for Denis?*, which the Thatchers, at the behest of their PR advisors, attended in the vein of being 'jolly good sports'. In fact, they both hated it.

'Denis's greatest value was that he was her link to "saloon bar Britain" – the heart of what she would have regarded as her critical supporters,' says Charles Powell.

> Through him, she learned what 'they' were thinking and how they would react to her policies. And then there was his stabilising role. We'd be on a foreign tour and it would be terribly hot and her hair would collapse – she'd worry about it terribly and he'd say, 'Now come on, old girl – it's nothing.' Then she would relax. He never interfered or lobbied. He expressed his own views and that was it.

Amongst Denis's well-known views were that the BBC was run by 'pinkoes and lefties' – he thought their coverage was biased and the staff were overpaid. 'Never watch it,' he said dismissively to one BBC board member who was introduced to him at a function. He was resistant to his own security detail and insisted on walking through London, whenever and wherever he could, striding out in his favourite black wool cape with a scarlet silk lining, looking, as his daughter Carol describes him, 'like a cross between Batman and Dracula'. He turned up on time at every function requested of him without complaint unless they clashed with a 'golf chums dinner' or a rugby match at his beloved Twickenham. He was notoriously fond of a drink and had no scruples about sending himself up. 'Mr Thatcher, how do you spend your time?' asked a fellow guest at a charity luncheon. 'Well, when I'm not completely pissed, I like to play a lot of golf,' he replied.

His reputation as a 'lady's man' preceded him. He was not good-looking, as his wife pointed out the moment she met him, but there was something about his stature, his energy and his impeccable manners which rendered him 'dashing'. 'Denis always kissed a lady's hand,' says a friend. 'This was actually a stroke of genius as it meant he didn't ever have to get in too close and kiss them on the cheek.' Springing to pull out a chair for a female dinner guest, whom he would frequently address as 'dear lady', and the purveyor of opinionated and lively small talk, he was adored by women on 'the circuit' such as Mary Wilson (wife of the former PM Harold) and the Queen Mother, who would, according to Charles Powell, say of him, 'Denis is such a splendid and sensible man. A national treasure.' Barbara Bush and he had a close friendship, and then there was, of course, Nancy Reagan, who always appeared (to the cameras at least) to be enjoying herself when paired with Denis – a rarity for this particular wife of the leader of the free world, who often went head-to-head with the other partners of global leaders, most notably Raisa Gorbachev and later Barbara Bush. 'I think that Denis and Nancy had a very good relationship, which was of course helped by the tremendous affection between Ronald Reagan and Mrs Thatcher,' said Sir Julian Seymour, former director of MT's private office. 'Denis was always a tremendous asset. I don't think she could have done it without him.'

Whilst her attachment to and dependence on Denis were never in question, writing a new book on Margaret Thatcher meant that interviewees I could comfortably describe as 'in the know' would often drop hints about the possibility of her having had affairs. At one dinner party, a CEO who had worked beside MT on a number of business-related projects buttonholed me in the hallway as I was leaving. 'If I were you,' he said quietly, 'I'd dig a little deeper on those rumours of affairs.'

This was easier said than done. Whilst many were willing to speculate, no one was prepared to go on the record. Except for Jonathan Aitken. 'Yes, I think she did have at least one affair very early on in her parliamentary career,' he says during our interview, 'but I can't for the life of me remember who it was – he was very boring, that's all I do remember.' And later? I float a name I've been given: Sir Humphrey Atkins? Aitken's eyes flicker. 'Quite possibly – there were knowledgeable rumours to that effect at the time. His good looks must have appealed to her, but his political brain was hopeless.' He'd previously been vague when the *Evening Standard* newspaper, in 2013, had suggested to him that Atkins, who had backed MT's leadership bid, was more than 'her poodle', notably during the time that Denis was in Africa. 'Well, I do think some of it was the drink talking,' he says. 'Ian Gow would always speak of her advances as "you know, when Margaret is in her cups."'

From his pictures, Atkins does appear to have been a perfect specimen. Tall, dark and dashingly handsome, he had been Conservative Chief Whip in 1973–9 and served MT as Secretary of State for Northern Ireland in 1979–81, after which MT appointed him Lord Privy Seal. Both he and Peter Carington resigned in 1982 over the Falklands invasion and she made him a Knight Commander (KCMG) in the 1983 Dissolution Honours. In 1987 he was granted a life peerage as Baron Colnbrook of Waltham St Lawrence. 'The joke about Atkins was that for someone who was not very good he kept getting promoted... now why was that?' asks another politician of the time. 'She was reckoned by her ministers to have a particular weakness for handsome men of a certain age who stood up straight and wore well-cut suits,' writes Hugo Young, 'a preference of which the most conspicuous beneficiary was widely agreed to have been Humphrey Atkins.'

When MT left office, the pressures on Denis to be 'present' for his demanding wife intensified. 'She was so used to making decisions, and when there were none to make, I think she leant on Denis and needed attention,' says Charles Powell. As a consequence, he sought distraction and solace during the day away from his wife and their home in Chester Square, busy with friends or retired golfing and rugby chums. It was at this point that he formed one of the most meaningful relationships of his later life, which would, quite justifiably, give MT cause for concern.

Marilyn or Mandy Foreman was better known in her earlier life as Mandy Rice-Davies. She was one third of the trio who brought down Minister for War John Profumo, and indirectly brought about the resignation of Conservative PM Harold Macmillan in 1963 and, in 1964, the dissolution of the entire Conservative government. Christine Keeler and osteopath Stephen Ward were also made notorious in the sex scandal. Rice-Davies was the architect of the well-known phrase 'Well, he would, wouldn't he?' which she used in her own defence in court, having been informed that hereditary peer and Conservative politician Lord Astor – the owner of the stately home of Cliveden, where the Profumo scandal began – categorically denied ever having had an affair with her. It has since taken on a life of its own, appearing in the *Oxford Dictionary of Quotations* since 1979 and generally held (according to Wikipedia) to be 'a British political phrase and aphorism that is commonly used as a retort to a self-interested denial'. These days, it is often shortened to 'MRDA': Mandy Rice-Davies applies.

By the time Denis Thatcher met former actress Rice-Davies, or Marilyn Foreman as she now was, she was on her third (and final) marriage, to billionaire Ken Foreman and living between Florida, the Bahamas, London and Virginia Water. Foreman was chairman of Attwood's, the waste management company, and Denis sat on the board. He and Mrs Foreman swiftly became friends and, according to Moore, he would often visit her at the couple's flat in London in Lowndes Square. 'He liked strong women, quite bossy women, which is why he liked me,' she said. For her part, she liked his turn of phrase, his military bearing and precision and sense of humour. They both had an interest in military history. He wrote her affectionate letters, according to Moore, which began 'Mandy dear'. The couples occasionally holidayed together and, when Foreman died, it was revealed that she kept two framed photographs of the Thatchers in her London flat. Foreman was a fan of MT, but she thought the former PM was distrustful of her: 'I could catch her looking at me when she thought I wasn't looking. She was working me out,' she said. MT's first words to the immaculately made-up, glamorously blonde Foreman, when they first met, were characteristically disarming: 'Tell me, how do you get your lipstick to stay on?' Was the relationship between Denis and Foreman sexual? 'No, I don't think it was, but there was a close friendship there,' allows Moore. But then, at the risk of sounding trite, he would say that, wouldn't he?

In December 1990, at MT's request, the Queen granted Denis the Thatcher Baronetcy as 1st Baronet of Scotney, the first hereditary title to be given to a non-royal in decades. He died in June 2003, from pancreatic cancer, holding her hand. MT paid an emotional tribute to her beloved husband at his funeral declaring: 'Being Prime Minister is a lonely job. In a sense, it ought to be: you cannot lead from the crowd. But with Denis there, I was never alone. What a man. What a husband. What a friend.'

Received wisdom (and perhaps an element of wishful thinking from some sectors) has it that MT never recovered from Denis's death. After a marriage of 51 years, adjusting to life without one's partner would take some doing for anyone, let alone someone whose monumental career was to a great extent predicated on the support of the departed other half. 'Of course, she had happy times after Denis, but we always knew that she would never be entirely the same,' says former secretary Amanda Ponsonby. 'How could she be?'

From then on, MT was buoyed by any number of her loyal circle, who took it upon themselves to visit, to entertain and to have her to stay. Most of us should be so lucky. The long list included the Reagans, the Hamiltons, the Wolfsons, the Butlers, the Barclays, the McAlpines, the Annenbergs, Jonathan Aitken, Jeffrey Archer, Bernard Ingham, Julian Seymour, Michael Forsyth and Tim Bell. She holidayed with her devoted Crawfie, who often stayed overnight with her in the same room, and took trips to visit her friend, the American socialite and philanthropist Carroll Petrie in the Hamptons.

The onset of dementia, which so famously ultimately felled Britain's first female PM, initially made itself felt in the early 2000s, although John Major had claimed erroneously and unkindly that it was behind her criticism of him, once he took office. As MT's life drew inexorably to a close, new strictures were placed upon her friends who wished to stop by. 'Towards the end Mark had banned visits from anyone other than family. I think he was embarrassed by her frailty. Charles Powell ruthlessly ignored him and I rather wish I'd done the same,' says Archie Hamilton. Powell, who would visit her every Sunday evening to sing with her the hymns from the TV programme *Songs of Praise*, was one of the last people to see her alive. He visited her at the Ritz Hotel on the evening of Sunday, 7 April 2013, where she was recuperating after a small operation, as a guest of the Barclay brothers. As Powell kissed her goodnight, he reflected that time was running out for his former boss and friend. He told his wife Carla as much when he arrived home.

The news that Margaret Thatcher had died quietly, peacefully and quite possibly in her sleep in the early morning of 8 April

2013 spawned a contrary narrative. It was, to borrow from an equally far-fetched but popular New York-based sitcom of the nineties, 'the one where Britain's most successful PM of the late twentieth century died an agonising, lonely death'. The story was promulgated by those who took a perverse delight in believing that someone whose policies they had disagreed with (or, in many cases, whose parents or grandparents had disagreed with them and who knew nothing about the woman herself) had somehow received a form of divine retribution. These were the same detractors who sent 'Ding Dong! The Witch Is Dead' to the top of the music charts that week and held street parties for the benefit of the cameras. 'People like the "lonely at the top" trope because it's a comfort to those who've wasted their potential or been lazy. But most of us will be lonely when we outlive the people we love,' says Julie Burchill. 'I'd far rather have a luxurious death at the Ritz, alone, than be surrounded by a bunch of sobbing idiots. A bit of loneliness is a small price to pay – and if you've got room service, so much the better.'

Whilst MT might not have put it quite like that, she would have agreed with Burchill and smiled wryly at the response of the haters. And then she would have turned her attentions to the positives, which were multitudinous. In a White House statement, American President Barack Obama said that

> the world has lost one of the great champions of freedom and liberty, and America has lost a true friend. As a grocer's daughter who rose to become Britain's first female Prime Minister, she stands as an example to our daughters that there is no glass ceiling that can't be shattered.

Former US Secretary of State Henry Kissinger told CNN that Thatcher was 'a tremendous prime minister. She was a great lady, she had very strong opinions. And to those of us who knew her over the decades, she was a very warm person, which is not the public image that is often given.' UN Secretary General Ban Ki-moon said the world owed a great deal to Thatcher's leadership: 'She was a pioneering leader for her contribution to peace and security, particularly at the height of the Cold War,' he said. Meanwhile NATO Secretary General Anders Fogh Rasmussen's statement included the sentence: 'Baroness Thatcher was an extraordinary politician who was a staunch defender of freedom, a powerful advocate of NATO and the transatlantic bond.'

Male-dominated plaudits aside, MT's greatest delight and satisfaction would have been the attendance at her funeral of the living person she had most revered. Queen Elizabeth II had let it be known, the day after the announcement of MT's death, that she would like to be present. This was not required of the monarch; more it was a mark of respect from one female leader to another, and the gesture elevated the funeral to a state occasion, in all but name. The rumour that HM and MT did not get along had already been dispelled by the fact that the Queen had awarded her former PM the Order of the Garter in 1995 – the most prestigious honour in the Queen's personal gift. The Queen had also attended both her seventieth and eightieth birthday parties. At the latter, they circulated side by side, beaming. When the Queen bade MT farewell that night with the words, 'I'm afraid I must go now,' MT replied, 'What a good idea, I think I'll go too.' 'You'd better not,' retorted the monarch, according to Charles Moore. 'It's your party.'

Queen Elizabeth II had only ever attended one other funeral service amongst those held for the eight Prime Ministers of her seventy-year reign who had died. It was, and could only be, that of the man whom Margaret Thatcher regularly acknowledged throughout her life as her greatest inspiration: Sir Winston Churchill.

# ACKNOWLEDGEMENTS

I should like to thank everyone quoted in this book and also the very many people who spoke to me off the record. Your time and generosity are hugely appreciated.

George Owers, formerly of Swift Press, is the editor who first saw the potential in this book and Karen Farrington ably stepped into his shoes a little later. My thanks to you both.

Thanks are also due in no particular order to: Diana Broccardo and Mark Richards of Swift Press, Ian Howe for his excellent copy-editing, peripatetic research assistants Jasmine Benham and Felix Naylor, my agent Eugenie Furniss and her associate Emily MacDonald. Friends are a lifeline for the solitary biographer and I'd like to thank all of mine for never failing to utter the eternally painful question: 'So how's the book going?' In particular: Deborah Mattinson – now Baroness Mattinson of Darlington – who opened up her contacts book, overlooking her political allegiance, and Jan Hall and Libby Purves, who did the same; the Witches of Walberswick – you know who you are. To Cecily Engle, Kate Muir and Julie Myerson for moral support; and AC, PP, BM, CB, AV, JB, LT, JH, JM, HMP, AP, RE, GF, WA, MS, BR, SP, LG&PW for the longevity of love and friendship. To my sister MG for always lending a sympathetic ear. My beloved friend Tine (Christine) Ward died during the writing of this book and I'd like to pay tribute to both her warrior spirit and her wicked sense of humour.

My sons Ethan and Truman were readers and willing critics of this manuscript. I'd like to thank Ethan for his unerring ability to adeptly rephrase a dodgy paragraph and Truman for having the sheer nerve to utter the resoundingly humbling phrase: 'But Mum, that's not how Simon Schama would have done it.'

TINA GAUDOIN
*Walberswick, April 2025*

# BIBLIOGRAPHY

## BOOKS

Abse, Leo, *Margaret, Daughter of Beatrice: A Politician's Psycho-Biography of Margaret Thatcher*, Jonathan Cape, 1989

Agar, Jon, *Science Policy under Thatcher*, UCL Press, 2019

Aitken, Jonathan, *Margaret Thatcher: Power and Personality*, Bloomsbury, 2013

Anderson, Oliver, *Rotten Borough: The Real Story of Mrs Thatcher's Grantham*, Fourth Estate, 1989

Beard, Mary, *Women & Power: A Manifesto*, Profile Books, 2017

Bell, Tim, *Right or Wrong: The Memoirs of Lord Bell*, Bloomsbury, 2014

Berlinski, Claire, *'There Is No Alternative': Why Margaret Thatcher Matters*, Basic Books, 2008

Booth, Cherie, and Cate Haste, *The Goldfish Bowl: Married to the Prime Minister 1955–1997*, Chatto & Windus, 2004

Brunson, Michael, *A Ringside Seat: The Autobiography of Michael Brunson*, Coronet, 2000

Burley, Rob, *Why Is This Lying Bastard Lying to Me? Searching for the Truth on Political TV*, Mudlark, 2024

Butler, Judith, *Gender Trouble: Feminism and the Subversion of Identity*, Routledge, 1990

Campbell, Beatrix, *The Iron Ladies: Why Do Women Vote Tory?* Virago Press, 1987

Campbell, John, *Margaret Thatcher*, i: *The Grocer's Daughter*, Jonathan Cape, 2000

Campbell, John, *Margaret Thatcher*, ii: *The Iron Lady*, Jonathan Cape, 2003

Cannadine, David, *Margaret Thatcher: A Life and Legacy*, Oxford University Press, 2017

Carroll, Rory, *Killing Thatcher: The IRA, the Manhunt and the Long War on the Crown*, Mudlark, 2023

Clarke, Ken, *Kind of Blue: A Political Memoir*, Macmillan, 2016

Cosgrave, Patrick, *Thatcher: The First Term*, Bodley Head, 1985

Cradock, Sir Percy, *In Pursuit of British Interests: Reflections on Foreign Policy under Margaret Thatcher and John Major*, John Murray, 1997

Dale, Iain, *Margaret Thatcher: In Her Own Words*, Biteback, 2010

Dale, Iain, and Jacqui Smith, eds, *The Honourable Ladies*, i: *Profiles of Women MPs 1918–1996*, Biteback, 2018

Farr, Diana, *Five at 10: Prime Ministers' Consorts since 1957*, André Deutsch, 1985

Filby, Eliza, *God and Mrs Thatcher: The Battle for Britain's Soul*, Biteback, 2015

Genz, Stéphanie, and Benjamin A. Brabon, *Postfeminism: Cultural Texts and Theories*, Edinburgh University Press, 2009

Gorman, Teresa, *No, Prime Minister!*, John Blake Publishing, 2001

Harris, John, *The Last Party: Britpop, Blair and the Demise of English Rock*, Fourth Estate, 2003

# BIBLIOGRAPHY

Harris, Robin, *Not for Turning: The Life of Margaret Thatcher*, Bantam Press, 2013

Hennessy, Peter, *The Prime Minister: The Office and Its Holders since 1945*, Penguin, 2001

Hollinghurst, Alan, *The Swimming-Pool Library*, Chatto & Windus, 1988

Hollingsworth, Mark, *The Ultimate Spin Doctor: The Life and Fast Times of Tim Bell*, Coronet, 1997

Howe, Geoffrey, *Conflict of Loyalty*, Macmillan, 1994

Ingham, Bernard, *Kill the Messenger*, HarperCollins, 1991

Ingham, Bernard, *The Slow Downfall of Margaret Thatcher: The Diaries of Bernard Ingham*, Biteback, 2019

Ingrams, Richard, and John Wells, *Bottoms Up! Further Letters of Denis Thatcher*, Private Eye, 1984

Jackson, Ben, and Robert Saunders, eds, *Making Thatcher's Britain*, Cambridge University Press, 2012

Jordanova, Ludmilla, *The Look of the Past: Visual and Material Evidence in Historical Practice*, Cambridge University Press, 2012

Junor, Penny, *Margaret Thatcher: Wife, Mother, Politician*, Sidgwick & Jackson, 1983

Kwarteng, Kwasi, *Thatcher's Trial: Six Months That Defined a Leader*, Bloomsbury, 2015

Letwin, Oliver, *Hearts and Minds: The Battle for the Conservative Party from Thatcher to the Present*, Biteback, 2017

Levin, Angela, *Margaret Thatcher*, Hamish Hamilton, 1981

Lewis, Helen, *Difficult Women: A History of Feminism in 11 Fights*, Jonathan Cape, 2020

McCormack, Catherine, *Women in the Picture: Women, Art and the Power of Looking*, Icon 2021

Maitland, Olga, *Margaret Thatcher: The First Ten Years*, Sidgwick & Jackson, 1989

Mattinson, Deborah, *Talking to a Brick Wall: How New Labour Stopped Listening to the Voter and Why We Need a New Politics*, Biteback, 2011

Millar, Ronald, *A View from the Wings: West End, West Coast, Westminster*, Weidenfeld & Nicolson, 1993

Moore, Charles, *Margaret Thatcher: The Authorized Biography*, i: *Not for Turning*, Penguin, 2013

Moore, Charles, *Margaret Thatcher: The Authorized Biography*, ii: *Everything She Wants*, Penguin, 2015

Moore, Charles, *Margaret Thatcher: The Authorized Biography*, iii: *Herself Alone*, Penguin, 2019

Morgan, Piers, *The Insider: The Private Diaries of a Scandalous Decade*, Ebury Press, 2005

Mount, Ferdinand, *Cold Cream: My Early Life and Other Mistakes*, Bloomsbury, 2008

Murray, Patricia, *Margaret Thatcher*, W.H. Allen, 1980

Nunn, Heather, *Thatcher, Politics and Fantasy: The Political Culture of Gender and Nation*, Lawrence & Wishart, 2002

Phillips, Melanie, *The Divided House: Women at Westminster*, Sidgwick & Jackson, 1980

Pugh, Martin, *Women and the Women's Movement in Britain: 1914–1959*, Macmillan Education, 1992

Reeves, Rachel, *Women of Westminster: The MPs Who Changed Politics*, I.B. Tauris, 2019

Rose, Kenneth, *Who Loses, Who Wins: The Journals of Kenneth Rose*, i: *1944–1979*, ed. R.D. Thorpe, Weidenfeld & Nicholson 2018

Rose, Kenneth, *Who Loses, Who Wins: The Journals of Kenneth Rose*, ii: *1979–2014*, ed. R.D. Thorpe, Weidenfeld & Nicholson 2019

# BIBLIOGRAPHY

Roy, Subroto, and John Clarke, eds, *Margaret Thatcher's Revolution: How It Happened and What It Meant*, Continuum, 2005

Seaton, Jean, *Pinkoes and Traitors: The BBC and the Nation 1974–1987*, Profile Books, 2015

Slocock, Caroline, *People Like Us: Margaret Thatcher and Me*, Biteback, 2018

Stothard, Peter, *The Senecans: Four Men and Margaret Thatcher*, Overlook Duckworth, 2016

Tebbit, Norman, *Unfinished Business*, Weidenfeld & Nicolson, 1991

Thatcher, Carol, *Diary of an Election: With Margaret Thatcher on the Campaign Trail: A Personal Account*, Sidgwick & Jackson, 1983

Thatcher, Carol, *Below the Parapet: The Biography of Denis Thatcher*, Harper Collins, 1996

Thatcher, Carol, *A Swim-on Part in the Goldfish Bowl*, Headline, 2008

Thatcher, Margaret, *The Downing Street Years*, HarperCollins, 1993

Thatcher, Margaret, *The Path to Power*, HarperCollins, 1995

Thatcher, Margaret, *The Autobiography 1925–2013 (Commemorative Edition)*, Harper Press, 2013

Thatcher, Margaret, *Statecraft: Strategies for a Changing World*, HarperCollins, 2002

Urban, George R., *Diplomacy and Disillusion at the Court of Margaret Thatcher: An Insider's View*, I.B. Tauris, 1996

Walter, Natasha, *The New Feminism*, Little, Brown, 1998

Walter, Natasha, ed., *On the Move*, Virago, 1999

Wapshott, Nicholas, *Ronald Reagan and Margaret Thatcher: A Political Marriage*, Sentinel 2007

Wapshott, Nicholas, and George Brock, *Thatcher*, Futura, 1983

Webster, Wendy, *Not a Man to Match Her: The Marketing of a Prime Minister*, The Women's Press, 1990

Wilkinson, Helen, *No Turning Back: Generations and the Genderquake*, Demos, 1994

Wyatt, Woodrow, *The Journals of Woodrow Wyatt*, ii, ed. Sarah Curtis, Macmillan, 1999

Young, Hugo, *One of Us: A Biography of Margaret Thatcher*, Macmillan, 1989

Young, Hugo, and Anne Sloman, *The Thatcher Phenomenon*, BBC Books, 1986

Young, Robb, *Power Dressing: First Ladies, Women Politicians and Fashion*, Merrell, 2011

## OTHER SOURCES/RESOURCES

Beauvallet, Anne, 'Thatcher and education in England: a one-way street?', *L'héritage du thatchérisme* (*The Thatcher Legacy*), no. 17, 2015, pp. 97–114, https://journals.openedition.org/osb/1771

Campbell, Beatrix, 'Margaret Thatcher: to be or not to be a woman', *British Politics*, vol. 10, no. 1, 2015

*The Gender Pay Gap Report*, University of Manchester, 2018, https://documents.manchester.ac.uk/display.aspx?DocID=35986

Gottlieb, Julie, and Beatrix Campbell, 'The Iron Ladies revisited', *Women's History Review*, vol. 28, no. 2, June 2018, pp. 337–49

Prestidge, Jessica Dawn, 'Margaret Thatcher's politics: the cultural and ideological forces of domestic femininity', doctoral thesis, Durham University, 2017

# BIBLIOGRAPHY

Sutcliffe-Braithwaite, Florence, 'Margaret Thatcher, individualism and the welfare state', History & Policy [website], April 2013

Wilson, Elizabeth, 'Thatcherism and women: after seven years', Socialist Register, vol. 23, 1987, pp. 199–235

# TELEVISION

*The Long Walk to Finchley*, dir. Niall MacCormick, BBC Four, 2008

*Margaret: Death of a Revolutionary*, dir. Martin Durkin, Wag TV, Channel 4, 2013

*Margaret Thatcher in the Soviet Union*, ITN, 1987

*Thatcher: A Very British Revolution*, BBC2, 2019

*Woman to Woman*, Yorkshire TV interview with Miriam Stoppard, 2 October 1985

# INDEX

20 July Group 247

abortion 101, 230
Abse, Leo 74–5, 89
Agar, Jon 235–6
AIDS crisis 33, 92, 249–251
Aitken, Jonathan
   on Airey Neave 276
   Falklands War 206, 211
   on Heseltine 291
   during miners' strike 224
   on Thatcher as a mother 80
   Thatcher meets Gorbachev 271–2
   on Thatcher's appearance 269
   on Thatcher's election 116–117
   on Thatcher's emotions 198
   on Thatcher's possible affairs 320
   on Thatcher's sense of humour 30
Allen, Paul 36
Ambitious About Autism 32
Amis, Kingsley 246, 290
Anderson, Oliver 73
Anglo-Irish Agreement of 1985 277

Archer, Jeffrey, Baron Archer of Weston-Super-Mare 282, 284, 286, 288–9, 324
Archer, Mary 288
Armstrong, Lisa 44
Arnold, Thomas 107
Asperger's Syndrome 25
Astor, Nancy Witcher Langhorne 141
Astor, William, 3rd Viscount Astor 322
Atkins, Humphrey, Baron Colnbrook of Waltham St Lawrence 204, 320–1
Atomic Weapons Establishment (AWE) 157
Attlee, Clement 215
Autism Spectrum Disorder 24–35

Baker, Kenneth 265
Balfour, Howard, 1st Baron Balfour 115
Ban, Ki-moon 326
Band Aid 260–1

Bandaranaike, Sirimavo 37, 133
Barnett, Emma 139
Battle of Orgreave 218
Bawden, Nina 110
BBC 207–8
Beard, Mary 160
Beauvoir, Simone de 142
Bell, Tim
   advises Thatcher on language 30
   arranges Thatcher's funeral 189–190
   bearer of bad news 188–9
   campaigns 185–8
   coal strikes 219
   and Gordon Reece 183
   meets Margaret Thatcher 183–4
   personal scandals 188
   as PR man 170–2, 182–3
   as private advisor 189–190
   relationship with Thatcher 282–3
   Thatcher tells Bell to be nice to Millar 178
   on Thatcher's accent 119
   on Thatcher's clothes 38–9
   on Thatcher's leadership 191
   on Thatcher's tears during Falklands War 90–1
Berry, Anthony 221
Bidisha 161
Billington, Michael 255
birth control pill 151, 201
Blair, Cherie 132, 316
Blair, Tony 131, 196–7, 228, 240, 269, 280
Blatch, Bertie 117
Blatch, Haden 117
Bondfield, Margaret 139
Bossom, Alfred 114
Bottomley, Virginia 37, 133, 161, 163
Boyle, Edward 108
Brabon, Benjamin A. 164
Braddock, Bessie 147
Bray, Tony 300–4
Brighton bombing 47, 93, 170, 220–1, 316
British Nationality Act 142
British Xylonite (BX) Plastics 31, 234, 304, 308, 392
Brittain, Jon 196
Brock, George 111
Brown, Gordon 126
Brown, Tina 56
Budgen, Nick 204
Burchill, Julie 134, 137, 140, 248–9, 253, 325
Burgdorf, Diane 33
Bush, Barbara 194, 319
Bush, George H.W. 181, 239, 290
Butler, Robin
   Brighton bombing 220, 221, 316
   on loss of HMS *Sheffield* 210–211
   on misogyny 120
   on Thatcher as a mother 82
   on Thatcher as an ordinary woman 94
   on Thatcher's female support 168
   on Thatcher's isolation during Falklands War 203, 206–7

# INDEX

on Thatcher's love of fashion  80
on Thatcher's relationship with the Queen  97
on unions  216

Callaghan, James  29–30, 145, 155, 165, 187, 213
Cameron, David  37, 40, 120
Cameron, Samantha  40
Campaign for Science and Engineering (CaSE)  236
Campbell, Alastair  172, 228
Campbell, Beatrix  63, 76, 160, 163, 196, 285
Campbell, John  66, 110, 225
Cannadine, David  155
caricaturists  46, 193
Carington, Peter, 6th Baron Carrington  96, 203–4, 214, 321
Carlton Club  119, 177
Carter, Angela  247
Carter, Jimmy  122
Carter, Violet Bonham  145
Cartland, Barbara  44, 57
Castle, Barbara, Baroness Castle of Blackburn  21, 43–4, 131–2, 139, 142–4
Catherine, Princess of Wales  45
Chalker, Lynda  163
Chalmers, Judith  77
Charles, Prince of Wales  259, 290
Chequers  56, 222, 272–3, 275, 317
Chorley, Matt  82

Churchill, Winston  98, 122, 196, 270, 274, 327
Churchill College, Cambridge  48–9, 242
Clark, Alan, Baron Parkinson of Carnforth
describes Michael Heseltine  292
diaries  193
on Nott  204
Clark, Jane  287
Clarke, Ken  121, 154, 192, 286
class, social
changes under Thatcher  124–7, 173, 223–4
'class ceiling'  118
and education  105
and feminism  151–2, 165
at Oxford  108, 113, 142
in pop culture  248
Thatcher from 'wrong' class  18, 38, 46, 71, 96, 101, 114, 204, 227, 262
Thatcher made fun of  62
Thatcher's discomfort with  97, 99
upper class  46, 89, 100–1, 111, 122–3
climate change, global  239–240
Clinton, Hillary  37, 56, 161
coal industry, privatisation of  222–4
Coghlan, Monica  288–9
Coleman, Brian  195
Coogan, Tim Pat  199
Cooke, Rachel  265
Cosgrave, Patrick  155

341

Cradock, Percy 280
Crawford, Cynthia 43, 47, 168–170, 221, 324
Crick, Bernard 74
Crowder, John 116
Cullen, Jane 79
Cullen, Muriel
  allegations about Thatcher's parentage 100
  career and accomplishments 69
  death 69
  leaves home to study 103
  letters to, about boys 31–2
  letters to, about clothes 34–5
  letters to, about films 22
  letters to, during Blitz 24
  letters to, highly detailed 26–9
  nurses mother 70
  temperament 68–70
  on Thatcher's romantic life 299–312
Cullen, Willie 304–9
Currie, Aggie 159
Currie, Edwina 163, 224
Cust, Peregrine, 6th Baron Brownlow 100

Dally, Anne 110
Darling, Jesse 264–5
Day, Robin 108
Diamond, Anne 41, 44–5
Dickson, Sally 168
Dobbs, Michael 183, 189
Dworkin, Andrea 164

Eden, Anthony, 1st Earl of Avon 285
Eden, Nicholas, 2nd Earl of Avon 250
education
  cuts in 240–1, 263
  nursery education promised 165
Education Act 1979 241
Education Act 1980 241
Elizabeth I 43, 140, 192–3, 199–200, 202, 259
Elizabeth II 17, 21, 43, 96, 209, 250, 326–7
Elizabeth the Queen Mother 98, 101, 290, 319
Enterprise Allowance Scheme 255
Esteve-Coll, Elizabeth 245–6

Fairweather, Eileen 130
Falkender, Marcia 44
Falklands War
  beginning of 200
  cabinet 284
  criticism for 136–156
  effect on Thatcher's re-election 212–213
  emotional effect on Thatcher 210–211
  grief over lost life 90, 170
  Ronald Reagan and 270–1
  Thatcher's gender 202
  Thatcher's isolation during 203–4
  Thatcher's leadership style 206–9
  unit commanders 205

# INDEX

Faludi, Susan 164
Family Allowances Act 142
Fawcett, Millicent 141
feminism 129–132
  history of 141
  and the left wing 138–9, 142
  Margaret Thatcher and 133–7, 141–8, 155–6, 165–6, 209
  response to Thatcher 160–4, 192, 197
  second wave 150–2
  and socialism 152
  'two-role solution' 145–6
Ferry, Georgina 238
Filby, Eliza 228–9
Fleming, Kate 179
Flint, Caroline 78
Fluck, Peter 46, 193
Flynn, Paul Philip 195
Fookes, Janet 163
Foreman, Amanda 118, 122, 136
Foreman, Ken 322–3
Foss, May 114
Fowler, Norman 122, 251
Franks Report on the Falklands 204
Fraser, Antonia 247
Friedan, Betty 75–6, 150–1
Frost, David 38

Gandhi, Indira 37, 133, 145, 196
gay culture 194–6
gender, performance of 45, 191–3, 252–4

Genz, Stéphanie 164
Getty, John Paul Jr 220
Gilbert and George 246
Glacier, John 41
Goodrich, Margaret 104, 107–9
Gorbachev, Mikhail 52–3, 56, 271–4
Gorbachev, Raisa 272, 319
Gordon, Bryony 88
Gorman, Teresa 151, 201
Gottlieb, Julie 63, 163
Gow, Ian 123, 277–8, 320
Gow, Jane 277–8
Grant, Hamilton 39
Grass, Marco 87
Green, Joe 219
Greenham protests 156–8
Greer, Fergus 67
Greer, Germaine 152
Grenada, US invasion of 271
Gross, Miriam 263–4
Groucho Club 249
Gummer, John 71–2, 239

Haig, Alexander 209
Hall, Peter 263
Halliwell, Geri 264
Hamilton, Anne 33, 82–3
Hamilton, Archie 33, 82, 124, 168, 324
Hamnett, Katharine 42
Harkess Affair 287
Harman, Harriet 138
Harris, John 248, 254
Harris, Kamala 37, 40, 161

Harris, Robin  26, 87–8, 154, 165
Hart, David  219–220
Healey, Denis  185, 198, 211
Heath, Edward
  and 'class ceiling'  118–119
  defeated 1974  171
  lost confidence in  121
  and milk scandal  155
  parties  120
  power cuts  177
  and unions  213, 215–216
Henderson, Robert  299, 308–312
Herbison, Peggy  142
Heseltine, Michael
  background  96
  on class  118
  on Greenham protests  157
  relationship with Thatcher  291–5
  resignation  236
  on unions  213
Hickman, Margaret  36, 313
Hodgkin, Dorothy  113, 237–8
Hodgson, Sharon  78
Hoggart, Simon  172
Hollingsworth, Mark  186, 188
homosexuality
  AIDS crisis  249–251
  decriminalisation of  177, 229
  Section 28  177, 196, 251–2
Hoskyns, John  180–1
housewives  75–6, 80, 89, 148–151, 172, 174
Howe, Geoffrey  54, 96, 121, 291

Howell, David  28, 90, 120–1, 123–4, 176, 214, 217
hunger strikes  199
Hunter-Tilney, Juliet  39–40
Hurd, Douglas  221

infected blood scandal, effects of  233–4, 251
Ingham, Bernard
  on Gorbachev  273
  as press secretary  52, 57, 175, 280–1, 324
  relationship with Thatcher  123
  on Thatcher and Reagan  270
  on Thatcher's lack of tact  31
Institute for Fiscal Studies  225
Irish National Liberation Army (INLA)  276
Irish Republican Army (IRA)  47, 93, 199, 221–2, 257, 277

J. Lyons and Co.  234, 308
Jack, Claire  30
Jackson, Glenda  132
Jenkins, Simon  212–13
John Wesley Society  112
Johnson, Boris  50
Johnson, Paul  129, 144
Jones, David  219
Jopling, Michael  96, 278
Jordanova, Ludmilla  46, 48–9
Joseph, Keith  93, 124–5, 151, 229
Junor, Penny  26, 63, 107, 109

# INDEX

Kealey, Terence 242
Keay, Douglas 230–1
Keays, Flora 285
Keays, Sara 284–5
Keeler, Christine 322
Kennedy, Helena, Baroness
    Kennedy of the Shaws 223
Kershaw, Anthony 115
Kesteven and Grantham Girls'
    School 24, 61, 66, 102–3, 105
King, Margaret
    closeness to Thatcher 21, 169
    on fashion 35, 39, 42, 50–5
    Thatcher and Heseltine 292, 294
    on Thatcher as a scientist 235
    on Thatcher's appearance 269
King, Oona, Baroness King of
    Bow 134–5
Kinnock, Neil 160, 200, 216, 218, 267
Kissinger, Henry 326
Kremlin 53, 222
Kristeva, Julia 73
Kureishi, Hanif 248

Ladbrokes 121
Lagarde, Christine 45
Laing, Hector 220
Lamb, Larry 186
Lamb, William 28
Langstaff, Brian 233–4
Larkin, Philip 246
Laski, Marghanita 143
Launer London (company) 47–8
Law, Roger 46, 193

Lawrence, Jon 99, 124–6
Lawson, Nigel 131, 291
Leach, Henry 205
Letwin, Oliver 33, 47, 67, 93, 114
Lewis, C.S. 142
Lewis, Helen 154
Libya 206, 222
Live Aid 259–261
London Fashion Week 41
London Weekend Television 80
Luce, Richard 204

McFarlane, Robert 271
MacGregor, Ian 217, 219
Maclean, Muriel 221
Macmillan, Harold 150, 215, 322
MacShane, Denis 275
Madonna 247, 255, 264
Maitlis, Emily 45
Major, John 78, 118, 163, 188, 289,
    295, 324
Major, Norma 92
Mallinson, Mary 114
Mann, Jean 142
Manning, Leah 147
*Margaret Thatcher, Queen of
    Soho* 195–6
Marr, Andrew 287
Married Women's Property Act of
    1870 131
Matrix Churchill 286
Maudling, Reginald 122
May, Theresa 94, 136
Meir, Golda 37, 133, 196

Meloni, Giorgia 41, 45
Menkes, Suzy 59–60
menopause 200–1
men's clubs 119–120
Merkel, Angela 41, 45, 160, 234
Met Office Hadley Centre for Climate Science and Services 240
Millar, Ronald
  campaigns 186–8
  homosexuality 250
  inspired by Peggy Noonan 181
  part of Three Marketeers 170
  relationship with Thatcher 177–8
  sinking of HMS *Sheffield* 210
  as speechwriter 176–7, 180–1
  Thatcher's sense of humour 29–30
  on Thatcher's voice 178–9
Mills, David 229
miners' strike of 1984 158–160
mining, coal 213–220
Mirren, Helen 259
misogyny *see* sexism
Mitterrand, François 43, 193, 208, 210, 274–5
Moore, Charles
  on allegations of vote rigging 117
  on campaign for working-class women 173
  on death of Muriel Cullen 69
  on Denis Thatcher's relationship with Mandy Rice-Davies 322–3
  on Falklands War 202, 204–5, 210
  on fashion 22–3
  on Thatcher and feminism 130
  on Thatcher's Grantham classmates 110
  on Parkinson 284
  quotes Richard Vinen on Powell 280
  on Roberts family 79
  on rumours about Alfred Roberts 74
  quotes John Vincent on snobbishness 95
  on Thatcher and Reagan 270
  on Thatcher as a chemist 111, 237
  on Thatcher as not easy to know 32
  quotes Gordon Reece on Thatcher on television 175
  on Thatcher and women's power 89–90
  on Thatcher's 80th birthday party 326
  on Thatcher's appeal to Conservatives 122
  on Thatcher's boyfriend Papillon 303
  on Thatcher's boyfriend Tony Bray 301–2, 304
  on Thatcher's first relationships 300–4, 307
  on Thatcher's friendship with Caroline Cush 100
  on Thatcher's literal-mindedness 29
  on Thatcher's love of central London 103

# INDEX

on Thatcher's love of Denis
  Thatcher 300
on Thatcher's love of Robert
  Henderson 304, 310, 312, 314
on Vicki Woods 58
on William Whitelaw 278
Moore, Suzanne 137
Mount, Ferdinand 30, 33
Murdoch, Rupert 91, 186, 290
Murray, Patricia 65, 69, 103–5,
  112
Murray, Pete 69

Naipaul, V.S. 247
Nallon, Steve 195
National Association of Colliery
  Overmen, Deputies and
  Shotfirers (NACODS) 220
National Autistic Society 24, 29, 32
National Coal Board (NCB) 216–
  217
National Health Service (NHS) 32
National Union of Mine-
  workers 213, 215, 220, 222
Neave, Airey 123, 275–7
New Romantic movement 252–3
Noble, Denis 236–7
Noonan, Peggy 181
Nott, John 91, 202–4, 211

Obama, Barack 45, 132, 325
Obama, Michelle 37, 45
O'Grady, Frances 159, 224
Oppenheim, Sally 122, 163

Orbach, Susie 162
Organisation of Women of
  African and Asian Descent
  (OWAAD) 152
Oxford University Conservative
  Association (OUCA) 22, 34,
  108–110, 112, 142, 301

Pankhurst, Emmeline 137, 141
Pankhurst, Sylvia 141
Papillon, David 303–4
Park, Daphne 241
Parkinson, Cecil 279, 282, 283–5
Parris, Matthew 194–6, 282
Paterson, Tessa Jardine 167
perestroika 274
Pershing missiles 42
Phillips, Melanie 143
Pine, Julian (pseudonym)
  *see* Anderson, Oliver
Pinter, Harold 247
Plowden Report 78
Ponsonby, Amanda 35–6, 167,
  323
popular culture
  Band Aid 260–1
  criticism of Thatcher 262–5
  Live Aid 259–261
  musical theatre 255
  novels 256–7
  pop music 247–9
  television 257–9
  women in 253–4
Portillo, Michael 185

Powell, Anthony 246
Powell, Carla 21
Powell, Charles
  on Gorbachev 273
  influence on Thatcher 279–280
  on Oxford University honorary degree 241
  Thatcher and Reagan 269, 271
  Thatcher on women's issues 144
  Thatcher's admiration for Dorothy Hodgkin 113, 237
  Thatcher's analytical abilities 72
  Thatcher's children 80, 83
  Thatcher's love of opera 262
  Thatcher's poise 31
  Thatcher's relationship with Denis Thatcher 318–319, 321
  Thatcher's relationship with the Queen 97–8
  Thatcher's relationships with male politicians 83
  visit from Mitterrand 275
  visited Thatcher at end of life 324
Powell, Enoch 208
Powell, Jonathan 279–280
Prior, Jim 96
Prodger, Michael 246
Profumo, John 321–2
Pugh, Martin 142–3, 156
Pym, Francis 96, 203–4

Rasmussen, Fogh 326
Rayner, Angela 41, 45, 268

Reagan, Nancy 40, 59, 319
Reagan, Ronald 21–2, 181, 199, 203–4, 209–210, 238, 256, 269–274, 320, 324
Redwood, John 155
Reece, Gordon
  advice about television appearances 170–4
  advises Thatcher on debate 155
  business activities 189–190
  campaigns 185–8
  choice of Saatchi & Saatchi 182
  PM election 174–6
  relationship with Thatcher 30
  risk-taking 182
  on Thatcher's voice 178–9
  on Thatcher's voice and dress 38
  and Tim Bell 183
Rees-Mogg, William 108
Reeves, Rachel 45, 147, 166
Representation of the People Act 1918 141
Research Assessment Exercise (RAE) 241–2
Riley, Andrew 49
Roantree, Barra 225
Roberts, Alfred 62–3, 65, 69–74, 106–7, 142, 311–313
Roberts, Beatrice 61, 63–6, 70–3, 75–6, 79–80
Robilliard, Joy 167, 168
Rook, Jean 186
Rothschild, Jacob, 4th Baron Rothschild 235

# INDEX

Rushdie, Salman  247, 257
Rutherford, Andy  184

Saatchi, Charles  182
Saatchi, Maurice  182–3
Saatchi & Saatchi  170, 184–5, 189, 246
Sandberg, Sheryl  45
Sands, Bobby  199
Saunders, Robin  37
Scarfe, Gerald  193
Scargill, Anne  159
Scargill, Arthur  159–160, 214–220, 222, 225
school milk scandal  152–4
Seaton, Jean  207
Section 28  177, 196, 250–2
sexism
  after Second World War  120
  from the BBC  207
  cartoonists  43
  female protestors  157–8
  and feminism  138–9
  at Oxford  108–9
  in Parliament  147–8
  in politics  144
  by striking miners  215
  against Thatcher  35–6, 154, 189
  Thatcher's work to enter politics  116–117
Seymour, Julian  22, 320, 324
Sharkey, John  189
Shattock, Jeanne  221
Sheehy, Gail  56–8, 62, 193

Shephard, Gillian
  appointed as junior minister  136
  class  123
  closing of mines  223
  on Mitterrand  274
  Thatcher and feminism  133, 136
  Thatcher and menopause  200
  Thatcher's isolation during the Falklands War  210
  Thatcher's upbringing  65, 112
Sherbourne, Stephen
  on Denis Thatcher  316
  on Powell and Ingham  281
  on pre-Thatcher Britain  140
  secretaries at 10 Downing St  92–3
  Thatcher's deliberation  217
  Thatcher's family  79
  Thatcher's fitting in  119
  Thatcher's relationship with the Queen  98
Sherman, Alfred  124–5
Shriver, Lionel  140–1
Sloanes  261–2
Slocock, Caroline  33, 62, 91–2, 98, 136–7, 144, 232, 239
Smith, Marie  194
Soames, Christopher  96, 123
Somerville College, Oxford  62, 106, 108–9, 111, 142, 196, 237, 241
Soskin, Shirley  37, 46
Spencer, Diana  40, 259, 261, 290
Spice, Betty  32

Spicer, Michael 79
*Spitting Image* (TV show) 46, 193
Steinem, Gloria 150
Stephens, Caroline 167, 183
Stephenson, Phoebe 64–5, 75
Stoppard, Miriam 67, 72
Strategic Defence Initiative (SDI) "Star Wars" 238–9, 273
Straw, Jack 131
Strong, Roy 245
Summerskill, Edith 147–8
Sutcliffe-Braithwaite, Florence 99, 124–6, 229
Swain, Jon 222

Taylor, Eric 221
Tebbit, Margaret 221
Tebbit, Norman
  on Airey Neave 276–7
  on Bell's conviction in 1977 188
  on Falklands War 206
  injured in Brighton bombing 221
  Thatcher's cabinet 123
  Thatcher's 'off days' 200
  Thatcher's political persona 192
  Thatcher's religious beliefs 198, 227–8
  Thatcher's strategists 275
  view of the 1960s 151
  on women in politics 179
Tedford, Matt 196
Thatcher, Carol
  after bombing 222
  birth 18
  comforts Thatcher 91
  dates Jonathan Aitken 198
  describes her father 154, 319
  learns of father's first marriage 314
  pressure on Thatcher's children 80–3
  sent to Mymwood 77
  Thatcher's effects on Carol 85–8
  on Thatcher's goals as a mother 79
Thatcher, Denis, 1st Baronet of Scotney
  advice on Falklands War 205
  calls on King to help Thatcher 35
  closeness with Carol 83
  dating relationship with Thatcher 297–300, 307, 310–313
  death 323
  decision not to have more children 201
  family photos for press 174
  first marriage 313–314
  first sight of children 149
  introduces Thatcher to Guinevere Tilney 39
  nervous breakdown 314–315
  as perfect consort 315–320
  preferred blondes 36
  relationship with his mother 89
  relationship with Mandy Rice-Davies 321–3

# INDEX

relationship with Thatcher 282
religious beliefs 232
resisted child care 81–2, 85
tax returns 131
Thatcher's closeness to Denis 55
and Thatcher's inner circle 168
Thatcher's marriage as escape 61
on Thatcher's temper 187
wedding 115
Thatcher, Diane 84–5
Thatcher, Margaret
auction of clothes 49–50
Ayurvedic treatments 57
becomes Prime Minister 130
birth 64
blouses 40–2
caricatures of 193
class roots 99–101
death 324–5
dementia at end of life 324
dressing for success 36–45, 176
Falklands War 202–213
fascination with upper class 95–6
and feminism 129–130
  see also feminism
handbag 46–9
hormone replacement therapy 201
identity as scientist 227
Iron Lady 209
love of chocolate 306
love of fashion 21–8, 34
love of music 66
love of sycophants 282–3

'milk snatcher' 152–5
model of female leadership 197–8
Oxford 105–111
papers 49
personal religious beliefs 227–33
political strategy 171–6
popular culture 262–5
preference in men 267–9
relationship with Elizabeth II 96–9
sexist commentaries on 35–6, 43, 138–9, 147–8 see also sexism
stereotypes 140
support for science 236–7
temperament 66–7, 187
vanity 58–9
views of women 77–8
wearing hats 37–8
wedding 115
on welfare state 231–2
Thatcher, Mark 76, 79, 80–5, 232, 281
Thatcherism 124–7
Thorneycroft, Peter 185
Thorpe, Jeremy 187
Tickell, Crispin 239–240
Tilney, Guinevere 21, 38–40, 51
trade unions 90, 137, 160, 213–215, 273
Trounce, Beverley 158–9
Trump, Melania 40–1, 161
Truss, Liz 41, 94, 136
Turner, Graham 263

Union of Democratic
    Mineworkers 219

*Vanity Fair* magazine 56, 62, 193–4
Vaughan, Janet 111
Victoria and Albert Museum 49–50, 245–6
Vincent, John 95
Vinen, Richard 280
Vira, Kartik 225
*Vogue* magazine 34–5, 40
von der Leyen, Ursula 45

Wakeham, Roberta 221
Waldegrave, William 126–7
Walden, Brian 123, 206, 242
Walker, Peter 217, 219
Wallace, Mary 74
Walter, Natasha 135–6, 147, 196–7
Walters, Ben 191
Wapshott, Nicholas 111, 271, 274
Ward, Alison 167, 183
Ward, Irene 76
Ward, Stephen 322
Warnock, Mary 111–112
Waugh, Auberon 158
Webb, Iain R. 248–9, 251–2
Webber, Andrew Lloyd 178, 255
Webster, Wendy 38, 64, 76, 89, 149, 162, 172
Weldon, Fay 130
Wells, John 116
West, Alan, Lord West of Spithead 205–6

Westland Affair 292
Westwood, Vivienne 50
Whitelaw, William, Viscount Whitelaw 119, 123–4, 174, 203, 278–9
Wickstead, Margaret 62
Wilkie, David 219
Wilkinson, Helen 147, 209, 224
Willetts, David 242
Williams, Shirley 139, 143–4, 166, 195
Willink, Rachel 110
Wilmers, Mary-Kay 75
Wilson, Harold 121, 153, 215
Windsor, Roger 222
Winfrey, Oprah 161
Wolfson, David 43, 169
Wollstonecraft, Mary 141
Women for Life on Earth 156
Wood, Heather 158
Woods, Vicki 58
Wyatt, Petronella 290–1
Wyatt, Verushka 291
Wyatt, Woodrow, Baron Wyatt of Weeford 193, 282, 289–291

Young, George 77
Young, Hugo 182, 198, 234–5, 238–9
Young, Janet, Baroness Young 96, 162

Zamyatin, Leonid 274